By Robert Lowell

Land of Unlikeness (1944)

Lord Weary's Castle (1946)

The Mills of the Kavanaughs (1951)

Life Studies (1959)

Phaedra (translation) (1961)

Imitations (1961)

For the Union Dead (1964)

The Old Glory (plays) (1965)

Near the Ocean (1967)

The Voyage & Other Versions of Poems by Baudelaire (1969)

Prometheus Bound (translation) (1969)

Notebook 1967–68 (revised and expanded edition, *Notebook*, 1970)

History (1973)

For Lizzie and Harriet (1973)

The Dolphin (1973)

Selected Poems (1976) (revised edition, 1977)

Day by Day (1977)

The Oresteia of Aeschylus (translation) (1978)

Collected Prose (1987)

Collected Poems (2003)

The Letters of Robert Lowell (2005)

Selected Poems

Robert Lowell

Selected Poems

EXPANDED EDITION

FARRAR, STRAUS AND GIROUX / NEW YORK

Farrar, Straus and Giroux
19 Union Square West, New York 10003

The first edition of *Selected Poems* by Robert Lowell was published in 1976, and a revised edition was published in 1977.

Grateful acknowledgment is made to the following for permission to reprint copyrighted material: Poems from *Lord Weary's Castle*, copyright © 1946 and renewed 1974 by Robert Lowell, reprinted by permission of Harcourt, Inc.; poems from *The Mills of the Kavanaughs*, copyright © 1951, 1950, 1948, 1947, 1946 by Robert Lowell, renewed 1979, 1978 by Harriet W. Lowell, renewed 1976, 1975, 1974 by Robert Lowell, reprinted by permission of Harcourt, Inc.; "Chronology" from *The Critical Response to Robert Lowell*, edited by Steven Gould Axelrod, copyright © by Steven Gould Axelrod, reprinted by permission of the Greenwood Publishing Group Inc., Westport, Conn.

Library of Congress Cataloging-in-Publication Data
Lowell, Robert, 1917–1977.
    Selected poems / Robert Lowell.— 1st expanded ed.
      p.   cm.
    Includes index.
    ISBN-13: 978-0-374-53006-8 (pbk. : alk. paper)
    ISBN-10: 0-374-53006-8 (pbk. : alk. paper)
    I. Title.

  PS3523.O89 A6 2006
  811'.52—dc22

                              2005054313

www.fsgbooks.com

10 9 8 7 6 5 4 3 2 1

Contents

FROM **For the Union Dead** (1964)

FROM Near the Ocean (1967)

FROM History (1973)

FROM **For Lizzie and Harriet** (1973)

FROM The Dolphin (1973)

FROM Selected Poems (1976)

Foreword

Robert Lowell was a transgressive artist—his art again and again broke taboos, both thematic and formal. Like the most ambitious transgressive artists, he was also at heart a moralist.

·

From the thrilling, bursting-at-the-seams formality of his first trade book, to the autobiographical dense-with-novelistic-detail free verse of *Life Studies*, the return to formal verse (now modeled on Marvell) in *Near the Ocean*—then the attempt to swallow the whole world in the sonnets, followed by the nearly transparent free verse of his final book—the progress of Lowell's formal inventions had the quality of allegory. Watching these shifts during his lifetime many readers felt something central was at stake in them in the way that many have felt with Picasso and Stravinsky. Like Picasso and Stravinsky, each new turn infuriated or disappointed or bored some previous partisans. With Lowell, this process is still going on.

·

He writes in *History*:

> Cézanne left his spine sticking in the landscape,
> his slow brush sucked the resin from the pines;
> Picasso's bullfighter's wrist for foil and flare—
> they cannot fill the crack in everything God made. (228)

The last line quotes a sentence from Emerson: "There is a crack in everything God has made." Lowell's immense work attempts to make us see the cracks in what we or the culture have thought of as whole. It makes us yearn to fill the cracks—even as we perceive that the present is irremediable, the result of the collapse of all our previous ambitions.

•

Lowell is the poet of the irremediable. His poems start when things are past essential change. This does not mean the poems are unconcerned with moral response, what we should do, how we should act in the unimaginable future—but any response that is moral must be made in the full light of a landscape haunted by the failure of our earlier desires, hopes, ambitions. Therefore huge energy and invention are spent on giving us, showing us what the present holds. "The Vanity of Human Wishes," Lowell's version of Juvenal's Tenth Satire, ends with a line that is not in Juvenal: "I give you simply what you have already" (203). We have it already but we have not seen it, not made it the ground of how we live. Like Baudelaire and Eliot (both moralists), Lowell conceives the poet as someone who brings back news of what the world is to a world that has been blind to it.

•

Let me make a little collage of quotations.

> Christ lost, our only king without a sword,
> turning the word *forgiveness* to a sword. (280)

The injunction to forgive haunts and chastises us. Our parents are, perhaps, hardest to forgive, just as they find us hardest to forgive. Home and childhood were chaos:

> when hurting others was as necessary as breathing,
> hurting myself more necessary than breathing. (217)

> always inside me is the child who died,
> always inside me is his will to die— (177)

> childhood, closer to me than what I love. (282)

Lowell finds that the Lord's Prayer fits his feeling only when he twists and inverts it:

> Father, forgive me
> my injuries,
> as I forgive

those I
have injured!

You never climbed
Mount Sion, yet left
dinosaur
death-steps on the crust,
where I must walk. (141)

Just as the injunction to forgive haunts and chastises us, the body politic mocks our ideals:

This house, this pioneer democracy, built
on foundations, not of rock, but blood as hard as rock. (223)

The passage from lower to upper middle age
is quicker than the sigh of a match in the water—
we too were students, and betrayed our hand. (225)

•

In Lowell, we must rediscover everything from the ground up—no received wisdom has purchase on what our actual experience is. Traditional religion, unlike secular culture, is right about what it insists are the essential issues of human life—but Lowell is deeply skeptical about traditional religious response to those issues, its answers:

all those settings out
that never left the ground,
beginning in wisdom, dying in doubt. (164)

The artist in his ambition to see and write the whole is himself mocked:

Even if I should indiscreetly write
the perfect sentence, it isn't English—
I go to bed Lord Byron, and wake up bald. (226)

•

Out of this moment that is close to nihilism, in Lowell a countermovement always arises. The brute need to act and make reaches for the language of religion, language that insists on our neediness and inadequacy, on help from mystery. In the final poem in the main body of Lowell's final book, he writes:

> Yet why not say what happened?
> Pray for the grace of accuracy
> Vermeer gave to the sun's illumination
> stealing like the tide across a map
> to his girl solid with yearning.
> We are poor passing facts,
> warned by that to give
> each figure in the photograph
> his living name. (338)

Elizabeth Hardwick, looking over the draft of a poem, once said to him: "Why not say what really happened?" Lowell's whole work, in its transgressive, almost barbaric immediacy, testifies to his unsuppressible wish to fulfill that plea. Fulfilling it is beyond his will: "accuracy" about us is not possible without the gift of numinous powers beyond us, "grace" for which we must "pray." To give each figure a "living name" is to resolve an inherent contradiction, to square the circle: a "name" is a sign that itself is fixed; precisely because it doesn't change it is useful. Whatever is "living" is at every second full of change. Art is the place where what is full of change and what achieves fixed formal shape become (this is art's mortal plea) one: an ideal for which even an artist as deeply gifted as Lowell needs grace.

●

The present volume is an enlargement of the *Selected Poems* Lowell himself made and revised in the year before his death. Now *Life Studies*—perhaps his most perfectly shaped large project—is complete, including the crucial prose memoir "91 Revere Street." Poems from his final volume, *Day by Day*, are present for the first time. There is a larger selection from *For the Union Dead* and *History*. The notes have been adapted from *The Collected Poems of Robert Lowell* (2003), edited by myself and David Gewanter.

FRANK BIDART

from

Lord Weary's Castle
(1946)

The Exile's Return

There mounts in squalls a sort of rusty mire,
Not ice, not snow, to leaguer the Hôtel
De Ville, where braced pig-iron dragons grip
The blizzard to their rigor mortis. A bell
Grumbles when the reverberations strip
The thatching from its spire,
The search-guns click and spit and split up timber
And nick the slate roofs on the Holstenwall
Where torn-up tilestones crown the victor. Fall
And winter, spring and summer, guns unlimber
And lumber down the narrow gabled street
Past your gray, sorry and ancestral house
Where the dynamited walnut tree
Shadows a squat, old, wind-torn gate and cows
The Yankee commandant. You will not see
Strutting children or meet
The peg-leg and reproachful chancellor
With a forget-me-not in his button-hole
When the unseasoned liberators roll
Into the Market Square, ground arms before
The Rathaus; but already lily-stands
Burgeon the risen Rhineland, and a rough
Cathedral lifts its eye. Pleasant enough,
Voi ch'entrate, and your life is in your hands.

The Holy Innocents

Listen, the hay-bells tinkle as the cart
Wavers on rubber tires along the tar
And cindered ice below the burlap mill
And ale-wife run. The oxen drool and start
In wonder at the fenders of a car,
And blunder hugely up St. Peter's hill.
These are the undefiled by woman—their
Sorrow is not the sorrow of this world:
King Herod shrieking vengeance at the curled
Up knees of Jesus choking in the air,

A king of speechless clods and infants. Still
The world out-Herods Herod; and the year,
The nineteen-hundred forty-fifth of grace,
Lumbers with losses up the clinkered hill
Of our purgation; and the oxen near
The worn foundations of their resting-place,
The holy manger where their bed is corn
And holly torn for Christmas. If they die,
As Jesus, in the harness, who will mourn?
Lamb of the shepherds, Child, how still you lie.

Colloquy in Black Rock

Here the jack-hammer jabs into the ocean;
My heart, you race and stagger and demand
More blood-gangs for your nigger-brass percussions,
Till I, the stunned machine of your devotion,
Clanging upon this cymbal of a hand,
Am rattled screw and footloose. All discussions

End in the mud-flat detritus of death.
My heart, beat faster, faster. In Black Mud
Hungarian workmen give their blood
For the martyre Stephen, who was stoned to death.

Black Mud, a name to conjure with: O mud
For watermelons gutted to the crust,
Mud for the mole-tide harbor, mud for mouse,
Mud for the armored Diesel fishing tubs that thud
A year and a day to wind and tide; the dust
Is on this skipping heart that shakes my house,

House of our Savior who was hanged till death.
My heart, beat faster, faster. In Black Mud
Stephen the martyre was broken down to blood:
Our ransom is the rubble of his death.

Christ walks on the black water. In Black Mud
Darts the kingfisher. On Corpus Christi, heart,
Over the drum-beat of St. Stephen's choir
I hear him, *Stupor Mundi*, and the mud
Flies from his hunching wings and beak—my heart,
The blue kingfisher dives on you in fire.

The Quaker Graveyard in Nantucket

(FOR WARREN WINSLOW, DEAD AT SEA)

Let man have dominion over the fishes of the sea and the fowls of the air and the beasts
and the whole earth, and every creeping creature that moveth upon the earth.

I.
A brackish reach of shoal off Madaket,—
The sea was still breaking violently and night
Had steamed into our North Atlantic Fleet,
When the drowned sailor clutched the drag-net. Light
Flashed from his matted head and marble feet,
He grappled at the net
With the coiled, hurdling muscles of his thighs:
The corpse was bloodless, a botch of reds and whites,
Its open, staring eyes
Were lustreless dead-lights
Or cabin-windows on a stranded hulk
Heavy with sand. We weight the body, close
Its eyes and heave it seaward whence it came,
Where the heel-headed dogfish barks its nose
On Ahab's void and forehead; and the name
Is blocked in yellow chalk.
Sailors, who pitch this portent at the sea
Where dreadnaughts shall confess
Its hell-bent deity,
When you are powerless
To sand-bag this Atlantic bulwark, faced
By the earth-shaker, green, unwearied, chaste
In his steel scales: ask for no Orphean lute
To pluck life back. The guns of the steeled fleet
Recoil and then repeat
The hoarse salute.

II.

Whenever winds are moving and their breath
Heaves at the roped-in bulwarks of this pier,
The terns and sea-gulls tremble at your death
In these home waters. Sailor, can you hear
The Pequod's sea wings, beating landward, fall
Headlong and break on our Atlantic wall
Off 'Sconset, where the yawing S-boats splash
The bellbuoy, with ballooning spinnakers,
As the entangled, screeching mainsheet clears
The blocks: off Madaket, where lubbers lash
The heavy surf and throw their long lead squids
For blue-fish? Sea-gulls blink their heavy lids
Seaward. The winds' wings beat upon the stones,
Cousin, and scream for you and the claws rush
At the sea's throat and wring it in the slush
Of this old Quaker graveyard where the bones
Cry out in the long night for the hurt beast
Bobbing by Ahab's whaleboats in the East.

III.

All you recovered from Poseidon died
With you, my cousin, and the harrowed brine
Is fruitless on the blue beard of the god,
Stretching beyond us to the castles in Spain,
Nantucket's westward haven. To Cape Cod
Guns, cradled on the tide,
Blast the eelgrass about a waterclock
Of bilge and backwash, roil the salt and sand
Lashing earth's scaffold, rock
Our warships in the hand
Of the great God, where time's contrition blues
Whatever it was these Quaker sailors lost
In the mad scramble of their lives. They died
When time was open-eyed,
Wooden and childish; only bones abide
There, in the nowhere, where their boats were tossed
Sky-high, where mariners had fabled news

Of IS, the whited monster. What it cost
Them is their secret. In the sperm-whale's slick
I see the Quakers drown and hear their cry:
"If God himself had not been on our side,
If God himself had not been on our side,
When the Atlantic rose against us, why,
Then it had swallowed us up quick."

IV.
This is the end of the whaleroad and the whale
Who spewed Nantucket bones on the thrashed swell
And stirred the troubled waters to whirlpools
To send the Pequod packing off to hell:
This is the end of them, three-quarters fools,
Snatching at straws to sail
Seaward and seaward on the turntail whale,
Spouting out blood and water as it rolls,
Sick as a dog to these Atlantic shoals:
Clamavimus, O depths. Let the sea-gulls wail

For water, for the deep where the high tide
Mutters to its hurt self, mutters and ebbs.
Waves wallow in their wash, go out and out,
Leave only the death-rattle of the crabs,
The beach increasing, its enormous snout
Sucking the ocean's side.
This is the end of running on the waves;
We are poured out like water. Who will dance
The mast-lashed master of Leviathans
Up from this field of Quakers in their unstoned graves?

V.
When the whale's viscera go and the roll
Of its corruption overruns this world
Beyond tree-swept Nantucket and Woods Hole
And Martha's Vineyard, Sailor, will your sword
Whistle and fall and sink into the fat?

In the great ash-pit of Jehoshaphat
The bones cry for the blood of the white whale,
The fat flukes arch and whack about its ears,
The death-lance churns into the sanctuary, tears
The gun-blue swingle, heaving like a flail,
And hacks the coiling life out: it works and drags
And rips the sperm-whale's midriff into rags,
Gobbets of blubber spill to wind and weather,
Sailor, and gulls go round the stoven timbers
Where the morning stars sing out together
And thunder shakes the white surf and dismembers
The red flag hammered in the mast-head. Hide
Our steel, Jonas Messias, in Thy side.

VI.

OUR LADY OF WALSINGHAM

There once the penitents took off their shoes
And then walked barefoot the remaining mile;
And the small trees, a stream and hedgerows file
Slowly along the munching English lane,
Like cows to the old shrine, until you lose
Track of your dragging pain.
The stream flows down under the druid tree,
Shiloah's whirlpools gurgle and make glad
The castle of God. Sailor, you were glad
And whistled Sion by that stream. But see:

Our Lady, too small for her canopy,
Sits near the altar. There's no comeliness
At all or charm in that expressionless
Face with its heavy eyelids. As before,
This face, for centuries a memory,
Non est species, neque decor,
Expressionless, expresses God: it goes
Past castled Sion. She knows what God knows,
Not Calvary's Cross nor crib at Bethlehem
Now, and the world shall come to Walsingham.

VII.
The empty winds are creaking and the oak
Splatters and splatters on the cenotaph,
The boughs are trembling and a gaff
Bobs on the untimely stroke
Of the greased wash exploding on a shoal-bell
In the old mouth of the Atlantic. It's well;
Atlantic, you are fouled with the blue sailors,
Sea-monsters, upward angel, downward fish:
Unmarried and corroding, spare of flesh
Mart once of supercilious, wing'd clippers,
Atlantic, where your bell-trap guts its spoil
You could cut the brackish winds with a knife
Here in Nantucket, and cast up the time
When the Lord God formed man from the sea's slime
And breathed into his face the breath of life,
And blue-lung'd combers lumbered to the kill.
The Lord survives the rainbow of His will.

In Memory of Arthur Winslow

DEATH FROM CANCER

This Easter, Arthur Winslow, less than dead,
Your people set you up in Phillips House
To settle off your wrestling with the crab—
The claws drop flesh upon your yachting blouse
Until longshoreman Charon come and stab
Through your adjusted bed
And crush the crab. On Boston Basin, shells
Hit water by the Union Boat Club wharf:
You ponder why the coxes' squeakings dwarf
The *resurrexit dominus* of all the bells.

Grandfather Winslow, look, the swanboats coast
That island in the Public Gardens, where
The bread-stuffed ducks are brooding, where with tub
And strainer the mid-Sunday Irish scare
The sun-struck shallows for the dusky chub
This Easter, and the ghost
Of risen Jesus walks the waves to run
Arthur upon a trumpeting black swan
Beyond Charles River to the Acheron
Where the wide waters and their voyager are one.

Mary Winslow

Her Irish maids could never spoon out mush
Or orange-juice enough; the body cools
And smiles as a sick child
Who adds up figures, and a hush
Grips at the poised relations sipping sherry
And tracking up the carpets of her four
Room kingdom. On the rigid Charles, in snow,
Charon, the Lubber, clambers from his wherry,
And stops her hideous baby-squawks and yells,
Wit's clownish afterthought. Nothing will go
Again. Even the gelded picador
Baiting the twinned runt bulls
With walrus horns before the Spanish Belles
Is veiled with all the childish bibelots.

Mary Winslow is dead. Out on the Charles
The shells hold water and their oarblades drag,
Littered with captivated ducks, and now
The bell-rope in King's Chapel Tower unsnarls
And bells the bestial cow
From Boston Common; she is dead. But stop,
Neighbor, these pillows prop
Her that her terrified and child's cold eyes
Glass what they're not: our Copley ancestress,
Grandiloquent, square-jowled and worldly-wise,
A Cleopatra in her housewife's dress;
Nothing will go again. The bells cry: "Come,
Come home," the babbling Chapel belfry cries:
"Come, Mary Winslow, come; I bell thee home."

The Drunken Fisherman

Wallowing in this bloody sty,
I cast for fish that pleased my eye
(Truly Jehovah's bow suspends
No pots of gold to weight its ends);
Only the blood-mouthed rainbow trout
Rose to my bait. They flopped about
My canvas creel until the moth
Corrupted its unstable cloth.

A calendar to tell the day;
A handkerchief to wave away
The gnats; a couch unstuffed with storm
Pouching a bottle in one arm;
A whiskey bottle full of worms;
And bedroom slacks: are these fit terms
To mete the worm whose molten rage
Boils in the belly of old age?

Once fishing was a rabbit's foot—
O wind blow cold, O wind blow hot,
Let suns stay in or suns step out:
Life danced a jig on the sperm-whale's spout—
The fisher's fluent and obscene
Catches kept his conscience clean.
Children, the raging memory drools
Over the glory of past pools.

Now the hot river, ebbing, hauls
Its bloody waters into holes;
A grain of sand inside my shoe
Mimics the moon that might undo
Man and Creation too; remorse,
Stinking, has puddled up its source;

Here tantrums thrash to a whale's rage.
This is the pot-hole of old age.

Is there no way to cast my hook
Out of this dynamited brook?
The Fisher's sons must cast about
When shallow waters peter out.
I will catch Christ with a greased worm,
And when the Prince of Darkness stalks
My bloodstream to its Stygian term . . .
On water the Man-Fisher walks.

Between the Porch and the Altar

I.

MOTHER AND SON

Meeting his mother makes him lose ten years,
Or is it twenty? Time, no doubt, has ears
That listen to the swallowed serpent, wound
Into its bowels, but he thinks no sound
Is possible before her, he thinks the past
Is settled. It is honest to hold fast
Merely to what one sees with one's own eyes
When the red velvet curves and haunches rise
To blot him from the pretty driftwood fire's
Façade of welcome. Then the son retires
Into the sack and selfhood of the boy
Who clawed through fallen houses of his Troy,
Homely and human only when the flames
Crackle in recollection. Nothing shames
Him more than this uncoiling, counterfeit
Body presented as an idol. It
Is something in a circus, big as life,
The painted dragon, a mother and a wife
With flat glass eyes pushed at him on a stick;
The human mover crawls to make them click.
The forehead of her father's portrait peels
With rosy dryness, and the schoolboy kneels
To ask the benediction of the hand,
Lifted as though to motion him to stand,
Dangling its watch-chain on the Holy Book—
A little golden snake that mouths a hook.

II.

ADAM AND EVE

The Farmer sizzles on his shaft all day.
He is content and centuries away
From white-hot Concord, and he stands on guard.
Or is he melting down like sculptured lard?
His hand is crisp and steady on the plough.
I quarrelled with you, but am happy now
To while away my life for your unrest
Of terror. Never to have lived is best;
Man tasted Eve with death. I taste my wife
And children while I hold your hands. I knife
Their names into this elm. What is exempt?
I eye the statue with an awed contempt
And see the puritanical façade
Of the white church that Irish exiles made
For Patrick—that Colonial from Rome
Had magicked the charmed serpents from their home,
As though he were the Piper. Will his breath
Scorch the red dragon of my nerves to death?
By sundown we are on a shore. You walk
A little way before me and I talk,
Half to myself and half aloud. They lied,
My cold-eyed seedy fathers when they died,
Or rather threw their lives away, to fix
Sterile, forbidding nameplates on the bricks
Above a kettle. Jesus rest their souls!
You cry for help. Your market-basket rolls
With all its baking apples in the lake.
You watch the whorish slither of a snake
That chokes a duckling. When we try to kiss,
Our eyes are slits and cringing, and we hiss;
Scales glitter on our bodies as we fall.
The Farmer melts upon his pedestal.

III.

It must have been a Friday. I could hear
The top-floor typist's thunder and the beer
That you had brought in cases hurt my head;
I'd sent the pillows flying from my bed,
I hugged my knees together and I gasped.
The dangling telephone receiver rasped
Like someone in a dream who cannot stop
For breath or logic till his victim drop
To darkness and the sheets. I must have slept,
But still could hear my father who had kept
Your guilty presents but cut off my hair.
He whispers that he really doesn't care
If I am your kept woman all my life,
Or ruin your two children and your wife;
But my dishonor makes him drink. Of course
I'll tell the court the truth for his divorce.
I walk through snow into St. Patrick's yard.
Black nuns with glasses smile and stand on guard
Before a bulkhead in a bank of snow,
Whose charred doors open, as good people go
Inside by twos to the confessor. One
Must have a friend to enter there, but none
Is friendless in this crowd, and the nuns smile.
I stand aside and marvel; for a while
The winter sun is pleasant and it warms
My heart with love for others, but the swarms
Of penitents have dwindled. I begin
To cry and ask God's pardon of our sin.
Where are you? You were with me and are gone.
All the forgiven couples hurry on
To dinner and their nights, and none will stop.
I run about in circles till I drop
Against a padlocked bulkhead in a yard
Where faces redden and the snow is hard.

IV.

I sit at a gold table with my girl
Whose eyelids burn with brandy. What a whirl
Of Easter eggs is colored by the lights,
As the Norwegian dancer's crystalled tights
Flash with her naked leg's high-booted skate,
Like Northern Lights upon my watching plate.
The twinkling steel above me is a star;
I am a fallen Christmas tree. Our car
Races through seven red-lights—then the road
Is unpatrolled and empty, and a load
Of ply-wood with a tail-light makes us slow.
I turn and whisper in her ear. You know
I want to leave my mother and my wife,
You wouldn't have me tied to them for life . . .
Time runs, the windshield runs with stars. The past
Is cities from a train, until at last
Its escalating and black-windowed blocks
Recoil against a Gothic church. The clocks
Are tolling. I am dying. The shocked stones
Are falling like a ton of bricks and bones
That snap and splinter and descend in glass
Before a priest who mumbles through his Mass
And sprinkles holy water; and the Day
Breaks with its lightning on the man of clay,
Dies amara valde. Here the Lord
Is Lucifer in harness: hand on sword,
He watches me for Mother, and will turn
The bier and baby-carriage where I burn.

The Ghost

(After Sextus Propertius)

A ghost is someone: death has left a hole
For the lead-colored soul to beat the fire:
   Cynthia leaves her dirty pyre
   And seems to coil herself and roll
     Under my canopy,
Love's stale and public playground, where I lie
And fill the run-down empire of my bed.
I see the street, her potter's field, is red
And lively with the ashes of the dead;

But she no longer sparkles off in smoke:
It is the body carted to the gate
   Last Friday, when the sizzling grate
   Left its charred furrows on her smock
     And ate into her hip.
A black nail dangles from a finger-tip
And Lethe oozes from her nether lip.
Her thumb-bones rattle on her brittle hands,
As Cynthia stamps and hisses and demands:

"Sextus, has sleep already washed away
Your manhood? You forget the window-sill
   My sliding wore to slivers? Day
   Would break before the Seven Hills
     Saw Cynthia retreat
And climb your shoulders to the knotted sheet.
You shouldered me and galloped on bare feet
To lay me by the crossroads. Have no fear:
Notus, who snatched your promise, has no ear.

"But why did no one call in my deaf ear?
Your calling would have gained me one more day.
   Sextus, although you ran away
   You might have called and stopped my bier

A second by your door.
No tears drenched a black toga for your whore
When broken tilestones bruised her face before
The Capitol. Would it have strained your purse
To scatter ten cheap roses on my hearse?

"The State will make Pompilia's Chloris burn:
I knew her secret when I kissed the skull
    Of Pluto in the tainted bowl.
    Let Nomas burn her books and turn
        Her poisons into gold;
The finger-prints upon the potsherd told
Her love. You let a slut, whose body sold
To Thracians, liquefy my golden bust
In the coarse flame that crinkled me to dust.

"If Chloris' bed has left you with your head,
Lover, I think you'll answer my arrears:
    My nurse is getting on in years,
    See that she gets a little bread—
        She never clutched your purse;
See that my little humpback hears no curse
From her close-fisted friend. But burn the verse
You bellowed half a lifetime in my name:
Why should you feed me to the fires of fame?

"I will not hound you, much as you have earned
It, Sextus: I shall reign in your four books—
    I swear this by the Hag who looks
    Into my heart where it was burned:
        Propertius, I kept faith;
If not, may serpents suck my ghost to death
And spit it with their forked and killing breath
Into the Styx where Agamemnon's wife
Founders in the green circles of her life.

"Beat the sycophant ivy from my urn,
That twists its binding shoots about my bones
    Where apple-sweetened Anio drones

Through orchards that will never burn
    While honest Herakles,
My patron, watches. Anio, you will please
Me if you whisper upon sliding knees:
'Propertius, Cynthia is here:
She shakes her blossoms when my waters clear.'

"You cannot turn your back upon a dream,
For phantoms have their reasons when they come:
    We wander midnights: then the numb
    Ghost wades from the Lethean stream;
        Even the foolish dog
Stops its hell-raising mouths and casts its clog;
At cock-crow Charon checks us in his log.
Others can have you, Sextus; I alone
Hold: and I grind your manhood bone on bone."

In the Cage

The lifers file into the hall,
According to their houses—twos
Of laundered denim. On the wall
A colored fairy tinkles blues
And titters by the balustrade;
Canaries beat their bars and scream.
We come from tunnels where the spade
Pick-axe and hod for plaster steam
In mud and insulation. Here
The Bible-twisting Israelite
Fasts for his Harlem. It is night,
And it is vanity, and age
Blackens the heart of Adam. Fear,
The yellow chirper, beaks its cage.

At the Indian Killer's Grave

Here, also, are the veterans of King Philip's War, who burned villages and slaughtered young and old, with pious fierceness, while the godly souls throughout the land were helping them with prayer. —HAWTHORNE

Behind King's Chapel what the earth has kept
Whole from the jerking noose of time extends
Its dark enigma to Jehoshaphat;
Or will King Philip plait
The just man's scalp in the wailing valley! Friends,
Blacker than these black stones the subway bends
About the dirty elm roots and the well
For the unchristened infants in the waste
Of the great garden rotten to its root;
Death, the engraver, puts forward his bone foot
And Grace-with-wings and Time-on-wings compel
All this antique abandon of the disgraced
To face Jehovah's buffets and his ends.

The dusty leaves and frizzled lilacs gear
This garden of the elders with baroque
And prodigal embellishments but smoke,
Settling upon the pilgrims and their grounds,
Espouses and confounds
Their dust with the off-scourings of the town;
The libertarian crown
Of England built their mausoleum. Here
A clutter of Bible and weeping willows guards
The stern Colonial magistrates and wards
Of Charles the Second, and the clouds
Weep on the just and unjust as they will,—
For the poor dead cannot see Easter crowds
On Boston Common or the Beacon Hill
Where strangers hold the golden Statehouse dome
For good and always. Where they live is home:
A common with an iron railing: here
Frayed cables wreathe the spreading cenotaph

Of John and Mary Winslow and the laugh
Of Death is hacked in sandstone, in their year.

A green train grinds along its buried tracks
And screeches. When the great mutation racks
The Pilgrim Fathers' relics, will these placques
Harness the spare-ribbed persons of the dead
To battle with the dragon? Philip's head
Grins on the platter, fouls in pantomime
The fingers of kept time:
"Surely, this people is but grass,"
He whispers, "this will pass;
But, Sirs, the trollop dances on your skulls
And breaks the hollow noddle like an egg
That thought the world an eggshell. Sirs, the gulls
Scream from the squelching wharf-piles, beg a leg
To crack their crops. The Judgment is at hand;
Only the dead are poorer in this world
Where State and elders thundered *raca*, hurled
Anathemas at nature and the land
That fed the hunter's gashed and green perfection—
Its settled mass concedes no outlets for your puns
And verbal Paradises. Your election,
Hawking above this slime
For souls as single as their skeletons,
Flutters and claws in the dead hand of time."

When you go down this man-hole to the drains,
The doorman barricades you in and out;
You wait upon his pleasure. All about
The pale, sand-colored, treeless chains
Of T-squared buildings strain
To curb the spreading of the braced terrain;
When you go down this hole, perhaps your pains
Will be rewarded well; no rough-cast house
Will bed and board you in King's Chapel. Here
A public servant putters with a knife
And paints the railing red
Forever, as a mouse

Cracks walnuts by the headstones of the dead
Whose chiselled angels peer
At you, as if their art were long as life.

I ponder on the railing at this park:
Who was the man who sowed the dragon's teeth,
That fabulous or fancied patriarch
Who sowed so ill for his descent, beneath
King's Chapel in this underworld and dark?
John, Matthew, Luke and Mark,
Gospel me to the Garden, let me come
Where Mary twists the warlock with her flowers—
Her soul a bridal chamber fresh with flowers
And her whole body an ecstatic womb,
As through the trellis peers the sudden Bridegroom.

Mr. Edwards and the Spider

I saw the spiders marching through the air,
Swimming from tree to tree that mildewed day
  In latter August when the hay
   Came creaking to the barn. But where
    The wind is westerly,
Where gnarled November makes the spiders fly
Into the apparitions of the sky,
  They purpose nothing but their ease and die
Urgently beating east to sunrise and the sea;

What are we in the hands of the great God?
It was in vain you set up thorn and briar
  In battle array against the fire
   And treason crackling in your blood;
    For the wild thorns grow tame
And will do nothing to oppose the flame;
Your lacerations tell the losing game
  You play against a sickness past your cure.
How will the hands be strong? How will the heart endure?

A very little thing, a little worm,
Or hourglass-blazoned spider, it is said,
  Can kill a tiger. Will the dead
   Hold up his mirror and affirm
    To the four winds the smell
And flash of his authority? It's well
If God who holds you to the pit of hell,
  Much as one holds a spider, will destroy,
Baffle and dissipate your soul. As a small boy

On Windsor Marsh, I saw the spider die
When thrown into the bowels of fierce fire:
  There's no long struggle, no desire
   To get up on its feet and fly—

It stretches out its feet
And dies. This is the sinner's last retreat;
   Yes, and no strength exerted on the heat
   Then sinews the abolished will, when sick
And full of burning, it will whistle on a brick.

But who can plumb the sinking of that soul?
Josiah Hawley, picture yourself cast
   Into a brick-kiln where the blast
   Fans your quick vitals to a coal—
      If measured by a glass,
How long would it seem burning! Let there pass
A minute, ten, ten trillion; but the blaze
Is infinite, eternal: this is death,
To die and know it. This is the Black Widow, death.

After the Surprising Conversions

September twenty-second, Sir: today
I answer. In the latter part of May,
Hard on our Lord's Ascension, it began
To be more sensible. A gentleman
Of more than common understanding, strict
In morals, pious in behavior, kicked
Against our goad. A man of some renown,
An useful, honored person in the town,
He came of melancholy parents; prone
To secret spells, for years they kept alone—
His uncle, I believe, was killed of it:
Good people, but of too much or little wit.
I preached one Sabbath on a text from Kings;
He showed concernment for his soul. Some things
In his experience were hopeful. He
Would sit and watch the wind knocking a tree
And praise this countryside our Lord has made.
Once when a poor man's heifer died, he laid
A shilling on the doorsill; though a thirst
For loving shook him like a snake, he durst
Not entertain much hope of his estate
In heaven. Once we saw him sitting late
Behind his attic window by a light
That guttered on his Bible; through that night
He meditated terror, and he seemed
Beyond advice or reason, for he dreamed
That he was called to trumpet Judgment Day
To Concord. In the latter part of May
He cut his throat. And though the coroner
Judged him delirious, soon a noisome stir
Palsied our village. At Jehovah's nod
Satan seemed more let loose amongst us: God
Abandoned us to Satan, and he pressed
Us hard, until we thought we could not rest

Till we had done with life. Content was gone.
All the good work was quashed. We were undone.
The breath of God had carried out a planned
And sensible withdrawal from this land;
The multitude, once unconcerned with doubt,
Once neither callous, curious nor devout,
Jumped at broad noon, as though some peddler groaned
At it in its familiar twang: "My friend,
Cut your own throat. Cut your own throat. Now! Now!"
September twenty-second, Sir, the bough
Cracks with the unpicked apples, and at dawn
The small-mouth bass breaks water, gorged with spawn.

The Death of the Sheriff

"forsitan et Priami fuerint quae fata, requiras?"

NOLI ME TANGERE

We park and stare. A full sky of the stars
Wheels from the pumpkin setting of the moon
And sparks the windows of the yellow farm
Where the red-flannelled madmen look through bars
At windmills thrashing snowflakes by an arm
Of the Atlantic. Soon
The undertaker who collects antiques
Will let his motor idle at the door
And set his pine-box on the parlor floor.
Our homicidal sheriff howled for weeks;

We kiss. The State had reasons: on the whole,
It acted out of kindness when it locked
Its servant in this place and had him watched
Until an ordered darkness left his soul
A *tabula rasa*; when the Angel knocked
The sheriff laid his notched
Revolver on the table for the guest.
Night draws us closer in its bearskin wrap
And our loved sightless smother feels the tap
Of the blind stars descending to the west

To lay the Devil in the pit our hands
Are draining like a windmill. Who'll atone
For the unsearchable quicksilver heart
Where spiders stare their eyes out at their own
Spitting and knotted likeness? We must start:
Our aunt, his mother, stands
Singing *O Rock of Ages*, as the light
Wanderers show a man with a white cane
Who comes to take the coffin in his wain,
The thirsty Dipper on the arc of night.

Where the Rainbow Ends

I saw the sky descending, black and white,
Not blue, on Boston where the winters wore
The skulls to jack-o'-lanterns on the slates,
And Hunger's skin-and-bone retrievers tore
The chickadee and shrike. The thorn tree waits
Its victim and tonight
The worms will eat the deadwood to the foot
Of Ararat: the scythers, Time and Death,
Helmed locusts, move upon the tree of breath;
The wild ingrafted olive and the root

Are withered, and a winter drifts to where
The Pepperpot, ironic rainbow, spans
Charles River and its scales of scorched-earth miles.
I saw my city in the Scales, the pans
Of judgment rising and descending. Piles
Of dead leaves char the air—
And I am a red arrow on this graph
Of Revelations. Every dove is sold
The Chapel's sharp-shinned eagle shifts its hold
On serpent-Time, the rainbow's epitaph.

In Boston serpents whistle at the cold.
The victim climbs the altar steps and sings:
"Hosannah to the lion, lamb, and beast
Who fans the furnace-face of IS with wings:
I breathe the ether of my marriage feast."
At the high altar, gold
And a fair cloth. I kneel and the wings beat
My cheek. What can the dove of Jesus give
You now but wisdom, exile? Stand and live,
The dove has brought an olive branch to eat.

from

The Mills of the Kavanaughs
(1951)

The Mills of the Kavanaughs

The heron warps its neck, a broken pick,
To study its reflection on the scales,
Or knife-bright shards of water lilies, quick
In the dead autumn water with their snails
And water lice. Her ballet glasses hold
Him twisted by a fist of spruce, as dry
As flint and steel. She thinks: "The bird is old,
A cousin to all scholars; that is why
He will abet my thoughts of Kavanaugh,
Who gave the Mills its lumberyard and weir
In eighteen hundred, when our farmers saw
John Adams bring their Romish church a bell,
Cast—so the records claim—by Paul Revere.
The sticks of *Kavanaugh* are buried here—
Many of them, too many, Love, to tell—
Faithful to where their virgin forest fell."

And now the mussed blue-bottles bead her float:
Bringers of luck. Of luck? At worst, a rest
From counting blisters on her metal boat,
That spins and staggers. North and south and west:
A scene, perhaps, of Fragonard—her park,
Whose planted poplars scatter penny-leaves,
White underneath, like mussels to the dark
Chop of the shallows. Extirpation grieves
The sunken martyred laughter of the loon,
Where Harry's mother bathed in navy-blue
Stockings and skirts. But now, the afternoon
Is sullen, it is all that she can do
To lift the anchor. She can hardly row
Against these whitecaps—surely never lulled
For man and woman. Washing to and fro,
The floorboards bruise the lilies that she pulled.

"Even in August it was autumn—all
A pond could harbor." Now her matches fall
In dozens by her bobber to expire
As target-circles on the mirrored fire-
Escapes of *Kavanaugh*. She sees they hold
Her mirror to her—just a little cold;
A ground hog's looking glass. "The day is sharp
And short, Love, and its sun is like this carp,
Or goldfish, almost twenty inches long,
Panting, a weak old dog, below a prong
Of deadwood fallen from my copper beech;
The settling leaves embower its warmth. They reach
For my reflection, but it glides through shoal
Aground, to where the squirrel held its roots
And freehold, Love, unsliding, when our boots
Pattered—a life ago once—on its hole.

"I think we row together, for the stern
Jumps from my weaker stroke, and down the cove
Our house is floating, and the windows burn,
As if its underpinnings fed the stove.
Her window's open; look, she waits for us,
And types, until the clattering tin bell
Upon her room-large table tolls for us.
Listen, your mother's asking, *is it well*?
Yes, very well. He died outside the church
Like Harry Tudor. Now we near the sluice
And burial ground above the burlap mill;
I see you swing a string of yellow perch
About your head to fan off gnats that mill
And wail, as your disheartened shadow tries
The buried bedstead, where your body lies—
Time out of mind—a failing stand of spruce.

"God knows!" she marvels. "Harry, *Kavanaugh*
Was lightly given. Soon enough we saw
Death like the Bourbon after Waterloo,
Who learning and forgetting nothing, knew

Nothing but ruin. Why must we mistrust
Ourselves with Death who takes the world on trust?
Although God's brother, and himself a god,
Death whipped his horses through the startled sod;
For neither conscience nor omniscience warned
Him from his folly, when the virgin scorned
His courtship, and the quaking earth revealed
Death's desperation to the Thracian field.
And yet we think the virgin took no harm:
She gave herself because her blood was warm—
And for no other reason, Love, I gave
Whatever brought me gladness to the grave."

Falling Asleep over the Aeneid

An old man in Concord forgets to go to morning service. He falls asleep, while reading Vergil, and dreams that he is Aeneas at the funeral of Pallas, an Italian prince.

The sun is blue and scarlet on my page,
And *yuck-a, yuck-a, yuck-a, yuck-a,* rage
The yellowhammers mating. Yellow fire
Blankets the captives dancing on their pyre,
And the scorched lictor screams and drops his rod.
Trojans are singing to their drunken God,
Ares. Their helmets catch on fire. Their files
Clank by the body of my comrade—miles
Of filings! Now the scythe-wheeled chariot rolls
Before their lances long as vaulting poles,
And I stand up and heil the thousand men,
Who carry Pallas to the bird-priest. Then
The bird-priest groans, and as his birds foretold,
I greet the body, lip to lip. I hold
The sword that Dido used. It tries to speak,
A bird with Dido's sworded breast. Its beak
Clangs and ejaculates the Punic word
I hear the bird-priest chirping like a bird.
I groan a little. "Who am I, and why?"
It asks, a boy's face, though its arrow-eye
Is working from its socket. "Brother, try,
O Child of Aphrodite, try to die:
To die is life." His harlots hang his bed
With feathers of his long-tailed birds. His head
Is yawning like a person. The plumes blow;
The beard and eyebrows ruffle. Face of snow,
You are the flower that country girls have caught,
A wild bee-pillaged honey-suckle brought
To the returning bridegroom—the design

Has not yet left it, and the petals shine;
The earth, its mother, has, at last, no help:
It is itself. The broken-winded yelp
Of my Phoenician hounds, that fills the brush
With snapping twigs and flying, cannot flush
The ghost of Pallas. But I take his pall,
Stiff with its gold and purple, and recall
How Dido hugged it to her, while she toiled,
Laughing—her golden threads, a serpent coiled
In cypress. Now I lay it like a sheet;
It clinks and settles down upon his feet,
The careless yellow hair that seemed to burn
Beforehand. Left foot, right foot—as they turn,
More pyres are rising: armored horses, bronze,
And gagged Italians, who must file by ones
Across the bitter river, when my thumb
Tightens into their wind-pipes. The beaks drum;
Their headman's cow-horned death's-head bites its tongue,
And stiffens, as it eyes the hero slung
Inside his feathered hammock on the crossed
Staves of the eagles that we winged. Our cost
Is nothing to the lovers, whoring Mars
And Venus, father's lover. Now his car's
Plumage is ready, and my marshals fetch
His squire, Acoetes, white with age, to hitch
Aethon, the hero's charger, and its ears
Prick, and it steps and steps, and stately tears
Lather its teeth; and then the harlots bring
The hero's charms and baton—but the King,
Vain-glorious Turnus, carried off the rest.
"I was myself, but Ares thought it best
The way it happened." At the end of time,
He sets his spear, as my descendants climb
The knees of Father Time, his beard of scalps,
His scythe, the arc of steel that crowns the Alps.
The elephants of Carthage hold those snows,
Turms of Numidian horse unsling their bows,
The flaming turkey-feathered arrows swarm
Beyond the Alps. "Pallas," I raise my arm

And shout, "Brother, eternal health. Farewell
Forever." Church is over, and its bell
Frightens the yellowhammers, as I wake
And watch the whitecaps wrinkle up the lake.
Mother's great-aunt, who died when I was eight,
Stands by our parlor sabre. "Boy, it's late.
Vergil must keep the Sabbath." Eighty years!
It all comes back. My Uncle Charles appears.
Blue-capped and bird-like. Phillips Brooks and Grant
Are frowning at his coffin, and my aunt,
Hearing his colored volunteers parade
Through Concord, laughs, and tells her English maid
To clip his yellow nostril hairs, and fold
His colors on him. . . . It is I. I hold
His sword to keep from falling, for the dust
On the stuffed birds is breathless, for the bust
Of young Augustus weighs on Vergil's shelf:
It scowls into my glasses at itself.

Her Dead Brother

The Lion of St. Mark's upon the glass
Shield in my window reddens, as the night
Enchants the swinging dories to its terrors,
And dulls your distant wind-stung eyes; alas,
Your portrait, coiled in German-silver hawsers, mirrors
The sunset as a dragon. Enough light
Remains to see you through your varnish. Giving
Your life has brought you closer to your friends;
Yes, it has brought you home. All's well that ends:
Achilles dead is greater than the living;

My mind holds you as I would have you live,
A wintering dragon. Summer was too short
When we went picnicking with telescopes
And crocking leather handbooks to that fort
Above the lank and heroned Sheepscot, where its slopes
Are clutched by hemlocks—spotting birds. I give
You back that idyll, Brother. Was it more?
Remember riding, scotching with your spur
That four-foot milk-snake in a juniper?
Father shellacked it to the ice-house door.

Then you were grown; I left you on your own.
We will forget that August twenty-third,
When Mother motored with the maids to Stowe,
And the pale summer shades were drawn—so low
No one could see us; no, nor catch your hissing word,
As false as Cressid! Let our deaths atone:
The fingers on your sword-knot are alive,
And Hope, that fouls my brightness with its grace,
Will anchor in the narrows of your face.
My husband's Packard crunches up the drive.

Mother Marie Therese

(Drowned in 1912)

The speaker is a Canadian nun stationed in New Brunswick.

Old sisters at our Maris Stella House
Remember how the Mother's strangled grouse
And snow-shoe rabbits matched the royal glint
Of Pio Nono's vestments in the print
That used to face us, while our aching ring
Of stationary rockers saw her bring
Our cake. Often, when sunset hurt the rocks
Off Carthage, and surprised us knitting socks
For victims of the Franco-Prussian War,
Our scandal'd set her frowning at the floor;
And vespers struck like lightning through the gloom
And oaken ennui of her sitting room.
It strikes us now, but cannot re-inspire;
False, false and false, I mutter to my fire.
The good old times, ah yes! But good, that all's
Forgotten like our Province's cabals;
And Jesus, smiling earthward, finds it good;
For we were friends of Cato, not of God.
This sixtieth Christmas, I'm content to pray
For what life's shrinkage leaves from day to day;
And it's a sorrow to recall our young
Raptures for Mother, when her trophies hung,
Fresh in their blood and color, to convince
Even Probationers that Heaven's Prince,
Befriending, whispered: "Is it then so hard?
Tarry a little while, O disregard
Time's wings and armor, when it flutters down
Papal tiaras and the Bourbon crown;
For quickly, priest and prince will stand, their shields
Before each other's faces, in the fields,
Where, as I promised, virtue will compel

Michael and all his angels to repel
Satan's advances, till his forces lie
Beside the Lamb in blissful fealty."
Our Indian summer! Then, our skies could lift,
God willing; but an Indian brought the gift.
"A sword," said Father Turbot, "not a saint";
Yet He who made the Virgin without taint
Chastised our Mother to the Rule's restraint.
Was it not fated that the sweat of Christ
Would wash the worldly serpent? Christ enticed
Her heart that fluttered, while she whipped her hounds
Into the quicksands of her manor grounds,
A lordly child, her habit fleur-de-lys'd—
There she dismounted, sick; with little heed,
Surrendered. Like Proserpina, who fell
Six months a year from earth to flower in hell;
She half-renounced by Candle, Book and Bell
Her flowers and fowling pieces for the Church.
She never spared the child and spoiled the birch;
And how she'd chide her novices, and pluck
Them by the ears for gabbling in Canuck,
While she was reading Rabelais from her chaise,
Or parroting the *Action Française*.
Her letter from the soi-disant French King,
And the less treasured golden wedding ring
Of her shy Bridegroom, yellow; and the regal
Damascus shot-guns, pegged upon her eagle
Emblems from Hohenzollern standards, rust.
Our world is passing; even she, whose trust
Was in its princes, fed the gluttonous gulls,
That whiten our Atlantic, when like skulls
They drift for sewage with the emerald tide.
Perpetual novenas cannot tide
Us past that drowning. After Mother died,
"An émigrée in this world and the next,"
Said Father Turbot, playing with his text.
Where is he? Surely, he is one of those,
Whom Christ and Satan spew! But no one knows
What's happened to that porpoise-bellied priest.

He lodged with us on Louis Neuvième's Feast,
And celebrated her memorial mass.
His bald spot tapestried by colored glass,
Our angels, Prussian blue and flaking red,
He squeaked and stuttered: "N-n-nothing is so d-dead
As a dead s-s-sister." Off Saint Denis' Head,
Our Mother, drowned on an excursion, sleeps.
Her billy goat, or its descendant, keeps
Watch on a headland, and I hear it bawl
Into this sixty-knot Atlantic squall,
"Mamamma's Baby," past Queen Mary's Neck,
The ledge at Carthage—almost to Quebec,
Where Monsieur de Montcalm, on Abraham's
Bosom, asleep, perceives our world that shams
His New World, lost—however it atones
For Wolfe, the Englishman, and Huron bones
And priests'. O Mother, here our snuffling crones
And cretins feared you, but I owe you flowers:
The dead, the sea's dead, has her sorrows, hours
On end to lie tossing to the east, cold,
Without bed-fellows, washed and bored and old,
Bilged by her thoughts, and worked on by the worms,
Until her fossil convent come to terms
With the Atlantic. Mother, there is room
Beyond our harbor. Past its wooden Boom
Now weak and waterlogged, that Frontenac
Once diagrammed, she welters on her back.
The bell-buoy, whom she called the Cardinal,
Dances upon her. If she hears at all,
She only hears it tolling to this shore,
Where our frost-bitten sisters know the roar
Of water, inching, always on the move
For virgins, when they wish the times were love,
And their hysterical hosannahs rouse
The loveless harems of the buck ruffed grouse,
Who drums, untroubled now, beside the sea—
As if he found our stern virginity
Contra naturam. We are ruinous;
God's Providence through time has mastered us:

Now all the bells are tongueless, now we freeze,
A later Advent, pruner of warped trees,
Whistles about our nunnery slabs, and yells,
And water oozes from us into wells;
A new year swells and stirs. Our narrow Bay
Freezes itself and us. We cannot say
Christ even sees us, when the ice floes toss
His statue, made by Hurons, on the cross,
That Father Turbot sank on Mother's mound—
A whirligig! Mother, we must give ground,
Little by little; but it does no good.
Tonight, while I am piling on more driftwood,
And stooping with the poker, you are here,
Telling your beads; and breathing in my ear,
You watch your orphan swording at her fears.
I feel you twitch my shoulder. No one hears
Us mock the sisters, as we used to, years
And years behind us, when we heard the spheres
Whirring *venite*; and we held our ears.
My mother's hollow sockets fill with tears.

The Fat Man in the Mirror

(After Werfel)

What's filling up the mirror? O, it is not I;
Hair-belly like a beaver's house? An old dog's eye?
    The forenoon was blue
    In the mad King's zoo
Nurse was swinging me so high, so high!

The bullies wrestled on the royal bowling green;
Hammers and sickles on their hoods of black sateen. . . .
    Sulking on my swing
    The tobacco King
Sliced apples with a pen-knife for the Queen.

This *I*, who used to mouse about the paraffined preserves,
And jammed a finger in the coffee-grinder, serves
    Time before the mirror.
    But this pursey terror . . .
Nurse, it is a person. *It is nerves.*

Where's the Queen-Mother waltzing like a top to staunch
The blood of Lewis, King of Faerie? Hip and haunch
    Lard the royal grotto;
    Straddling Lewis' motto,
Time, the Turk, its sickle on its paunch.

Nurse, Nurse, it rises on me . . . O, it starts to roll,
My apples, O, are ashes in the meerschaum bowl. . . .
    If you'd only come,
    If you'd only come,
Darling, if . . . The apples that I stole,

While Nurse and I were swinging in the Old One's eye . . .
Only a fat man with his beaver on his eye
    Only a fat man,
    Only a fat man
Bursts the mirror. O, it is not I!

Thanksgiving's Over

Thanksgiving night, 1942: a room on Third Avenue. Michael dreams of his wife, a German-American Catholic, who leapt from a window before she died in a sanatorium. The church is the Franciscan church on 31st Street.

Thanksgiving night: Third Avenue was dead;
My fowl was soupbones. Fathoms overhead,
Snow warred on the El's world in the blank snow.
"Michael," she whispered, "just a year ago,
Even the shoreleave from the *Normandie*
Were weary of Thanksgiving; but they'd stop
And lift their hats. I watched their arctics drop
Below the birdstoup of the Anthony
And Child who guarded our sodality
For lay-Franciscans, Michael, till I heard
The birds inside me, and I knew the Third
Person possessed me, for I was the bird
Of Paradise, the parrot whose absurd
Garblings are glory. *Cherry ripe, ripe, ripe . . .*"

Winter had come on horseback, and the snow,
Hostile and unattended, wrapped my feet
In sheepskins. Where I'd stumbled from the street,
A red cement Saint Francis fed a row
Of toga'd boys with birds beneath a Child.
His candles flamed in tumblers, and He smiled.
"Romans!" she whispered, "look, these overblown
And bootless Brothers tell us we must go
Barefooted through the snow where birds recite:
Come unto us, our burden's light—light, light,
This burden that our marriage turned to stone!
O Michael, must we join the deaf and dumb

Breadline for children? Sit and listen." So
I sat. I counted to ten thousand, wound
My cowhorn beads from Dublin on my thumb,
And ground them. *Miserere?* Not a sound.

Life Studies

(1959)

Part One

Beyond the Alps

(On the train from Rome to Paris. 1950, the year Pius XII defined the dogma of Mary's bodily assumption.)

Reading how even the Swiss had thrown the sponge
in once again and Everest was still
unscaled, I watched our Paris pullman lunge
mooning across the fallow Alpine snow.
O bella Roma! I saw our stewards go
forward on tiptoe banging on their gongs.
Life changed to landscape. Much against my will
I left the City of God where it belongs.
There the skirt-mad Mussolini unfurled
the eagle of Caesar. He was one of us
only, pure prose. I envy the conspicuous
waste of our grandparents on their grand tours—
long-haired Victorian sages accepted the universe,
while breezing on their trust funds through the world.

When the Vatican made Mary's Assumption dogma,
the crowds at San Pietro screamed *Papa*.
The Holy Father dropped his shaving glass,
and listened. His electric razor purred,
his pet canary chirped on his left hand.
The lights of science couldn't hold a candle
to Mary risen—at one miraculous stroke,
angel-wing'd, gorgeous as a jungle bird!
But who believed this? Who could understand?
Pilgrims still kissed Saint Peter's brazen sandal.
The Duce's lynched, bare, booted skull still spoke.
God herded his people to the *coup de grâce*—
the costumed Switzers sloped their pikes to push,
O Pius, through the monstrous human crush. . . .

Our mountain-climbing train had come to earth.
Tired of the querulous hush-hush of the wheels,
the blear-eyed ego kicking in my berth
lay still, and saw Apollo plant his heels
on terra firma through the morning's thigh . . .
each backward, wasted Alp, a Parthenon,
fire-branded socket of the Cyclops' eye.
There were no tickets for that altitude
once held by Hellas, when the Goddess stood,
prince, pope, philosopher and golden bough,
pure mind and murder at the scything prow—
Minerva, the miscarriage of the brain.

Now Paris, our black classic, breaking up
like killer kings on an Etruscan cup.

The Banker's Daughter

*(Marie de Medici, shortly after the assassination of her husband, Henri IV.
Later, she was exiled by her son and lived in a house lent to her by Rubens.)*

Once this poor country egg from Florence lay
at her accouchement, such a virtuous ton
of woman only women thought her one.
King Henry pirouetted on his heel
and jested, "Look, my cow's producing veal."

O cozy scuffles, soft obscenities,
wardrobes that dragged the exchequer to its knees,
cables of pearl and crazy lutes strung tight—
O tension, groin and backbone! Every night
I kicked the pillows and embroidered lies
to rob my husband's purse. I said his eyes
flew kiting to my dormer from the blue.
I was a sparrow. He was fifty-two.

Alas, my brutal girlish mood-swings drove
my husband, wrenched and giddy, from the Louvre,
to sleep in single lodgings on the town.

He feared the fate of kings who died in sport. . . .
Murder cut him short—
a kitchen-knife honed on a carriage-wheel.

Your great nerve gone, Sire, sleep without a care.
No Hapsburg galleon coasts off Finisterre
with bars of bullion now to subsidize
the pilfering, pillaging democracies,
the pin-head priest, the nihilist grandee.
Sleep, sleep, my husband. There at Saint Denis,
the chiselled bolster and Carrara hound

show no emotion when we kiss the ground.
Now seasons cycle to the laughing ring
of scything children; king must follow king
and walk the plank to his immortal leap.
Ring, ring, tired bells, the King of France is dead;
who'll give the lover of the land a bed?
My son is adding inches in his sleep.
I see his dimpled fingers clutch Versailles.
Sing lullaby, my son, sing lullaby.
I rock my nightmare son, and hear him cry
for ball and sceptre; he asks the queen to die. . . .
And so I press my lover's palm to mine;
I am his vintage, and his living vine
entangles me, and oozes mortal wine
moment to moment. By repeated crime,
even a queen survives her little time.
You too, my husband. How you used to look
for blood and pastime! If you ever took
unfair advantages by right of birth,
pardon the easy virtues of the earth.

Inauguration Day: January 1953

The snow had buried Stuyvesant.
The subways drummed the vaults. I heard
the El's green girders charge on Third,
Manhattan's truss of adamant,
that groaned in ermine, slummed on want. . . .
Cyclonic zero of the word,
God of our armies, who interred
Cold Harbor's blue immortals, Grant!
Horseman, your sword is in the groove!

Ice, ice. Our wheels no longer move.
Look, the fixed stars, all just alike
as lack-land atoms, split apart,
and the Republic summons Ike,
the mausoleum in her heart.

A Mad Negro Soldier Confined at Munich

"We're all Americans, except the Doc,
a Kraut DP, who kneels and bathes my eye.
The boys who floored me, two black maniacs, try
to pat my hands. Rounds, rounds! Why punch the clock?

In Munich the zoo's rubble fumes with cats;
hoydens with air-guns prowl the Koenigsplatz,
and pink the pigeons on the mustard spire.
Who but my girl-friend set the town on fire?

Cat-houses talk cold turkey to my guards;
I found my *Fräulein* stitching outing shirts
in the black forest of the colored wards—
lieutenants squawked like chickens in her skirts.

Her German language made my arteries harden—
I've no annuity from the pay we blew.
I chartered an aluminum canoe,
I had her six times in the English Garden.

Oh mama, mama, like a trolley-pole
sparking at contact, her electric shock—
the power-house! . . . The doctor calls our roll—
no knives, no forks. We file before the clock,

and fancy minnows, slaves of habit, shoot
like starlight through their air-conditioned bowl.
It's time for feeding. Each subnormal boot-
black heart is pulsing to its ant-egg dole."

Part Two

The account of him is platitudinous, worldly and fond, but he has no Christian name and is entitled merely Major *M.* Myers in my Cousin Cassie Mason Myers Julian-James's privately printed *Biographical Sketches: A Key to a Cabinet of Heirlooms in the Smithsonian Museum.* The name-plate under his portrait used to spell out his name bravely enough: he was Mordecai Myers. The artist painted Major Myers in his sanguine War of 1812 uniform with epaulets, white breeches, and a scarlet frogged waistcoat. His right hand played with the sword "now to be seen in the Smithsonian cabinet of heirlooms." The pose was routine and gallant. The full-lipped smile was good-humoredly pompous and embarrassed.

Mordecai's father, given neither name nor initial, is described with an air of hurried self-congratulation by Cousin Cassie as "a friend of the Reverend Ezra Styles, afterward President of Yale College." As a very young man the son, Mordecai, studied military tactics under a French émi-gré, "the Bourbons' celebrated Colonel De la Croix." Later he was "ma-tured" by six years' practical experience in a New York militia regiment organized by Colonel Martin Van Buren. After "the successful engage-ment against the British at Chrysler's Field, thirty shrapnel splinters were extracted from his shoulder." During convalescence, he wooed and won Miss Charlotte Bailey, "thus proving himself a better man than his rivals, the united forces of Plattsburg." He fathered ten children, sponsored an enlightened law exempting Quakers from military service in New York State, and died in 1870 at the age of ninety-four, "a Grand Old Man, who impressed strangers with the poise of his old-time manners."

Undoubtedly Major Mordecai had lived in a more ritualistic, gaudy, and animal world than twentieth-century Boston. There was something undecided, Mediterranean, versatile, almost double-faced about his bearing which suggested that, even to his contemporaries, he must have seemed gratuitously both *ci-devant* and *parvenu.* He was a dark man, a German Jew—no downright Yankee, but maybe such a fellow as Napoleon's mad, pomaded son-of-an-innkeeper general, Junot, Duc D'Abrantes; a man like mad George III's pomaded, disreputable son, "Prinny," the Prince Regent. Or he was one of those Moorish-looking dons painted by his contemporary, Goya—some leader of Spanish guerrillas against Bonaparte's occupation, who fled to South America. Our Major's suffering almond eye rested on his luxurious dawn-colored fingers ruffling an off-white glove.

Bailey-Mason-Myers! Easy-going, Empire State patricians, these relatives of my Grandmother Lowell seemed to have given my father his character. For he likewise lacked that granite *back-countriness* which Grandfather Arthur Winslow attributed to his own ancestors, the iconoclastic, mulish Dunbarton New Hampshire Starks. On the joint Mason-Myers bookplate, there are two merry and naked mermaids—lovely marshmallowy, boneless, Rubensesque butterballs, all burlesque-show bosoms and Flemish smiles. Their motto, *malo frangere quam flectere*, reads "I prefer to bend than to break."

Mordecai Myers was my Grandmother Lowell's grandfather. His life was tame and honorable. He was a leisured squire and merchant, a member of the state legislature, a mayor of Schenectady, a "president" of Kinderhook village. Disappointingly, his famous "blazing brown eye" seems in all things to have shunned the outrageous. After his death he was remembered soberly as a New York State gentleman, the friend and host of worldly men and politicians with Dutch names: De Witt Clinton, Vanderpoel, Hoes, and Schuyler. My mother was roused to warmth by the Major's scarlet vest and exotic eye. She always insisted that he was the one properly dressed and dieted ancestor in the lot we had inherited from my father's Cousin Cassie. Great-great-Grandfather Mordecai! Poor sheepdog in wolf's clothing! In the anarchy of my adolescent war on my parents, I tried to make him a true wolf, the wandering Jew! *Homo lupus homini!*

Major Mordecai Myers' portrait has been mislaid past finding, but out of my memories I often come on it in the setting of our Revere Street house, a setting now fixed in the mind, where it survives all the distortions of fantasy, all the blank befogging of forgetfulness. There, the vast number of remembered *things* remains rocklike. Each is in its place, each has its function, its history, its drama. There, all is preserved by that motherly care that one either ignored or resented in his youth. The things and their owners come back urgent with life and meaning—because finished, they are endurable and perfect.

Cousin Cassie only became a close relation in 1922. In that year she died. After some unpleasantness between Mother and a co-heiress, Helen Bailey, the estate was divided. Mother used to return frozen and thrilled from her property disputes, and I, knowing nothing of the rights and wrongs, would half-perversely confuse Helen Bailey with Helen of Troy and harden my mind against the monotonous *parti pris* of Mother's voice. Shortly after our move to Boston in 1924, a score of unwanted Myers portraits was delivered to our new house on Revere Street. These were later followed by "their dowry"—four moving vans groaning with heavy Edwardian furniture. My father began to receive his first quarterly payments from the Mason-Myers Julian-James Trust Fund, sums "not grand enough to corrupt us," Mother explained, "but sufficient to prevent Daddy from being entirely at the mercy of his salary." The Trust sufficed: our lives became tantalized with possibilities, and my father felt encouraged to take the risk—a small one in those boom years—of resigning from the Navy on the gamble of doubling his income in business.

I was in the third grade and for the first time becoming a little more popular at school. I was afraid Father's leaving the Navy would destroy my standing. I was a churlish, disloyal, romantic boy, and quite without hero worship for my father, whose actuality seemed so inferior to the photographs in uniform he once mailed to us from the Golden Gate. My real *love*, as Mother used to insist to all new visitors, was toy soldiers. For a few months at the flood tide of this infatuation, people were ciphers to me—valueless except as chances for increasing my armies of soldiers. Roger Crosby, a child in the second grade of my Brimmer Street School, had thousands—not mass-produced American stereotypes, but hand-painted solid lead soldiers made to order in Dijon, France. Roger's father had a still more artistic and adult collection; its ranks—each man at least six inches tall—marched in glass cases under the eyes of recognizable replicas of mounted Napoleonic captains: Kléber, Marshal Ney, Murat, King of Naples. One delirious afternoon Mr. Crosby showed me his toys and was perhaps the first grownup to talk to me not as a child but as an equal when he discovered how feverishly I followed his anecdotes on uniforms and the evolution of tactical surprise. Afterwards, full of high thoughts, I ran up to Roger's play room and hoodwinked him into believing that his own soldiers were "ballast turned out by central European sweatshops." He agreed I was being sweetly generous when I traded twenty-four worthless Jordan Marsh papier-mâché doughboys for whole companies of his gorgeous, imported Old Guards, Second Empire "red-legs," and modern *chasseurs d'Alpine* with sky-blue berets. The haul was so huge that I had to take a child's wheelbarrow to Roger's house at the top of Pinckney Street. When I reached home with my last load, Mr. Crosby was talking with my father on our front steps. Roger's soldiers were all returned; I had only the presence of mind to hide a single soldier, a peely-nosed black sepoy wearing a Shriner's fez.

Nothing consoled me for my loss, but I enjoyed being allowed to draw Father's blunt dress sword, and I was proud of our Major Mordecai. I used to stand dangerously out in the middle of Revere Street in order to see through our windows and gloat on this portrait's scarlet waistcoat blazing in the bare, Spartan whiteness of our den-parlor. Mordecai Myers lost his glory when I learned from my father that he was only a "major *pro tem.*" On a civilian, even a civilian soldier, the flamboyant waistcoat was stuffy and no more martial than officers' costumes in our elementary school musicals.

In 1924 people still lived in cities. Late that summer, we bought the 91 Revere Street house, looking out on an unbuttoned part of Beacon Hill bounded by the North End slums, though reassuringly only four blocks away from my Grandfather Winslow's brown pillared house at 18 Chestnut Street. In the decades preceding and following the First World War, old Yankee families had upset expectation by regaining this section of the Hill from the vanguards of the lace-curtain Irish. This was bracing news for my parents in that topsy-turvy era when the Republican Party and what were called "people of the right sort" were no longer dominant in city elections. Still, even in the palmy, laissez-faire '20s, Revere Street refused to be a straightforward, immutable residential fact. From one end to the other, houses kept being sanded down, repainted, or abandoned to the flaking of decay. Houses, changing hands, changed their language and nationality. A few doors to our south the householders spoke "Beacon Hill British" or the flat *nay nay* of the Boston Brahmin. The parents of the children a few doors north spoke mostly in Italian.

My mother felt a horrified giddiness about the adventure of our address. She once said, "We are barely perched on the outer rim of the hub of decency." We were less than fifty yards from Louisburg Square, the cynosure of old historic Boston's plain-spoken, cold roast elite—the Hub of the Hub of the Universe. Fifty yards!

As a naval ensign, Father had done postgraduate work at Harvard. He had also done postgraduate work at M.I.T., preferred the purely scientific college, and condescended to both. In 1924, however, his tone began to change; he now began to speak warmly of Harvard as his second alma mater. We went to football games at the Harvard Stadium, and one had the feeling that our lives were now being lived in the brutal, fashionable expectancy of the stadium: we had so many downs, so many minutes, and so many yards to go for a winning touchdown. It was just such a winning financial and social advance that my parents promised themselves would follow Father's resignation from the Navy and his acceptance of a sensible job offered him at the Cambridge branch of Lever Brothers' Soap.

The advance was never to come. Father resigned from the service in 1927, but he never had a civilian *career*; he instead had merely twenty-two years of the civilian *life*. Almost immediately he bought a larger and more stylish house; he sold his ascetic, stove-black Hudson and bought a plump brown Buick; later the Buick was exchanged for a high-toned, as-good-as-new Packard with a custom-designed royal blue and mahogany body. Without drama, his earnings more or less decreased from year to year.

But so long as we were on Revere Street, Father tried to come to terms with it and must have often wondered whether he on the whole liked or disliked the neighborhood's lack of side. He was still at this time rather truculently democratic in what might be described as an upper middle-class, naval, and Masonic fashion. He was a mumbler. His opinions were almost morbidly hesitant, but he considered himself a matter-of-fact man of science and had an unspoiled faith in the superior efficiency of northern nations. He modeled his allegiances and humor on the cockney imperialism of Rudyard Kipling's swearing Tommies, who did their job. Autochthonous Boston snobs, such as the Winslows or members of Mother's reading club, were alarmed by the brassy callousness of our naval visitors, who labeled the Italians they met on Revere Street as "grade-A" and "grade-B wops." The Revere Street "grade-B's" were Sicilian Catholics and peddled crummy second-hand furniture on Cambridge Street, not far from the site of Great-great-Grandfather Charles Lowell's disused West Church, praised in an old family folder as "a haven from the Sodom and Gomorrah of Trinitarian orthodoxy and the tyranny of the letter." Revere Street "grade-A's," good North Italians, sold fancy groceries and Colonial heirlooms in their shops near the Public Garden. Still other Italians were Father's familiars; they sold him bootleg Scotch and *vino rosso* in teacups.

The outside of our Revere Street house was a flat red brick surface unvaried by the slightest suggestion of purple panes, delicate bay, or triangular window-cornice—a sheer wall formed by the seamless conjunction of four inseparable façades, all of the same commercial and purgatorial design. Though placed in the heart of Old Boston, it was ageless and artless, an epitome of those "leveler" qualities Mother found most grueling about the naval service. 91 Revere Street was mass-produced, *regulation-issue*, and yet struck Boston society as stupidly out of the ordinary, like those white elephants—a mother-of-pearl scout knife or a tea-kettle barometer—which my father used to pick up on sale at an Army-Navy store.

The walls of Father's minute Revere Street den-parlor were bare and white. His bookshelves were bare and white. The den's one adornment was a ten-tube home-assembled battery radio set, whose loudspeaker had the shape and color of a Mexican sombrero. The radio's specialty was getting programs from Australia and New Zealand in the early hours of the morning.

My father's favorite piece of den furniture was his oak and "rhinoceros hide" armchair. It was ostentatiously a masculine, or rather a bachelor's, chair. It had a notched, adjustable back; it was black, cracked, hacked, scratched, splintered, gouged, initialed, gunpowder-charred and tumbler-ringed. It looked like pale tobacco leaves laid on dark tobacco leaves. I doubt if Father, a considerate man, was responsible for any of the marring. The chair dated from his plebe days at the Naval Academy, and had been bought from a shady, shadowy, roaring character, midshipman "Beauty" Burford. Father loved each disfigured inch.

My father had been born two months after his own father's death. At each stage of his life, he was to be forlornly fatherless. He was a deep boy brought up entirely by a mild widowed mother and an intense widowed grandmother. When he was fourteen and a half, he became a deep young midshipman. By the time he graduated from Annapolis, he had a high sense of abstract form, which he beclouded with his humor. He had reached, perhaps, his final mental possibilities. He was deep—not with profundity, but with the dumb depth of one who trusted in statistics and was dubious of personal experience. In his forties, Father's soul went underground: as a civilian he kept his high sense of form, his humor, his accuracy, but this accuracy was henceforth unimportant, recreational, *hors de combat*. His debunking grew myopic; his shyness grew evasive; he argued with a fumbling languor. In the twenty-two years Father lived after he resigned from the Navy, he never again deserted Boston and never became Bostonian. He survived to drift from job to job, to be displaced, to be grimly and literally that old cliché, a fish out of water. He gasped and wheezed with impotent optimism, took on new ideals with each new job, never ingeniously enjoyed his leisure, never even hid his head in the sand.

Mother hated the Navy, hated naval society, naval pay, and the trip-hammer rote of settling and unsettling a house every other year when Father was transferred to a new station or ship. She had been married nine or ten years and still suspected that her husband was savorless, unmasterful, merely considerate. Unmasterful—Father's specialized efficiency lacked utterly the flattering bossiness she so counted on from her father, my Grandfather Winslow. It was not Father's absence on sea-duty that mattered; it was the eroding necessity of moving *with* him, of keeping in step. When he was far away on the Pacific, she had her friends, her parents, a house to herself—Boston! Fully conscious of her uniqueness and normality she basked in the refreshing stimulation of dreams in which she imagined Father as suitably sublimed. She used to describe such a sublime man to me over tea and English muffins. He was Siegfried carried lifeless through the shining air by Brunnhilde to Valhalla, and accompanied by the throb of my Great Aunt Sarah playing his leitmotif in the released manner taught her by the Abbé Liszt. Or Mother's hero dove through the grottoes of the Rhine and slaughtered the homicidal and vulgar dragon coiled about the golden hoard. Mother seemed almost light-headed when she retold the romance of Sarah Bernhardt in *L'Aiglon*, the Eaglet, the weakling! She would speak the word *weakling* with such amused vehemence that I formed a grandiose and false image of L'Aiglon's Father, the *big* Napoleon: he was a strong man who scratched under his paunchy little white vest a torso all hair, muscle, and manliness. Instead of the dreams, Mother now had the insipid fatigue of keeping house. Instead of the *Eagle*, she had a twentieth-century naval commander interested in steam, radio, and "the fellows." To avoid naval yards, steam, and "the fellows," Mother had impulsively bought the squalid, impractical Revere Street house. Her marriage daily forced her to squander her subconsciously hoarded energies.

"*Weelawaugh, we-ee-eeelawaugh, weelawaugh,*" shrilled Mother's high voice. "*But-and, but-and, but-and!*" Father's low mumble would drone in answer. Though I couldn't be sure that I had caught the meaning of the words, I followed the sounds as though they were a movie. I felt drenched in my parents' passions.

91 Revere Street was the setting for those arthritic spiritual pains that

troubled us for the two years my mother spent in trying to argue my father into resigning from the Navy. When the majestic, hollow boredom of the second year's autumn dwindled to the mean boredom of a second winter, I grew less willing to open my mouth. I bored my parents, they bored me.

"Weelawaugh, we-ee-eelawaugh, weelawaugh!" "But-and, but-and, but-and!"

During the week ends I was at home much of the time. All day I used to look forward to the nights when my bedroom walls would once again vibrate, when I would awake with rapture to the rhythm of my parents arguing, arguing one another to exhaustion. Sometimes, without bathrobe or slippers, I would wriggle out into the cold hall on my belly and ambuscade myself behind the banister. I could often hear actual words. "Yes, yes, yes," Father would mumble. He was "backsliding" and "living in the fool's paradise of habitual retarding and retarded do-nothing inertia." Mother had violently set her heart on the resignation. She was hysterical even in her calm, but like a patient and forbearing strategist, she tried to pretend her neutrality. One night she said with murderous coolness, "Bobby and I are leaving for Papá's." This was an ultimatum to force Father to sign a deed placing the Revere Street house in Mother's name.

I writhed with disappointment on the nights when Mother and Father only lowed harmoniously together like cows, as they criticized Helen Bailey or Admiral De Stahl. Once I heard my mother say, "A *man* must make up his *own* mind. Oh Bob, if you are going to resign, do it *now* so I can at least plan for your son's *survival* and education on a single continent."

About this time I was being sent for my *survival* to Dr. Dane, a Quaker chiropractor with an office on Marlborough Street. Dr. Dane wore an old-fashioned light tan druggist's smock; he smelled like a healthy old-fashioned drugstore. His laboratory was free of intimidating technical equipment, and had only the conservative lay roughness and toughness that was so familiar and disarming to us in my Grandfather Winslow's country study or bedroom. Dr. Dane's rosy hands wrenched my shoulders with tremendous éclat and made me feel a hero; I felt unspeakable joy whenever an awry muscle fell back into serenity. My mother, who had no curiosity or imagination for cranky occultism, trusted Dr. Dane's clean, undrugged manliness—so like home. She believed that chiropractic had cured me of my undiagnosed asthma, which had defeated the expensive specialists.

"A penny for your thoughts, Schopenhauer," my mother would say.

"I am thinking about pennies," I'd answer.

"When *I* was a child I used to love telling Mamá everything I had done," Mother would say.

"But you're not a child," I would answer.

I used to enjoy dawdling and humming "Anchors Aweigh" up Revere Street after a day at school. "Anchors Aweigh," the official Navy song, had originally been the song composed for my father's class. And yet my mind always blanked and seemed to fill with a clammy hollowness when Mother asked prying questions. Like other tongue-tied, difficult children, I dreamed I was a master of cool, stoical repartee. "What have you been doing, Bobby?" Mother would ask. "I haven't," I'd answer. At home I thus saved myself from emotional exhaustion.

At school, however, I was extreme only in my conventional mediocrity, my colorless, distracted manner, which came from restless dreams of being admired. My closest friend was Eric Burckhard, the son of a professor of architecture at Harvard. The Burckhards came from Zurich and were very German, not like Ludendorff, but in the kindly, comical, nineteenth-century manner of Jo's German husband in *Little Men*, or in the manner of the crusading *sturm und drang* liberal scholars in second year German novels. "Eric's mother and father are *both* called Dr. Burckhard," my mother once said, and indeed there was something endearingly repellent about Mrs. Burckhard with her doctor's degree, her long, unstylish skirts, and her dramatic, dulling blond braids. Strangely the Burckhards' sober continental bourgeois house was without golden mean—everything was either hilariously old Swiss or madly modern. The Frau Doctor Burckhard used to serve mid-morning hot chocolate with rosettes of whipped cream, and receive her friends in a long, uncarpeted hall-drawing room with lethal ferns and a yellow beeswaxed hardwood floor shining under a central skylight. On the wall there were large expert photographs of what at a distance appeared to be Mont Blanc—they were in reality views of Frank Lloyd Wright's Japanese hotel.

I admired the Burckhards and felt at home in their house, and these feelings were only intensified when I discovered that my mother was always ill at ease with them. The heartiness, the enlightenment, and the bright, ferny greenhouse atmosphere were too much for her.

Eric and I were too young to care for books or athletics. Neither of our houses had absorbing toys or an elevator to go up and down in. We were inseparable, but I cannot imagine what we talked about. I loved Eric because he was more popular than I and yet absolutely *sui generis* at the Brimmer School. He had a chalk-white face and limp, fine, white-blond hair. He was frail, elbowy, started talking with an enthusiastic Mont Blanc chirp and would flush with bewilderment if interrupted. All the other boys at Brimmer wore little tweed golf suits with knickerbockers, but Eric always arrived in a black suit coat, a Byronic collar, and cuffless gray flannel trousers that almost hid his shoes. The long trousers were replaced on warm days by gray flannel shorts, such as were worn by children still in kindergarten. Eric's unenviable and freakish costumes were too old or too young. He accepted the whims of his parents with a buoyant tranquillity that I found unnatural.

My first and terminating quarrel with Eric was my fault. Eventually almost our whole class at Brimmer had whooping cough, but Eric's seizure was like his long trousers—untimely: he was sick a month too early. For a whole month he was in quarantine and forced to play by himself in a removed corner of the Public Garden. He was certainly conspicuous as he skiproped with his Swiss nurse under the out-of-the-way Ether Memorial Fountain far from the pond and the swan boats. His parents had decided that this was an excellent opportunity for Eric to brush up on his German, and so the absoluteness of his quarantine was monstrously exaggerated by the fact that child and nurse spoke no English but only a guttural, British-sounding, Swiss German. Round and round and round the Fountain, he played intensely, fraily, obediently, until I began to tease him. Though motioned away by him, I came close. I had attracted some of the most popular Brimmer School boys. For the first time I had gotten favorable attention from several little girls. I came close. I shouted. Was Eric afraid of girls? I imitated his German. *Ein, zwei, drei, BEER.* I imitated Eric's coughing. "He is afraid he will give you whooping cough if he talks or lets you come nearer," the nurse said in her musical Swiss-English voice. I came nearer. Eric flushed, grew white, bent double with coughing. He began to cry, and had to be led away from the Public Garden. For a whole week I routed Eric from the Garden daily, and for two or three days I was a center of interest. "Come see the Lake Geneva spider monkey!" I would shout. I don't know why I couldn't stop. Eric never told his father, I think, but when he recovered we no longer spoke. The breach was so unspoken and intense that our classmates were actually horrified. They even devised a solemn ritual for our reconciliation. We crossed our hearts, mixed spit, mixed blood. The reconciliation was hollow.

———

My parents' confidences and quarrels stopped each night at ten or eleven o'clock, when my father would hang up his tuxedo, put on his commander's uniform, and take a trolley back to the naval yard at Charlestown. He had just broken in a new car. Like a chauffeur, he watched this car, a Hudson, with an informed vigilance, always giving its engine hair-trigger little tinkerings of adjustment or friendship, always fearful lest the black body, unbeautiful as his boiled shirts, should lose its outline and gloss. He drove with flawless, almost instrumental, monotony. Mother, nevertheless, was forever encouraging him to walk or take taxis. She would tell him that his legs were growing vestigial from disuse and remind him of the time a jack had slipped and he had broken his leg while shifting a tire. "Alone and at night," she would say, "an amateur driver is unsafe in a car." Father sighed and obeyed—only, putting on a martyred and penny-saving face, he would keep his self-respect by taking the trolley rather than a taxi. Each night he shifted back into his uniform, but his departures from Revere Street were so furtive that several months passed before I realized what was happening—we had *two* houses! Our second house was the residence in the Naval Yard assigned to the third in command. It was large, had its own flagpole, and screen porches on three levels—yet it was something to be ashamed of. Whatever pomp or distinction its possession might have had for us was destroyed by an eccentric humiliation inflicted on Father by his superior, Admiral De Stahl, the commandant at Charlestown. De Stahl had not been consulted about our buying the 91 Revere Street house. He was outraged, stormed about "flaunting private fortunes in the face of naval tradition," and ordered my father to sleep on bounds at the Yard in the house provided for that purpose.

On our first Revere Street Christmas Eve, the telephone rang in the middle of dinner; it was Admiral De Stahl demanding Father's instant return to the Navy Yard. Soon Father was back in his uniform. In taking leave of my mother and grandparents he was, as was usual with him under pressure, a little evasive and magniloquent. "A woman works from sun to sun," he said, "but a sailor's watch is never done." He compared a naval officer's hours with a doctor's, hinted at surprise maneuvers, and explained away the uncommunicative arrogance of Admiral De Stahl: "The Old Man has to be hush-hush." Later that night, I lay in bed and tried to imagine that my father was leading his engineering force on a surprise maneuver through arctic wastes. A forlorn hope! "Hush-hush, hush-hush," whispered the snowflakes as big as street lamps as they broke on Father—broke and buried. Outside, I heard real people singing carols,

shuffling snow off their shoes, opening and shutting doors. I worried at
the meaning of a sentence I had heard quoted from the *Boston Evening
Transcript*: "On this Christmas Eve, as usual, the whole of Beacon Hill can
be expected to become a single old-fashioned open house—the names of
mine host the Hill, and her guests will read like the contents of the Social
Register." I imagined Beacon Hill changed to the snow queen's palace, as
vast as the north pole. My father pressed a cold finger to his lip: "hush-
hush," and led his surprise squad of sailors around an altar, but the altar
was a tremendous cash register, whose roughened nickel surface was
cheaply decorated with trowels, pyramids, and Arabic swirls. A great
drawer helplessly chopped back and forth, unable to shut because choked
with greenbacks. "Hush-hush!" My father's engineers wound about me
with their eye-patches, orange sashes, and curtain-ring earrings, like the
Gilbert and Sullivan pirates' chorus. . . . Outside on the streets of Beacon
Hill, it was night, it was dismal, it was raining. Something disturbing had
befallen the familiar and honorable Salvation Army band; its big drum
and accordion were now accompanied by drunken voices howling: *The
Old Gray Mare, she ain't what she used to be, when Mary went to milk the
cow*. A sound of a bosun's whistle. Women laughing. Someone repeatedly
rang our doorbell. I heard my mother talking on the telephone. "Your
inebriated sailors have littered my doorstep with the dregs of Scollay
Square." There was a gloating panic in her voice that showed she enjoyed
the drama of talking to Admiral De Stahl. "Sir," she shrilled, "you have
compelled my husband to leave me alone and defenseless on Christmas
Eve!" She ran into my bedroom. She hugged me. She said, "Oh Bobby,
it's such a comfort to have a man in the house." "I am not a man," I said,
"I am a boy."

Boy—at that time this word had private associations for me; it meant
weakness, outlawry, and yet was a status to be held onto. Boys were a side-
line at my Brimmer School. The eight superior grades were limited to
girls. In these grades, moreover, scholarship was made subservient to dis-
cipline, as if in contempt of the male's two idols: career and earning
power. The school's tone, its *ton*, was a blend of the feminine and the
military, a bulky reality governed in turn by stridency, smartness, and
steadiness. The girls wore white jumpers, black skirts, stockings, and
rectangular low-heeled shoes. An ex-West Pointer had been appointed to
teach drill; and, at the moment of my enrollment in Brimmer, our princi-
pal, the hitherto staid Miss Manice, was rumored to be showing signs of
age and of undermining her position with the school trustees by girlish,

quite out of character, rhapsodies on the varsity basketball team, winner of two consecutive championships. The lower four grades, peaceful and lackadaisical, were, on the other hand, almost a separate establishment. Miss Manice regarded these "coeducated" classes with amused carelessness, allowed them to wear their ordinary clothes, and . . . carelessness, however, is incorrect—Miss Manice, in her administration of the lower school, showed the inconsistency and euphoria of a dual personality. Here she mysteriously shed all her Prussianism. She quoted Emerson and Mencken, disparaged the English, threatened to break with the past, and boldly coquetted with the non-military American genius by displaying movies illustrating the careers of Edison and Ford. Favored lower school teachers were permitted to use us as guinea pigs for mildly radical experiments. At Brimmer I *un*learned writing. The script that I had mastered with much agony at my first school was denounced as illegible: I was taught to print according to the Dalton Plan—to this day, as a result, I have to print even my two middle names and can only really *write* two words: "Robert" and "Lowell." Our instruction was subject to bewildering leaps. The usual fall performance by the Venetian glass-blowers was followed by a tour of the Riverside Press. We heard Rudy Vallee, then heard spirituals sung by the Hampton Institute choir. We studied grammar from a formidable, unreconstructed textbook written by Miss Manice's father. There, I battled with figures of speech and Greek terminology: *Chiasmus*, the arrangement of corresponding words in opposite order; *Brachylogy*, the failure to repeat an element that is supplied in more or less modified form. Then all this pedantry was nullified by the introduction of a new textbook which proposed to lift the face of syntax by using game techniques and drawings.

Physical instruction in the lower school was irregular, spontaneous, and had nothing of that swept and garnished barrack-room cameraderie of the older girls' gymnasium exercises. On the roof of our school building, there was an ugly concrete area that looked as if it had been intended for the top floor of a garage. Here we played tag, drew lines with chalk, and chose up sides for a kind of kids' soccer. On bright spring days, Mr. Newell, a submerged young man from Boston University, took us on botanical hikes through the Arboretum. He had an eye for inessentials— read us Martha Washington's poems at the Old State House, pointed out the roof of Brimmer School from the top of the Customs House, made us count the steps of the Bunker Hill Monument, and one rainy afternoon broke all rules by herding us into the South Boston Aquarium in order to give an unhealthy, eager, little lecture on the sewage-consumption of the conger eel. At last Miss Manice seemed to have gotten wind of Mr. Newell's moods. For an afternoon or two she herself served as his substitute. We were walked briskly past the houses of Parkman and Dana, and assigned themes on the spunk of great persons who had overcome physical handicaps and risen to the top of the ladder. She talked about Elizabeth Barrett, Helen Keller; her pet theory, however, was that "women simply are not the equals of men." I can hear Miss Manice browbeating my white and sheepish father, "How can we stand up to you? Where are our Archimedeses, our Wagners, our Admiral Simses?" Miss Manice adored "Sir Walter Scott's *big bow-wow*," wished "Boston had banned the tubercular novels of the Brontës," and found nothing in the world "so simpatico" as the "strenuous life" lived by President Roosevelt. Yet the extravagant hysteria of Miss Manice's philanthropy meant nothing; Brimmer was entirely a woman's world—*dummkopf*, perhaps, but not in the least Quixotic, Brimmer was ruled by a woman's obvious aims and by her naive pragmatism. The quality of this regime, an extension of my mother's, shone out in full glory at general assemblies or when I sat with a handful of other boys on the bleachers of Brimmer's new Manice Hall. In unison our big girls sang "America"; back and forth our amazons tramped—their brows were wooden, their dress was black and white, and their columns followed standard-bearers holding up an American flag, the white flag of the Commonwealth of Massachusetts, and the green flag of Brimmer. At basketball games against Miss Lee's or Miss Winsor's, it was our upper-school champions who rushed onto the floor, as feline and fateful in their pace as lions. This was our own immediate and daily spectacle; in comparison such masculine displays as trips to battle cruisers commanded by comrades of my father seemed eyewash—the Navy moved in a realm as ghostlike and removed from my life as the elfin acrobatics of Douglas Fairbanks or Peter Pan. I wished I were an older girl. I wrote Santa Claus for a field hockey stick. To be a boy at Brimmer was to be small, denied, and weak.

I was promised an improved future and taken on Sunday afternoon drives through the suburbs to inspect the boys' schools: Rivers, Dexter, Country Day. These expeditions were stratagems designed to give me a chance to know my father; Mother noisily stayed behind and amazed me by pretending that I had forbidden her to embark on "men's work." Father, however, seldom insisted, as he should have, on seeing the headmasters in person, yet he made an astonishing number of friends; his trust begat trust, and something about his silences encouraged junior masters and even school janitors to pour out small talk that was detrimental to rival institutions. At each new school, however, all this gossip was easily refuted; worse still Mother was always ready to cross-examine Father in a manner that showed that she was asking questions for the purpose of giving, not of receiving, instruction; she expressed astonishment that a wishy-washy desire to be everything to everybody had robbed a naval man of any reliable concern for his son's welfare. Mother regarded the suburban schools as "gerrymandered" and middle-class; after Father had completed his round of inspections, she made her own follow-up visits and told Mr. Dexter and Mr. Rivers to their faces that she was looking for a "respectable stop-gap" for her son's "three years between Brimmer and Saint Mark's." Saint Mark's was the boarding school for which I had been enrolled at birth, and was due to enter in 1930. I distrusted change, knew each school since kindergarten had been more constraining and punitive than its predecessor, and believed the suburban country day schools were flimsily disguised fronts for reformatories. With the egotistic, slightly paranoid apprehensions of an only child, I wondered what became of boys graduating from Brimmer's fourth grade, feared the worst—we were darkly imperiled, like some annual bevy of Athenian youths destined for the Minotaur. And to judge from my father, men between the ages of six and sixty did nothing but meet new challenges, take on heavier responsibilities, and lose all freedom to explode. A ray of hope in the far future was my white-haired Grandfather Winslow, whose unchecked commands and demands were always upsetting people for their own good—he was all I could ever want to be: the bad boy, the problem child, the commodore of his household.

When I entered Brimmer I was eight and a half. I was distracted in my studies, assented to whatever I was told, picked my nose whenever no one was watching, and worried our third-grade teacher by organizing creepy little gangs of boys at recess. I was girl-shy. Thick-witted, narcissistic, thuggish, I had the conventional prepuberty character of my age; whenever a girl came near me, my whole person cringed like a sponge wrung dry by a clenching fist. I was less rather than more bookish than most children, but the girl I dreamed about continually had wheel-spoke black and gold eyelashes, double-length page-boy blond hair, a little apron, a bold, blunt face, a saucy, shivery way of talking, and . . . a paper body—she was the girl in John Tenniel's illustrations to *Alice in Wonderland*. The invigorating and symmetrical aplomb of my ideal Alice was soon enriched and nullified by a second face, when my father took me to the movies on the afternoon of one of Mother's headaches. An innocuous child's movie, the bloody, all-male *Beau Geste* had been chosen, but instead my father preferred a nostalgic tour of places he had enjoyed on shore leave. We went to the Majestic Theater where he had first seen Pola Negri—where we too saw Pola Negri, sloppy-haired, slack, yawning, ravaged, unwashed . . . an Anti-Alice.

Our class belles, the Norton twins, Elie and Lindy, fell far short of the Nordic Alice and the foreign Pola. Their prettiness, rather fluffy, freckled, bashful, might have escaped notice if they had been one instead of two, and if their manners had been less goodhumored, entertaining, and reliable. What mattered more than sex, athletics, or studies to us at Brimmer was our popularity; each child had an unwritten class-popularity poll inside his head. Everyone was ranked, and all day each of us mooned profoundly on his place, as it quivered like our blood or a compass needle with a thousand revisions. At nine character is, perhaps, too much *in ovo* for a child to be strongly disliked, but sitting next to Elie Norton, I glanced at her and gulped prestige from her popularity. We were not close at first; then nearness made us closer friends, for Elie had a gracious gift, the gift of gifts, I suppose, in a child: she forgot all about the popularity-rank of the classmate she was talking to. No moron could have seemed so uncritical as this airy, chatty, intelligent child, the belle of our grade. She noticed my habit of cocking my head on one side, shutting my eyes, and driving like a bull through opposition at soccer—wishing to amuse without wounding, she called me Buffalo Bull. At general assembly she would giggle with contented admiration at the upper-school girls in their penal black and white. "What bruisers, what beef-eaters! Dear girls," she would sigh, parroting her sophisticated mother, "we shall all become fodder for the governess classes before graduating from Brimmer." I felt that Elie Norton understood me better than anyone except my playful little Grandmother Winslow.

One morning there was a disaster. The boy behind me, no friend, had been tapping at my elbow for over a minute to catch my attention before I consented to look up and see a great golden puddle spreading toward me from under Elie's chair. I dared not speak, smile, or flicker an eyelash in her direction. She ran bawling from the classroom. Trying to catch every eye, yet avoid commitment, I gave sidelong and involuntary smirks at space. I began to feel manic with superiority to Elie Norton and struggled to swallow down a feeling of goaded hollowness—was I deserting her?

Our teacher left us on our honor and ran down the hall. The class milled about in a hesitant hush. The girls blushed. The boys smirked. Miss Manice, the principal, appeared. She wore her whitish-brown dress with darker brown spots. Shimmering in the sunlight and chilling us, she stood moth-like in the middle of the classroom. We rushed to our seats. Miss Manice talked about how there was "nothing laughable about a malaise." She broke off. Her face took on an expression of invidious disgust. She was staring at me. . . . In the absentmindedness of my guilt and excitement, I had taken the nearest chair, the chair that Elie Norton had just left. "Lowell," Miss Manice shrieked, "are you going to soak there all morning like a bump on a log?"

When Elie Norton came back, there was really no break in her friendliness toward me, but there was something caved in, something crippled in the way I stood up to her and tried to answer her disengaged chatter. I thought about her all the time; seldom meeting her eyes now, I felt rich and raw in her nearness. I wanted passionately to stay on at Brimmer, and told my mother a fib one afternoon late in May of my last year. "Miss Manice has begged me to stay on," I said, "and enter the fifth grade." Mother pointed out that there had never been a boy in the fifth grade. Contradicted, I grew excited. "If Miss Manice has begged me to stay," I said, "why can't I stay?" My voice rose, I beat on the floor with my open hands. Bored and bewildered, my mother went upstairs with a headache. "If you won't believe me," I shouted after her, "why don't you telephone Miss Manice or Mrs. Norton?"

Brimmer School was thrown open on sunny March and April afternoons and our teachers took us for strolls on the polite, landscaped walks of the Public Garden. There I'd loiter by the old iron fence and gape longingly across Charles Street at the historic Boston Common, a now largely wrong-side-of-the-tracks park. On the Common there were mossy bronze reliefs of Union soldiers, and a captured German tank filled with smelly wads of newspaper. Everywhere there were grit, litter, gangs of Irish, Negroes, Latins. On Sunday afternoons orators harangued about Sacco and Vanzetti, while others stood about heckling and blocking the sidewalks. Keen young policemen, looking for trouble, lolled on the benches. At nightfall a police lieutenant on horseback inspected the Common. In the Garden, however, there was only Officer Lever, a single white-haired and mustached dignitary, who had once been the doorman at the Union Club.

He now looked more like a member of the club. "Lever's a man about town," my Grandfather Winslow would say. "Give him Harris tweeds and a glass of Scotch, and I'd take him for Cousin Herbert." Officer Lever was without thoughts or deeds, but Back Bay and Beacon Hill parents loved him just for being. No one asked this hollow and leonine King Log to be clairvoyant about children.

One day when the saucer magnolias were in bloom, I bloodied Bulldog Binney's nose against the pedestal of George Washington's statue in full view of Commonwealth Avenue; then I bloodied Dopey Dan Parker's nose; then I stood in the center of a sundial tulip bed and pelted a little enemy ring of third-graders with wet fertilizer. Officer Lever was telephoned. Officer Lever telephoned my mother. In the presence of my mother and some thirty nurses and children, I was expelled from the Public Garden. I was such a bad boy, I was told, "that *even* Officer Lever had been forced to put his foot down."

New England winters are long. Sunday mornings are long. Ours were often made tedious by preparations for dinner guests. Mother would start airing at nine. Whenever the air grew so cold that it hurt, she closed the den windows; then we were attacked by sour kitchen odors winding up a clumsily rebuilt dumb-waiter shaft. The windows were again thrown open. We sat in an atmosphere of glacial purity and sacrifice. Our breath puffed whitely. Father and I wore sleeveless cashmere jerseys Mother had bought at Filene's Basement. A do-it-yourself book containing diagrams for the correct carving of roasts lay on the arm of Father's chair. At hand were Big Bill Tilden on tennis, Capablanca on chess, newspaper clippings from Sidney Lenz's bridge column, and a magnificent tome with photographs and some American's nationalist sketch of Sir Thomas Lipton's errors in the Cup Defender races. Father made little progress in these diversions, and yet one of the authors assured him that mastery demanded only willing readers who understood the meaning of English words. Throughout the winter a gray-whiteness glared through the single den window. In the apoplectic brick alley, a fire escape stood out against our sooty plank fence. Father believed that churchgoing was undignified for a naval man; his Sunday mornings were given to useful acts such as lettering his three new galvanized garbage cans: R.T.S. LOWELL—U.S.N.

Our Sunday dinner guests were often naval officers. Naval officers were not Mother's sort; very few people *were* her sort in those days, and that was her trouble—a very authentic, human, and plausible difficulty, which made Mother's life one of much suffering. She did not have the self-assurance for wide human experience; she needed to feel liked, admired, surrounded by the approved and familiar. Her haughtiness and chilliness came from apprehension. She would start talking like a *grande dame* and then stand back rigid and faltering, as if she feared being crushed by her own massively intimidating offensive.

Father's old Annapolis roommate, Commander Billy "Battleship Bilge" Harkness, was a frequent guest at Revere Street and one that always threw Mother off balance. Billy was a rough diamond. He made jokes about his "all-American family tree," and insisted that his name, pronounced H*a*rkness, should be spelled H*e*rkness. He came from Louisville, Kentucky, drank whisky to "renew his Bourbon blood," and still spoke with an accent that sounded—so his colleagues said—"like a bran-fed stallion." Like my father, however, Commander Billy had entered the Naval Academy when he was a boy of fourteen; his Southernisms had been thoroughly rubbed away. He was teased for knowing nothing about race horses, mountaineers, folk ballads, hams, sour mash, tobacco . . . Kentucky Colonels. Though hardly an officer and a gentleman in the old Virginian style, he was an unusual combination of clashing virtues: he had led his class in the sciences and yet was what his superiors called "a *mathmaddition* with the habit of command." He and my father, the youngest men in their class, had often been shipmates. Bilge's executive genius had given color and direction to Father's submissive tenacity. He drank like a fish at parties, but was a total abstainer on duty. With reason Commander Harkness had been voted the man most likely to make a four-star admiral in the class of '07.

Billy called his wife *Jimmy* or *Jeems*, and had a rough friendly way of saying, "Oh, Jimmy's bright as a penny." Mrs. Harkness was an unpleasant rarity: she was the only naval officer's wife we knew who was also a college graduate. She had a flat flapper's figure, and hid her intelligence behind a nervous twitter of vulgarity and toadyism. "Charlotte," she would almost scream at Mother, "is this mirAGE, this MIRacle your *own* dining room!"

Then Mother might smile and answer in a distant, though cosy and amused, voice, "I usually manage to make myself pretty comfortable."

Mother's comfort was chic, romantic, impulsive. If her silver service shone, it shone with hectic perfection to rebuke the functional domesticity of naval wives. She had determined to make her *ambiance* beautiful and luxurious, but wanted neither her beauty nor her luxury unaccompanied. Beauty pursued too exclusively meant artistic fatuity of a kind made farcical by her Aunt Sarah Stark Winslow, a beauty too lofty and original ever to marry, a prima donna on the piano, too high-strung ever to give a public recital. Beauty alone meant the maudlin ignominy of having one's investments managed by interfering relatives. Luxury alone, on the other hand, meant for Mother the "paste and fool's-gold polish" that one met with in the foyer of the new Statler Hotel. She loathed the "undernourishment" of Professor Burckhard's Bauhaus modernism, yet in moments of pique she denounced our pompous Myers mahoganies as "suitable for politicians at the Bellevue Hotel." She kept a middle-of-the-road position, and much admired Italian pottery with its fresh peasant colors and puritanical, clean-cut lines. She was fond of saying, "The French *do* have taste," but spoke with a double-edged irony which implied the French, with no moral standards to support their finish, were really no better than naval yahoos. Mother's beautiful house was dignified by a rich veneer of the useful.

"I have always believed carving to be *the* gentlemanly talent," Mother used to proclaim. Father, faced with this opinion, pored over his book of instructions or read the section on table carving in the Encyclopædia Britannica. Eventually he discovered among the innumerable small, specialized Boston "colleges" an establishment known as a carving school. Each Sunday from then on he would sit silent and erudite before his roast. He blinked, grew white, looked winded, and wiped beads of perspiration from his eyebrows. His purpose was to reproduce stroke by stroke his last carving lesson, and he worked with all the formal rightness and particular error of some shaky experiment in remote control. He enjoyed quiet witticisms at the expense of his carving master—"a philosopher who gave himself all the airs of a Mahan!" He liked to pretend that the carving master had stated that "No two cuts are identical," *ergo*: "each offers original problems for the *executioner*." Guests were appeased by Father's saying, "I am just a plebe at this guillotine. Have a hunk of my roast beef hash."

What angered Father was Mrs. Harkness's voice grown merciless with excitement, as she studied his hewing and hacking. She was sure to say something tactless about how Commander Billy was "a stingy artist at carving who could shave General Washington off the dollar bill."

Nothing could stop Commander Billy, that born carver, from reciting verses:

> *"By carving my way*
> *I lived on my pay;*
> *This* reeward, *though small,*
> *Beats none at all . . .*
>
> *My carving paper-thin*
> *Can make a guinea* hin,
> *All giblets, bones, and skin,*
> *Canteen a party of* tin.*"*

And I, furious for no immediate reason, blurted out, "Mother, how much does Grandfather Winslow have to fork up to pay for Daddy's carving school?"

These Sunday dinners with the Harknesses were always woundingly boisterous affairs. Father, unnaturally outgoing, would lead me forward and say, "Bilge, I want you to meet my first coupon from the bond of matrimony."

Commander Billy would answer, "So this is the range-finder you are raising for future wars!" They would make me salute, stand at attention, stand at ease. "Angel-face," Billy would say to me, "you'll skipper a flivver."

"Jimmy" Harkness, of course, knew that Father was anxiously negotiating with Lever Brothers' Soap, and arranging for his resignation from the service, but nothing could prevent her from proposing time and again her "hens' toast to the drakes." Dragging Mother to her feet, Jimmy would scream, "To Bob and Bilgy's next battleship together!"

What Father and Commander Billy enjoyed talking about most was their class of '07. After dinner, the ladies would retire to the upstairs sitting room. As a special privilege I was allowed to remain at the table with the men. Over and over, they would talk about their ensigns' cruise around the world, escaping the "reeport," gunboating on the upper Yangtze during the Chinese Civil War, keeping sane and sanitary at Guantanamo, patroling the Golfo del Papayo during the two-bit Nicaraguan Revolution, when water to wash in cost a dollar a barrel and was mostly "alkali and wrigglers." There were the class casualties: Holden and Holcomb drowned in a foundered launch off Hampton Roads; "Count" Bowditch, killed by the Moros and famous for his dying words to Commander Harkness: "I'm all right. Get on the job, Bilge."

They would speak about the terrible 1918 influenza epidemic, which had killed more of their classmates than all the skirmishes or even the World War. It was an honor, however, to belong to a class which included "Chips" Carpender, whose destroyer, the *Fanning*, was the only British or American warship to force a German submarine to break water and surrender. It was a feather in their caps that three of their classmates, Bellinger, Reade, and another, should have made the first trans-Atlantic seaplane flight. They put their faith in teamwork, and Lindbergh's solo hop to Paris struck them as unprofessional, a newspaper trick. What made Father and Commander Billy mad as hornets was the mare's-nest made of naval administration by "deserving Democrats." Hadn't Secretary of State Bryan ordered their old battlewagon the *Idaho* to sail on a goodwill mission to Switzerland? "Bryan, Bryan, Bryan," Commander Billy would boom, "the pious swab had been told that Lake Geneva had annexed the Adriatic." Another "guy with false gills," Josephus Daniels, "ordained by Divine Providence Secretary of the Navy," had refused to send Father and Billy to the war zone. "You are looking," Billy would declaim, "at martyrs in the famous victory of red tape. Our names are rubric." A man they had to take their hats off to was Theodore Roosevelt; Billy had been one of the lucky ensigns who had helped "escort the redoubtable Teddy to Panama." Perhaps because of his viciously inappropriate nickname, "Bilge," Commander Harkness always spoke with brutal facetiousness against the class *bilgers*, officers whose "services were no longer required by the service." In more Epicurean moods, Bilge would announce that he "meant to accumulate a lot of dough from complacent, well-meaning, although misguided West Point officers gullible enough to bet their shirts on the Army football team."

"Let's have a squint at your *figger* and waterline, Bob," Billy would say. He'd admire Father's trim girth and smile familiarly at his bald spot. "Bob," he'd say, "you've maintained your displacement and silhouette unmodified, except for somewhat thinner top chafing gear."

Commander Billy's drinking was a "pain in the neck." He would take possession of Father's sacred "rhino" armchair, sprawl legs astraddle, make the tried and true framework groan, and crucify Mother by roaring out verbose toasts in what he called "me boozy cockney-h'Irish." He would drink to our cocktail shaker. " 'Ere's to the 'older of the Lowell-dom nectar," he would bellow. "Hip, hip, hooray for señor Martino, h'our h'old hipmate, 'elpmate, and hhonorary member of '07—h'always h'able to navigate and never says dry." We never got through a visit without one of Billy's "Bottoms up to the 'ead of the Nation. 'Ere's to herb-garden

'Erb." This was a swaggering dig at Herbert Hoover's notoriously correct, but insular, refusal to "imbibe anything more potent than Bromo-Seltzer" at a war-relief banquet in Brussels. Commander Billy's bulbous, water-on-the-brain forehead would glow and trickle with fury. Thinking on Herbert Hoover and Prohibition, he was unable to contain himself. "What a hick! We haven't been steered by a gentleman of parts since the redoubtable Teddy." He recited *wet* verses, such as the following inserted in Father's class book:

> *"I tread the bridge with measured pace;*
> *Proud, yet anguish marks my face—*
> *What worries me like crushing sin*
> *Is where on the sea can I buy dry gin?"*

In his cups, Commander Bilge acted as though he owned us. He looked like a human ash-heap. Cigar ashes buried the heraldic hedgehog on the ash tray beside him; cigar ashes spilled over and tarnished the golden stork embroidered on the table-cover; cigar ashes littered his own shiny blue-black uniform. Greedily Mother's eyes would brighten, drop and brighten. She would say darkly, "I was brought up by Papá to be like a naval officer, to be ruthlessly neat."

Once Commander Billy sprawled back so recklessly that the armchair began to come apart. "You see, Charlotte," he said to Mother, "at the height of my *climacteric* I am breaking Bob's chair."

Harkness went in for tiresome, tasteless harangues against Amy Lowell, which he seemed to believe necessary for the enjoyment of his after-dinner cigar. He would point a stinking baby stogie at Mother. " 'Ave a peteeto cigareeto, Charlotte," he would crow. "Puff on this whacking black cheroot, and you'll be a match for any reeking señorita *femme fatale* in the spiggotty republics, where blindness from Bob's bathtub hooch is still unknown. When you go up in smoke, Charlotte, remember the *Maine*. Remember Amy Lowell, that cigar-chawing, guffawing, senseless and meterless, multimillion-heiress, heavyweight mascot on a floating fortress. Damn the *Patterns*! Full speed ahead on a cigareeto!"

Amy Lowell was never a welcome subject in our household. Of course, no one spoke disrespectfully of Miss Lowell. She had been so plucky, so *formidable, so beautifully and unblushingly immense*, as Henry James might have said. And yet, though irreproachably decent herself apparently, like Mae West she seemed to provoke indecorum in others.

There was an anecdote which I was too young to understand: it was about Amy's getting her migraine headaches from being kept awake by the exercises of honeymooners in an adjacent New York hotel room. Amy's relatives would have liked to have honored her as a *personage*, a personage a little *outrée* perhaps, but perfectly within the natural order, like Amy's girlhood idol, the Duse. Or at least she might have been unambiguously tragic, short-lived, and a classic, like her last idol, John Keats. My parents piously made out a case for Miss Lowell's *Life of Keats*, which had killed its author and was so much more manly and intelligible than her poetry. Her poetry! But was *poetry* what one could call Amy's loud, bossy, unladylike *chinoiserie*—her free verse! For those that could understand it, her matter was, no doubt, blameless, but the effrontery of her manner made my parents relish Robert Frost's remark that "writing free verse was like playing tennis without a net."

Whenever Amy Lowell was mentioned Mother bridled. Not distinguishing, not caring whether her relative were praised or criticized, she would say, "Amy had the courage of her convictions. She worked like a horse." Mother would conclude characteristically, "Amy did insist on doing everything the *hard* way. I think, perhaps, that her brother, the President of Harvard, did more for *other* people."

Often Father seemed to pay little attention to the conversation of his guests. He would smack his lips, and beam absentmindedly and sensuously, as if he were anticipating the comforts of civilian life—a perpetual shore leave in Hawaii. The Harknesses, however, cowed him. He would begin to feel out the subject of his resignation and observe in a wheedle obscurely loaded with significance that "certain *cits*, no brighter than you or I, pay income taxes as large as a captain's yearly salary."

Commander Harkness, unfortunately, was inclined to draw improper conclusions from such remarks. Disregarding the "romance of commerce," he would break out into ungentlemanly tirades against capital. "Yiss, old Bob," he would splutter, "when I consider the ungodly hoards garnered in by the insurance and broking gangs, it breaks my heart. Riches, reaches, overreaches! If Bob and I had half the swag that Harkness of Yale has just given Lowell of Harvard to build Georgian houses for Boston quee-eers with British accents!" He rumbled on morosely about retired naval officers "forced to live like coolies on their half-pay. Hurrah for the Bull Moose Party!" he'd shout. "Hurrah for Boss Curley! Hurrah for the Bolshies!"

Nothing prevented Commander Billy from telling about his diplomatic mission in 1918, when "his eyes had seen the Bolshie on his native heath." He had been in Budapest "during the brief sway of Béla Kun-Whon. Béla was giving those Hunkyland money-bags and educators the boot into the arms of American philanthropy!"

Then Mother would say, hopefully, "Mamá always said that the *old* Hungarians *did* have taste. Billy, your reference to Budapest makes me heartsick for Europe. I am dying for Bob and Bobby's permission to spend next summer at Etretat."

Commander Billy Harkness specialized in verses like "The Croix de Guerre":

> *"I toast the guy, who, crossing over,*
> *Abode in London for a year,*
> *The guy who to his wife and lover*
> *Returned with conscience clean and clear,*
> *Who nightly prowling Piccadilly*
> *Gave icy stares to floozies wild,*
> *And when approached said, 'Bilgy Billy*
> *Is mama's darling angel child—'*
> *Now he's the guy who rates the croy dee geer!"*

Mother, however, smiled mildly. "Billy," she would say, "my cousin, Admiral Ledyard Atkinson, always has a twinkle in his eye when he asks after your *vers de société.*"

" 'Tommy' Atkins!" snorted Commander Billy. "I know Tommy better than my own mother. He's the first chapter in a book I'm secretly writing and leaving to the archives called *Wild Admirals I Have Known.* And now my bodily presence may no longer grace the inner sanctum of the Somerset Club, for fear Admiral Tommy'll assault me with five new chapters of his *Who Won the Battle of Jutland?*"

After the heat and push of Commander Billy, it was pleasant to sit in the shade of the Atkinsons. Cousin Ledyard wasn't exactly an admiral: he had been promoted to this rank during the World War and had soon reverted back to his old rank of captain. In 1926 he was approaching the retiring age and was still a captain. He was in charge of a big, stately, comfortable, but anomalous warship, which seldom sailed further than hailing distance from its Charlestown drydock. He was himself stately and anomalous. Serene, silver-maned, and Spanish-looking, Cousin Ledyard liked full-dress receptions and crowed like a rooster in his cabin crowded with liveried Filipinos, Cuban trophies, and racks of experimental firearms, such as pepper-box pistols and a machine gun worked by electric batteries. He rattled off Spanish phrases, told first-hand adventure stories about service with Admiral Schley, and reminded one of some landsman and diplomat commanding a galleon in Philip II's Armada. With his wife's money he had bought a motor launch which had a teak deck and a newfangled diesel engine. While his warship perpetually rode at anchor, Cousin Ledyard was forever hurrying about the harbor in his launch. "Oh, Led Atkinson has dash and his own speedboat!" This was about the best my father could bring himself to say for his relative. Commander Billy, himself a man of action, was more sympathetic: "Tommy's about a hundred horse and buggy power." Such a dinosaur, however, had little to offer an '07 Annapolis graduate. Billy's final judgment was that Cousin Ledyard knew less *trig* than a schoolgirl, had been promoted through mistaken identity or merely as "window-dressing," and "was really plotting to put airplane carriers in square sails to stem the tide of our declining Yankee seamanship." Mother lost her enthusiasm for Captain Atkinson's stately chatter—he was "unable to tell one woman from another."

Cousin Ledyard's wife, a Schenectady Hoes distantly related to my still living Great-Grandmother Myers, was twenty years younger than her husband. This made her a trying companion; with the energy of youth she demanded the homage due to age. Once while playing in the Mattapoisett tennis tournament, she had said to her opponent, a woman her own age but married to a young husband, "I believe I'll call you Ruth; you can call me Mrs. Atkinson." She was a radiant Christian Scientist, darted about in smart serge suits and blouses frothing with lace. She filled her purse with Science literature and boasted without irony of "Boston's greatest grand organ" in the Christian Science mother temple on Huntington Avenue. As a girl, she had grown up with our Myers furniture. We dreaded Mrs. Atkinson's descents on Revere Street. She pooh-poohed Mother's taste, snorted at our ignorance of Myers family history, treated us as mere custodians of the Myers furniture, resented alterations, and had the memory of a mastodon for Cousin Cassie's associations with each piece. She wouldn't hear of my mother's distress from neuralgia, dismissed my asthma as "growing-pains," and sought to rally us by gossiping about healers. She talked a prim, sprightly babble. Like many Christian Scientists, she had a bloodless, euphoric, inexhaustible interest in her own body. In a discourse which lasted from her first helping of roast beef through her second demitasse, Mrs. Atkinson held us spellbound by telling how her healer had "surprised and evaporated a cyst inside a sac" inside her "major intestine."

I can hear my father trying to explain his resignation from the Navy to Cousin Ledyard or Commander Billy. Talking with an unnatural and importunate jocularity, he would say, "Billy Boy, it's a darned shame, but this State of Massachusetts doesn't approve of the service using its franchise and voting by mail. I haven't had a chance to establish residence since our graduation in '07. I think I'll put my blues in mothballs and become a *cit* just to prove I still belong to the country. The directors of Lever Brothers' Soap in Cambridge . . . I guess for *cits*, Billy, they've really got something on the ball, because they tell me they want me on their team."

Or Father, Cousin Ledyard, Commander Billy, and I would be sitting on after dinner at the dining-room table and talking man to man. Father would say, "I'm afraid I'll grow dull and drab with all this goldbricking ashore. I am too old for tennis singles, but too young for that confirmed state of senility known as golf."

Cousin Ledyard and Commander Billy would puff silently on their cigars. Then Father would try again and say pitifully, "I don't think a naval man can ever on the *outside* replace the friends he made during his years of wearing the blue."

Then Cousin Ledyard would give Father a polite, funereal look and say, "Speaking of golf, Bob, you've hit me below the belt. I've been flubbing away at the game for thirty years without breaking ninety."

Commander Billy was blunter. He would chaff Father about becoming a "beachcomber" or "purser for the Republican junior chamber of commerce." He would pretend that Father was in danger of being jailed for evading taxes to support "Uncle Sam's circus." *Circus* was Commander Billy's slang for the Navy. The word reminded him of a comparison, and once he stood up from the table and bellowed solemnly: "Oyez, oyez! Bob Lowell, our bright boy, our class baby, is now on a par with 'Rattle-Ass Rats' Richardson, who resigned from us to become press agent for Sells-Floto Circus, and who writes me: 'Bilgy Dear—Beating the drum ahead of the elephants and the spangled folk, I often wonder why I run into so few of my classmates.' "

Those dinners, those apologies! Perhaps I exaggerate their embarassment because they hover so grayly in recollection and seem to anticipate ominously my father's downhill progress as a civilian and Bostonian. It was to be expected, I suppose, that Father should be in irons for a year or two, while becoming detached from his old comrades and interests, while waiting for the new life.

I used to sit through the Sunday dinners absorbing cold and anxiety from the table. I imagined myself hemmed in by our new, inherited Victorian Myers furniture. In the bleak Revere Street dining room, none of these pieces had at all that air of unhurried condescension that had been theirs behind the summery veils of tissue paper in Cousin Cassie Julian-James's memorial volume. Here, table, highboy, chairs, and screen—mahogany, cherry, teak—looked nervous and disproportioned. They seemed to wince, touch elbows, shift from foot to foot. High above the highboy, our gold National Eagle stooped forward, plastery and doddering. The Sheffield silver-plate urns, more precious than solid sterling, peeled; the bodies of the heraldic mermaids on the Mason-Myers crest blushed a metallic copper tan. In the harsh New England light, the bronze sphinxes supporting our sideboard looked as though manufactured in Grand Rapids. All too clearly no one had worried about synchronizing the grandfather clock's minutes, days, and months with its mellow old Dutch seascape-painted discs for showing the phases of the moon. The stricken, but still striking gong made sounds like steam banging through pipes. Colonel Myers' monumental Tibetan screen had been impiously shortened to fit it for a low Yankee ceiling. And now, rough and gawky, like some Hindu water buffalo killed in mid-rush but still alive with mad momentum, the screen hulked over us . . . and hid the pantry sink.

Our real blue-ribbon-winning *bête noire* was of course the portrait of Cousin Cassie's father, Mordecai Myers' fourth and most illustrious son: Colonel Theodorus Bailey Myers. The Colonel, like half of our new portraits, was merely a collateral relation; though really as close to us as James Russell Lowell, no one called the Colonel "Great Grand Uncle," and Mother playfully pretended that her mind was overstrained by having to remember his full name, rank, and connection. In the portrait, Colonel Theodorus wore a black coat and gray trousers, an obsequiously conservative costume which one associated with undertakers and the musicians at Symphony Hall. His spats were pearl gray plush with pearl buttons. His mustache might have been modeled on the mustache of a bartender in a Western. The majestic Tibetan screen enclosed him as though he were an ancestor-god from Lhasa, a blasphemous yet bogus attitude. Mr. Myers' colonel's tabs were crudely stitched to a civilian coat; his New York Yacht Club button glowed like a carnation; his vainglorious picture frame was a foot and a half wide. Forever, his right hand hovered over a glass dome that covered a model locomotive. He was vaguely Middle-Eastern and waiting. A lady in Mother's sewing circle had pertly interpreted this portrait as, "King Solomon about to receive the Queen of Sheba's shares in the Boston and Albany Railroad." Gone now was the Colonel's place of honor at Cousin Cassie's Washington mansion; gone was his charming satire on the belles of 1850, entitled, *Nothing to Wear*, which had once been quoted "throughout the length and breadth of the land as generally as was Bret Harte's *Heathen Chinee*"; gone was his priceless collection of autographed letters of *all* the Signers of the Declaration of Independence—he had said once, "my letters will be my tombstone." Colonel Theodorus Bailey Myers had never been a New Englander. His family tree reached to no obscure Somersetshire yeoman named Winslowe or Lowle. He had never even, like his father, Mordecai, gloried in a scarlet War of 1812 waistcoat. His portrait was an indifferent example from a dull, bad period. The Colonel's only son had sheepishly changed his name from Mason-Myers to Myers-Mason.

Waiting for dinner to end and for the guests to leave, I used to lean forward on my elbows, support each cheekbone with a thumb, and make my fingers meet in a clumsy Gothic arch across my forehead. I would stare through this arch and try to make life stop. Out in the alley the sun shone irreverently on our three garbage cans lettered: R.T.S. LOWELL—U.S.N. When I shut my eyes to stop the sun, I saw first an orange disc, then a red disc, then the portrait of Major Myers apotheosized, as it were, by the sunlight lighting the blood smear of his scarlet waistcoat. Still there was no *coup de théâtre* about the Major as he looked down on us with his portly young man's face of a comfortable upper New York State patroon and the friend of Robert Livingston and Martin Van Buren. Great-great-Grandfather Myers had never frowned down in judgment on a Salem witch. There was no allegory in his eyes, no *Mayflower*. Instead he looked peacefully at his sideboard, his cut-glass decanters, his cellaret—the worldly bosom of the Mason-Myers mermaid engraved on a silver-plated urn. If he could have spoken, Mordecai would have said, "My children, my blood, accept graciously the loot of your inheritance. We are all dealers in used furniture."

The man who seems in my memory to sit under old Mordecai's

portrait is not my father, but Commander Billy—*the* Commander after Father had thrown in his commission. There Billy would sit glowing, perspiring, bragging. Despite his rowdiness, he even then breathed the power that would make him a vice-admiral and hero in World War II. I can hear him boasting in lofty language of how he had stood up for democracy in the day of Lenin and Béla Kun; of how he "practiced the sport of kings" (i.e., commanded a destroyer) and combed the Mediterranean, Adriatic, and Black Seas like gypsies—seldom knowing what admiral he served under or where his next meal or load of fuel oil was coming from.

It always vexed the Commander, however, to think of the strings that had been pulled to have Father transferred from Washington to Boston. He would ask Mother, "Why in God's name should a man with Bob's brilliant cerebellum go and mess up his record by actually *begging* for that impotent field nigger's job of second in command at the defunct Boston Yard!"

I would squirm. I dared not look up because I knew that the Commander abhorred Mother's dominion over my father, thought my asthma, supposedly brought on by the miasmal damp of Washington, a myth, and considered our final flight to Boston a scandal.

My mother, on the other hand, would talk back sharply and explain to Billy that there was nothing second-string about the Boston Yard except its commandant, Admiral De Stahl, who had gone into a frenzy when he learned that my parents, supposed to live at the naval yard, had set themselves up without his permission at 91 Revere Street. The Admiral had *commanded* Father to reside at the yard, but Mother had bravely and stubbornly held on at Revere Street.

"A really great person," she would say, "knows how to be courteous to his superiors."

Then Commander Harkness would throw up his hands in despair and make a long buffoonish speech. "Would you believe it?" he'd say. "De Stahl, the anile slob, would make Bob Lowell sleep seven nights a week and twice on Sundays in that venerable twenty-room pile provided for his third in command at the yard. 'Bobby me boy,' the Man says, 'henceforth I will that you sleep wifeless. You're to push your beauteous mug into me boudoir each night at ten-thirty and each morn at six. And don't mind me laying to alongside the Missus De Stahl,' the old boy squeaks; 'we're just two oldsters as weak as babies. But Robbie Boy,' he says, 'don't let me hear of you hanging on your telephone wire and bending off the ear of that forsaken frau of yours sojourning on Revere Street. I might have to phone you in a hurry, if I should happen to have me stroke.' "

Taking hold of the table with both hands, the Commander tilted his chair backwards and gaped down at me with sorrowing Gargantuan wonder: "I know why Young Bob is an only child."

Part Three

Ford Madox Ford

(1873–1939)

The lobbed ball plops, then dribbles to the cup. . . .
(a birdie Fordie!) But it nearly killed
the ministers. Lloyd George was holding up
the flag. He gabbled, "Hop-toad, hop-toad, hop-toad!
Hueffer has used a niblick on the green;
it's filthy art, Sir, filthy art!"
You answered, "What is art to me and thee?
Will a blacksmith teach a midwife how to bear?"
That cut the puffing statesman down to size,
Ford. You said, "Otherwise,
I would have been general of a division." Ah Ford!
Was it war, the sport of kings, that your *Good Soldier*,
the best French novel in the language, taught
those Georgian Whig magnificoes at Oxford,
at Oxford decimated on the Somme?
Ford, five times black-balled for promotion,
then mustard gassed voiceless some seven miles
behind the lines at Nancy or Belleau Wood:
you emerged in your "worn uniform,
gilt dragons on the revers of the tunic,"
a Jonah—O divorced, divorced
from the whale-fat of post-war London! Boomed,
cut, plucked and booted! In Provence, New York . . .
marrying, blowing . . . nearly dying
at Boulder, when the altitude
pressed the world on your heart,
and your audience, almost football-size,
shrank to a dozen, while you stood
mumbling, with fish-blue-eyes,
and mouth pushed out
fish-fashion, as if you gagged for air. . . .
Sandman! Your face, a childish *O*. The sun
is pernod-yellow and it gilds the heirs
of all the ages there on Washington

and Stuyvesant, your Lilliputian squares,
where writing turned your pockets inside out.
But master, mammoth mumbler, tell me why
the bales of your left-over novels buy
less than a bandage for your gouty foot.
Wheel-horse, O unforgetting elephant,
I hear you huffing at your old Brevoort,
Timon and Falstaff, while you heap the board
for publishers. Fiction! I'm selling short
your lies that made the great your equals. Ford,
you were a kind man and you died in want.

For George Santayana

(1863–1952)

In the heydays of 'forty-five,
bus-loads of souvenir-deranged
G.I.'s and officer-professors of philosophy
came crashing through your cell,
puzzled to find you still alive,
free-thinking Catholic infidel,
stray spirit, who'd found
the Church too good to be believed.
Later I used to dawdle
past Circus and Mithraic Temple
to *Santo Stefano* grown paper-thin
like you from waiting. . . .
There at the monastery hospital,
you wished those geese-girl sisters wouldn't bother
their heads and yours by praying for your soul:
"There is no God and Mary is His Mother."

Lying outside the consecrated ground
forever now, you smile
like Ser Brunetto running for the green
cloth at Verona—not like one
who loses, but like one who'd won . . .
as if your long pursuit of Socrates'
demon, man-slaying Alcibiades,
the demon of philosophy, at last had changed
those fleeting virgins into friendly laurel trees
at *Santo Stefano Rotondo*, when you died
near ninety,
still unbelieving, unconfessed and unreceived,
true to your boyish shyness of the Bride.
Old trooper, I see your child's red crayon pass,
bleeding deletions on the galleys you hold

under your throbbing magnifying glass,
that worn arena, where the whirling sand
and broken-hearted lions lick your hand
refined by bile as yellow as a lump of gold.

To Delmore Schwartz

(Cambridge 1946)

We couldn't even keep the furnace lit!
Even when we had disconnected it,
the antiquated
refrigerator gurgled mustard gas
through your mustard-yellow house,
and spoiled our long maneuvered visit
from T. S. Eliot's brother, Henry Ware. . . .

Your stuffed duck craned toward Harvard from my trunk:
its bill was a black whistle, and its brow
was high and thinner than a baby's thumb;
its webs were tough as toenails on its bough.
It was your first kill; you had rushed it home,
pickled in a tin wastebasket of rum—
it looked through us, as if it'd died dead drunk.
You must have propped its eyelids with a nail,
and yet it lived with us and met our stare,
Rabelaisian, lubricious, drugged. And there,
perched on my trunk and typing-table,
it cooled our universal
Angst a moment, Delmore. We drank and eyed
the chicken-hearted shadows of the world.
Underseas fellows, nobly mad,
we talked away our friends. "Let Joyce and Freud,
the Masters of Joy,
be our guests here," you said. The room was filled
with cigarette smoke circling the paranoid,
inert gaze of Coleridge, back
from Malta—his eyes lost in flesh, lips baked and black.
Your tiger kitten, *Oranges*,
cartwheeled for joy in a ball of snarls.
You said:
*"We poets in our youth begin in sadness;
thereof in the end come despondency and madness;*

Stalin has had two cerebral hemorrhages!"
The Charles
River was turning silver. In the ebb-
light of morning, we stuck
the duck
-'s web-
foot, like a candle, in a quart of gin we'd killed.

Words for Hart Crane

"When the Pulitzers showered on some dope
or screw who flushed our dry mouths out with soap,
few people would consider why I took
to stalking sailors, and scattered Uncle Sam's
phoney gold-plated laurels to the birds.
Because I knew my Whitman like a book,
stranger in America, tell my country: I,
Catullus redivivus, once the rage
of the Village and Paris, used to play my role
of homosexual, wolfing the stray lambs
who hungered by the Place de la Concorde.
My profit was a pocket with a hole.
Who asks for me, the Shelley of my age,
must lay his heart out for my bed and board."

Part Four

LIFE STUDIES

I

My Last Afternoon with Uncle Devereux Winslow

1922: the stone porch of my Grandfather's summer house

I.
"I won't go with you. I want to stay with Grandpa!"
That's how I threw cold water
on my Mother and Father's
watery martini pipe dreams at Sunday dinner.
. . . Fontainebleau, Mattapoisett, Puget Sound. . . .
Nowhere was anywhere after a summer
at my Grandfather's farm.
Diamond-pointed, athirst and Norman,
its alley of poplars
paraded from Grandmother's rose garden
to a scary stand of virgin pine,
scrub, and paths forever pioneering.

One afternoon in 1922,
I sat on the stone porch, looking through
screens as black-grained as drifting coal.
Tockytock, tockytock
clumped our Alpine, Edwardian cuckoo clock,
slung with strangled, wooden game.
Our farmer was cementing a root-house under the hill.
One of my hands was cool on a pile
of black earth, the other warm
on a pile of lime. All about me
were the works of my Grandfather's hands:
snapshots of his *Liberty Bell* silver mine;
his high school at *Stukkert am Neckar*;
stogie-brown beams; fools'-gold nuggets;
octagonal red tiles,
sweaty with a secret dank, crummy with ant-stale;
a Rocky Mountain chaise longue,

its legs, shellacked saplings.
A pastel-pale Huckleberry Finn
fished with a broom straw in a basin
hollowed out of a millstone.
Like my Grandfather, the décor
was manly, comfortable,
overbearing, disproportioned.

What were those sunflowers? Pumpkins floating shoulder-high?
It was sunset, Sadie and Nellie
bearing pitchers of ice-tea,
oranges, lemons, mint, and peppermints,
and the jug of shandygaff,
which Grandpa made by blending half and half
yeasty, wheezing homemade sarsaparilla with beer.
The farm, entitled *Char-de-sa*
in the Social Register,
was named for my Grandfather's children:
Charlotte, Devereux, and Sarah.
No one had died there in my lifetime . . .
Only Cinder, our Scottie puppy
paralyzed from gobbling toads.
I sat mixing black earth and lime.

II.
I was five and a half.
My formal pearl gray shorts
had been worn for three minutes.
My perfection was the Olympian
poise of my models in the imperishable autumn
display windows
of Rogers Peet's boys' store below the State House
in Boston. Distorting drops of water
pinpricked my face in the basin's mirror.
I was a stuffed toucan
with a bibulous, multicolored beak.

III.
Up in the air
by the lakeview window in the billiards-room,
lurid in the doldrums of the sunset hour,
my Great Aunt Sarah
was learning *Samson and Delilah.*
She thundered on the keyboard of her dummy piano,
with gauze curtains like a boudoir table,
accordionlike yet soundless.
It had been bought to spare the nerves
of my Grandmother,
tone-deaf, quick as a cricket,
now needing a fourth for "Auction,"
and casting a thirsty eye
on Aunt Sarah, risen like the phoenix
from her bed of troublesome snacks and Tauchnitz classics.

Forty years earlier,
twenty, auburn headed,
grasshopper notes of genius!
Family gossip says Aunt Sarah
tilted her archaic Athenian nose
and jilted an Astor.
Each morning she practiced
on the grand piano at Symphony Hall,
deathlike in the off-season summer—
its naked Greek statues draped with purple
like the saints in Holy Week. . . .
On the recital day, she failed to appear.

IV.
I picked with a clean finger nail at the blue anchor
on my sailor blouse washed white as a spinnaker.
What in the world was I wishing?
. . . A sail-colored horse browsing in the bulrushes . . .
A fluff of the west wind puffing
my blouse, kiting me over our seven chimneys,
troubling the waters. . . .

As small as sapphires were the ponds: *Quittacus, Snippituit,*
and *Assawompset,* halved by "the Island,"
where my Uncle's duck blind
floated in a barrage of smoke-clouds.
Double-barrelled shotguns
stuck out like bundles of baby crow-bars.
A single sculler in a camouflaged kayak
was quacking to the decoys. . . .

At the cabin between the waters,
the nearest windows were already boarded.
Uncle Devereux was closing camp for the winter.
As if posed for "the engagement photograph,"
he was wearing his severe
war-uniform of a volunteer Canadian officer.
Daylight from the doorway riddled his student posters,
tacked helter-skelter on walls as raw as a boardwalk.
Mr. Punch, a watermelon in hockey tights,
was tossing off a decanter of Scotch.
La Belle France in a red, white and blue toga
was accepting the arm of her "protector,"
the ingenu and porcine Edward VII.
The pre-war music hall belles
had goose necks, glorious signatures, beauty-moles,
and coils of hair like rooster tails.
The finest poster was two or three young men in khaki kilts
being bushwhacked on the veldt—
They were almost life-size. . . .

My Uncle was dying at twenty-nine.
"You are behaving like children,"
said my Grandfather,
when my Uncle and Aunt left their three baby daughters,
and sailed for Europe on a last honeymoon . . .
I cowered in terror.
I wasn't a child at all—
unseen and all-seeing, I was Agrippina
in the Golden House of Nero. . . .
Near me was the white measuring-door

my Grandfather had pencilled with my Uncle's heights.
In 1911, he had stopped growing at just six feet.
While I sat on the tiles,
and dug at the anchor on my sailor blouse,
Uncle Devereux stood behind me.
He was as brushed as Bayard, our riding horse.
His face was putty.
His blue coat and white trousers
grew sharper and straighter.
His coat was a blue jay's tail,
his trousers were solid cream from the top of the bottle.
He was animated, hierarchical,
like a gingersnap man in a clothes-press.
He was dying of the incurable Hodgkin's disease. . . .
My hands were warm, then cool, on the piles
of earth and lime,
a black pile and a white pile. . . .
Come winter,
Uncle Devereux would blend to the one color.

Dunbarton

My Grandfather found
his grandchild's fogbound solitudes
sweeter than human society.

When Uncle Devereux died,
Daddy was still on sea-duty in the Pacific;
it seemed spontaneous and proper
for Mr. MacDonald, the farmer,
Karl, the chauffeur, and even my Grandmother
to say, "your Father." They meant my Grandfather.

He was my Father. I was his son.
On our yearly autumn get-aways from Boston
to the family graveyard in Dunbarton,
he took the wheel himself—
like an admiral at the helm.
Freed from Karl and chuckling over the gas he was saving,
he let his motor roller-coaster
out of control down each hill.
We stopped at the *Priscilla* in Nashua
for brownies and root-beer,
and later "pumped ship" together in the Indian Summer. . . .

At the graveyard, a suave Venetian Christ
gave a sheepdog's nursing patience
to Grandfather's Aunt Lottie,
his Mother, the stone but not the bones
of his Father, Francis.
Failing as when Francis Winslow could count
them on his fingers,
the clump of virgin pine still stretched patchy ostrich necks
over the disused millpond's fragrantly woodstained water,
a reddish blur,
like the ever-blackening wine-dark coat

in our portrait of Edward Winslow
once sheriff for George the Second,
the sire of bankrupt Tories.

Grandfather and I
raked leaves from our dead forebears,
defied the dank weather
with "dragon" bonfires.

Our helper, Mr. Burroughs,
had stood with Sherman at Shiloh—
his thermos of shockless coffee
was milk and grounds;
his illegal home-made claret
was as sugary as grape jelly
in a tumbler capped with paraffin.

I borrowed Grandfather's cane
carved with the names and altitudes
of Norwegian mountains he had scaled—
more a weapon than a crutch.
I lanced it in the fauve ooze for newts.
In a tobacco tin after capture, the umber yellow mature newts
lost their leopard spots,
lay grounded as numb
as scrolls of candied grapefruit peel.
I saw myself as a young newt,
neurasthenic, scarlet
and wild in the wild coffee-colored water.

In the mornings I cuddled like a paramour
in my Grandfather's bed,
while he scouted about the chattering greenwood stove.

Grandparents

They're altogether otherworldly now,
those adults champing for their ritual Friday spin
to pharmacist and five-and-ten in Brockton.
Back in my throw-away and shaggy span
of adolescence, Grandpa still waves his stick
like a policeman;
Grandmother, like a Mohammedan, still wears her thick
lavender mourning and touring veil;
the Pierce Arrow clears its throat in a horse-stall.
Then the dry road dust rises to whiten
the fatigued elm leaves—
the nineteenth century, tired of children, is gone.
They're all gone into a world of light; the farm's my own.

The farm's my own!
Back there alone,
I keep indoors, and spoil another season.
I hear the rattley little country gramophone
racking its five foot horn:
"O Summer Time!"
Even at noon here the formidable
Ancien Régime still keeps nature at a distance. Five
green shaded light bulbs spider the billiards-table;
no field is greener than its cloth,
where Grandpa, dipping sugar for us both,
once spilled his demitasse.
His favorite ball, the number three,
still hides the coffee stain.

Never again
to walk there, chalk our cues,
insist on shooting for us both.
Grandpa! Have me, hold me, cherish me!
Tears smut my fingers. There

half my life-lease later,
I hold an *Illustrated London News*—;
disloyal still,
I doodle handlebar
mustaches on the last Russian Czar.

Commander Lowell

(1887–1950)

There were no undesirables or girls in my set,
when I was a boy at Mattapoisett—
only Mother, still her Father's daughter.
Her voice was still electric
with a hysterical, unmarried panic,
when she read to me from the Napoleon book.
Long-nosed Marie Louise
Hapsburg in the frontispiece
had a downright Boston bashfulness,
where she grovelled to Bonaparte, who scratched his navel,
and bolted his food—just my seven years tall!
And I, bristling and manic,
skulked in the attic,
and got two hundred French generals by name,
from *A* to *V*—from Augereau to Vandamme.
I used to dope myself asleep,
naming those unpronounceables like sheep.

Having a naval officer
for my Father was nothing to shout
about to the summer colony at "Matt."
He wasn't at all "serious,"
when he showed up on the golf course,
wearing a blue serge jacket and numbly cut
white ducks he'd bought
at a Pearl Harbor commissariat. . .
and took four shots with his putter to sink his putt.
"Bob," they said, "golf's a game you really ought to know how to play,
if you play at all."
They wrote him off as "naval,"
naturally supposed his sport was sailing.
Poor Father, his training was engineering!
Cheerful and cowed

among the seadogs at the Sunday yacht club,
he was never one of the crowd.

"Anchors aweigh," Daddy boomed in his bathtub,
"Anchors aweigh,"
when Lever Brothers offered to pay
him double what the Navy paid.
I nagged for his dress sword with gold braid,
and cringed because Mother, new
caps on all her teeth, was born anew
at forty. With seamanlike celerity,
Father left the Navy,
and deeded Mother his property.

He was soon fired. Year after year,
he still hummed "Anchors aweigh" in the tub—
whenever he left a job,
he bought a smarter car.
Father's last employer
was Scudder, Stevens and Clark, Investment Advisors,
himself his only client.
While Mother dragged to bed alone,
read Menninger,
and grew more and more suspicious,
he grew defiant.
Night after night,
à la clarté déserte de sa lampe,
he slid his ivory Annapolis slide rule
across a pad of graphs—
piker speculations! In three years
he squandered sixty thousand dollars.

Smiling on all,
Father was once successful enough to be lost
in the mob of ruling-class Bostonians.
As early as 1928,
he owned a house converted to oil,
and redecorated by the architect

of St. Mark's School. . . . Its main effect
was a drawing room, "longitudinal as Versailles,"
its ceiling, roughened with oatmeal, was blue as the sea.
And once
nineteen, the youngest ensign in his class,
he was "the old man" of a gunboat on the Yangtze.

Terminal Days at Beverly Farms

At Beverly Farms, a portly, uncomfortable boulder
bulked in the garden's center—
an irregular Japanese touch.
After his Bourbon "old fashioned," Father,
bronzed, breezy, a shade too ruddy,
swayed as if on deck-duty
under his six pointed star-lantern—
last July's birthday present.
He smiled his oval Lowell smile,
he wore his cream gabardine dinner-jacket,
and indigo cummerbund.
His head was efficient and hairless,
his newly dieted figure was vitally trim.

Father and Mother moved to Beverly Farms
to be a two minute walk from the station,
half an hour by train from the Boston doctors.
They had no sea-view,
but sky-blue tracks of the commuters' railroad shone
like a double-barrelled shotgun
through the scarlet late August sumac,
multiplying like cancer
at their garden's border.

Father had had two coronaries.
He still treasured underhand economies,
but his best friend was his little black *Chevie*,
garaged like a sacrificial steer
with gilded hooves,
yet sensationally sober,
and with less side than an old dancing pump.
The local dealer, a "buccaneer,"
had been bribed a "king's ransom"
to quickly deliver a car without chrome.

Each morning at eight-thirty,
inattentive and beaming,
loaded with his "calc" and "trig" books,
his clipper ship statistics,
and his ivory slide rule,
Father stole off with the *Chevie*
to loaf in the Maritime Museum at Salem.
He called the curator
"the commander of the Swiss Navy."

Father's death was abrupt and unprotesting.
His vision was still twenty-twenty.
After a morning of anxious, repetitive smiling,
his last words to Mother were:
"I feel awful."

Father's Bedroom

In my Father's bedroom:
blue threads as thin
as pen-writing on the bedspread,
blue dots on the curtains,
a blue kimono,
Chinese sandals with blue plush straps.
The broad-planked floor
had a sandpapered neatness.
The clear glass bed-lamp
with a white doily shade
was still raised a few
inches by resting on volume two
of Lafcadio Hearn's
Glimpses of Unfamiliar Japan.
Its warped olive cover
was punished like a rhinoceros hide.
In the flyleaf:
"Robbie from Mother."
Years later in the same hand:
"This book has had hard usage
on the Yangtze River, China.
It was left under an open
porthole in a storm."

For Sale

Poor sheepish plaything,
organized with prodigal animosity,
lived in just a year—
my Father's cottage at Beverly Farms
was on the market the month he died.
Empty, open, intimate,
its town-house furniture
had an on tiptoe air
of waiting for the mover
on the heels of the undertaker.
Ready, afraid
of living alone till eighty,
Mother mooned in a window,
as if she had stayed on a train
one stop past her destination.

Sailing Home from Rapallo

(February 1954)

Your nurse could only speak Italian,
but after twenty minutes I could imagine your final week,
and tears ran down my cheeks. . . .

When I embarked from Italy with my Mother's body,
the whole shoreline of the *Golfo di Genova*
was breaking into fiery flower.
The crazy yellow and azure sea-sleds
blasting like jack-hammers across
the *spumante*-bubbling wake of our liner,
recalled the clashing colors of my Ford.
Mother travelled first-class in the hold;
her *Risorgimento* black and gold casket
was like Napoleon's at the *Invalides*. . . .

While the passengers were tanning
on the Mediterranean in deck-chairs,
our family cemetery in Dunbarton
lay under the White Mountains
in the sub-zero weather.
The graveyard's soil was changing to stone—
so many of its deaths had been midwinter.
Dour and dark against the blinding snowdrifts,
its black brook and fir trunks were as smooth as masts.
A fence of iron spear-hafts
black-bordered its mostly Colonial grave-slates.
The only "unhistoric" soul to come here
was Father, now buried beneath his recent
unweathered pink-veined slice of marble.
Even the Latin of his Lowell motto:
Occasionem cognosce,
seemed too businesslike and pushing here,
where the burning cold illuminated
the hewn inscriptions of Mother's relatives:

twenty or thirty Winslows and Starks.
Frost had given their names a diamond edge. . . .

In the grandiloquent lettering on Mother's coffin,
Lowell had been misspelled *LOVEL*.
The corpse
was wrapped like *panettone* in Italian tinfoil.

During Fever

All night the crib creaks;
home from the healthy country to the sick city,
my daughter in fever
flounders in her chicken-colored sleeping bag.
"Sorry," she mumbles like her dim-bulb father, "sorry."

Mother, Mother!
as a gemlike undergraduate,
part criminal and yet a Phi Bete,
I used to barge home late.
Always by the bannister
my milk-tooth mug of milk
was waiting for me on a plate
of Triskets.
Often with unadulterated joy,
Mother, we bent by the fire
rehashing Father's character—
when he thought we were asleep,
he'd tiptoe down the stairs
and chain the door.

Mother, your master-bedroom
looked away from the ocean.
You had a window-seat,
an electric blanket,
a silver hot water bottle
monogrammed like a hip-flask,
Italian china fruity
with bunches and berries
and proper *putti*.
Gold, yellow and green,
the nuptial bed
was as big as a bathroom.

Born ten years and yet an aeon
too early for the twenties,
Mother, you smile
as if you saw your Father
inches away yet hidden, as when he groused behind a screen
over a National Geographic Magazine,
whenever young men came to court you
back in those settled years of World War One.
Terrible that old life of decency
without unseemly intimacy
or quarrels, when the unemancipated woman
still had her Freudian papá and maids!

Waking in the Blue

The night attendant, a B.U. sophomore,
rouses from the mare's-nest of his drowsy head
propped on *The Meaning of Meaning*.
He catwalks down our corridor.
Azure day
makes my agonized blue window bleaker.
Crows maunder on the petrified fairway.
Absence! My heart grows tense
as though a harpoon were sparring for the kill.
(This is the house for the "mentally ill.")

What use is my sense of humor?
I grin at Stanley, now sunk in his sixties,
once a Harvard all-American fullback,
(if such were possible!)
still hoarding the build of a boy in his twenties,
as he soaks, a ramrod
with the muscle of a seal
in his long tub,
vaguely urinous from the Victorian plumbing.
A kingly granite profile in a crimson golf-cap,
worn all day, all night,
he thinks only of his figure,
of slimming on sherbet and ginger ale—
more cut off from words than a seal.

This is the way day breaks in Bowditch Hall at McLean's;
the hooded night lights bring out "Bobbie,"
Porcellian '29,
a replica of Louis XVI
without the wig—
redolent and roly-poly as a sperm whale,
as he swashbuckles about in his birthday suit
and horses at chairs.

These victorious figures of bravado ossified young.

In between the limits of day,
hours and hours go by under the crew haircuts
and slightly too little nonsensical bachelor twinkle
of the Roman Catholic attendants.
(There are no Mayflower
screwballs in the Catholic Church.)

After a hearty New England breakfast,
I weigh two hundred pounds
this morning. Cock of the walk,
I strut in my turtle-necked French sailor's jersey
before the metal shaving mirrors,
and see the shaky future grow familiar
in the pinched, indigenous faces
of these thoroughbred mental cases,
twice my age and half my weight.
We are all old-timers,
each of us holds a locked razor.

Home After Three Months Away

Gone now the baby's nurse,
a lioness who ruled the roost
and made the Mother cry.
She used to tie
gobbets of porkrind in bowknots of gauze—
three months they hung like soggy toast
on our eight foot magnolia tree,
and helped the English sparrows
weather a Boston winter.

Three months, three months!
Is Richard now himself again?
Dimpled with exaltation,
my daughter holds her levee in the tub.
Our noses rub,
each of us pats a stringy lock of hair—
they tell me nothing's gone.
Though I am forty-one,
not forty now, the time I put away
was child's-play. After thirteen weeks
my child still dabs her cheeks
to start me shaving. When
we dress her in her sky-blue corduroy,
she changes to a boy,
and floats my shaving brush
and washcloth in the flush. . . .
Dearest, I cannot loiter here
in lather like a polar bear.

Recuperating, I neither spin nor toil.
Three stories down below,
a choreman tends our coffin's length of soil,
and seven horizontal tulips blow.
Just twelve months ago,

these flowers were pedigreed
imported Dutchmen; now no one need
distinguish them from weed.
Bushed by the late spring snow,
they cannot meet
another year's snowballing enervation.

I keep no rank nor station.
Cured, I am frizzled, stale and small.

II

Memories of West Street and Lepke

Only teaching on Tuesdays, book-worming
in pajamas fresh from the washer each morning,
I hog a whole house on Boston's
"hardly passionate Marlborough Street,"
where even the man
scavenging filth in the back alley trash cans,
has two children, a beach wagon, a helpmate,
and is a "young Republican."
I have a nine months' daughter,
young enough to be my granddaughter.
Like the sun she rises in her flame-flamingo infants' wear.

These are the tranquillized *Fifties*,
and I am forty. Ought I to regret my seedtime?
I was a fire-breathing Catholic C.O.,
and made my manic statement,
telling off the state and president, and then
sat waiting sentence in the bull pen
beside a Negro boy with curlicues
of marijuana in his hair.

Given a year,
I walked on the roof of the West Street Jail, a short
enclosure like my school soccer court,
and saw the Hudson River once a day
through sooty clothesline entanglements
and bleaching khaki tenements.
Strolling, I yammered metaphysics with Abramowitz,
a jaundice-yellow ("it's really tan")
and fly-weight pacifist,
so vegetarian,
he wore rope shoes and preferred fallen fruit.
He tried to convert Bioff and Brown,
the Hollywood pimps, to his diet.

Hairy, muscular, suburban,
wearing chocolate double-breasted suits,
they blew their tops and beat him black and blue.

I was so out of things, I'd never heard
of the Jehovah's Witnesses.
"Are you a C.O.?" I asked a fellow jailbird.
"No," he answered, "I'm a J.W."
He taught me the "hospital tuck,"
and pointed out the T-shirted back
of *Murder Incorporated's* Czar Lepke,
there piling towels on a rack,
or dawdling off to his little segregated cell full
of things forbidden the common man:
a portable radio, a dresser, two toy American
flags tied together with a ribbon of Easter palm.
Flabby, bald, lobotomized,
he drifted in a sheepish calm,
where no agonizing reappraisal
jarred his concentration on the electric chair—
hanging like an oasis in his air
of lost connections. . . .

Man and Wife

Tamed by *Miltown*, we lie on Mother's bed;
the rising sun in war paint dyes us red;
in broad daylight her gilded bed-posts shine,
abandoned, almost Dionysian.
At last the trees are green on Marlborough Street,
blossoms on our magnolia ignite
the morning with their murderous five days' white.
All night I've held your hand,
as if you had
a fourth time faced the kingdom of the mad—
its hackneyed speech, its homicidal eye—
and dragged me home alive. . . . Oh my *Petite*,
clearest of all God's creatures, still all air and nerve:
you were in your twenties, and I,
once hand on glass
and heart in mouth,
outdrank the Rahvs in the heat
of Greenwich Village, fainting at your feet—
too boiled and shy
and poker-faced to make a pass,
while the shrill verve
of your invective scorched the traditional South.

Now twelve years later, you turn your back.
Sleepless, you hold
your pillow to your hollows like a child;
your old-fashioned tirade—
loving, rapid, merciless—
breaks like the Atlantic Ocean on my head.

"To Speak of Woe That Is in Marriage"

"It is the future generation that presses into being by means of these exuberant feelings and supersensible soap bubbles of ours." SCHOPENHAUER

"The hot night makes us keep our bedroom windows open.
Our magnolia blossoms. Life begins to happen.
My hopped up husband drops his home disputes,
and hits the streets to cruise for prostitutes,
free-lancing out along the razor's edge.
This screwball might kill his wife, then take the pledge.
Oh the monotonous meanness of his lust. . . .
It's the injustice . . . he is so unjust—
whiskey-blind, swaggering home at five.
My only thought is how to keep alive.
What makes him tick? Each night now I tie
ten dollars and his car key to my thigh. . . .
Gored by the climacteric of his want,
he stalls above me like an elephant."

Skunk Hour

(FOR ELIZABETH BISHOP)

Nautilus Island's hermit
heiress still lives through winter in her Spartan cottage;
her sheep still graze above the sea.
Her son's a bishop. Her farmer
is first selectman in our village;
she's in her dotage.

Thirsting for
the hierarchic privacy
of Queen Victoria's century,
she buys up all
the eyesores facing her shore,
and lets them fall.

The season's ill—
we've lost our summer millionaire,
who seemed to leap from an L. L. Bean
catalogue. His nine-knot yawl
was auctioned off to lobstermen.
A red fox stain covers Blue Hill.

And now our fairy
decorator brightens his shop for fall;
his fishnet's filled with orange cork,
orange, his cobbler's bench and awl;
there is no money in his work,
he'd rather marry.

One dark night,
my Tudor Ford climbed the hill's skull;
I watched for love-cars. Lights turned down,
they lay together, hull to hull,
where the graveyard shelves on the town. . . .
My mind's not right.

A car radio bleats,
"Love, O careless Love. . . ." I hear
my ill-spirit sob in each blood cell,
as if my hand were at its throat. . . .
I myself am hell;
nobody's here—

only skunks, that search
in the moonlight for a bite to eat.
They march on their soles up Main Street:
white stripes, moonstruck eyes' red fire
under the chalk-dry and spar spire
of the Trinitarian Church.

I stand on top
of our back steps and breathe the rich air—
a mother skunk with her column of kittens swills the garbage pail.
She jabs her wedge-head in a cup
of sour cream, drops her ostrich tail,
and will not scare.

from

For the Union Dead

(1964)

Water

It was a Maine lobster town—
each morning boatloads of hands
pushed off for granite
quarries on the islands,

and left dozens of bleak
white frame houses stuck
like oyster shells
on a hill of rock,

and below us, the sea lapped
the raw little match-stick
mazes of a weir,
where the fish for bait were trapped.

Remember? We sat on a slab of rock.
From this distance in time,
it seems the color
of iris, rotting and turning purpler,

but it was only
the usual gray rock
turning the usual green
when drenched by the sea.

The sea drenched the rock
at our feet all day,
and kept tearing away
flake after flake.

One night you dreamed
you were a mermaid clinging to a wharf-pile,
and trying to pull
off the barnacles with your hands.

We wished our two souls
might return like gulls
to the rock. In the end,
the water was too cold for us.

The Old Flame

My old flame, my wife!
Remember our lists of birds?
One morning last summer, I drove
by our house in Maine. It was still
on top of its hill—

Now a red ear of Indian maize
was splashed on the door.
Old Glory with thirteen stars
hung on a pole. The clapboard
was old-red schoolhouse red.

Inside, a new landlord,
a new wife, a new broom!
Atlantic seaboard antique shop
pewter and plunder
shone in each room.

A new frontier!
No running next door
now to phone the sheriff
for his taxi to Bath
and the State Liquor Store!

No one saw your ghostly
imaginary lover
stare through the window,
and tighten
the scarf at his throat.

Health to the new people,
health to their flag, to their old
restored house on the hill!

Everything had been swept bare,
furnished, garnished and aired.

Everything's changed for the best—
how quivering and fierce we were,
there snowbound together,
simmering like wasps
in our tent of books!

Poor ghost, old love, speak
with your old voice
of flaming insight
that kept us awake all night.
In one bed and apart,

we heard the plow
groaning up hill—
a red light, then a blue,
as it tossed off the snow
to the side of the road.

Middle Age

Now the midwinter grind
is on me, New York
drills through my nerves,
as I walk
the chewed-up streets.

At forty-five,
what next, what next?
At every corner,
I meet my Father,
my age, still alive.

Father, forgive me
my injuries,
as I forgive
those I
have injured!

You never climbed
Mount Sion, yet left
dinosaur
death-steps on the crust,
where I must walk.

The Mouth of the Hudson

(FOR ESTHER BROOKS)

A single man stands like a bird-watcher,
and scuffles the pepper and salt snow
from a discarded, gray
Westinghouse Electric cable drum.
He cannot discover America by counting
the chains of condemned freight-trains
from thirty states. They jolt and jar
and junk in the siding below him.
He has trouble with his balance.
His eyes drop,
and he drifts with the wild ice
ticking seaward down the Hudson,
like the blank sides of a jig-saw puzzle.

The ice ticks seaward like a clock.
A Negro toasts
wheat-seeds over the coke-fumes
of a punctured barrel.
Chemical air
sweeps in from New Jersey,
and smells of coffee.

Across the river,
ledges of suburban factories tan
in the sulphur-yellow sun
of the unforgivable landscape.

Fall 1961

Back and forth, back and forth
goes the tock, tock, tock
of the orange, bland, ambassadorial
face of the moon
on the grandfather clock.

All autumn, the chafe and jar
of nuclear war;
we have talked our extinction to death.
I swim like a minnow
behind my studio window.

Our end drifts nearer,
the moon lifts,
radiant with terror.
The state
is a diver under a glass bell.

A father's no shield
for his child.
We are like a lot of wild
spiders crying together,
but without tears.

Nature holds up a mirror.
One swallow makes a summer.
It's easy to tick
off the minutes,
but the clockhands stick.

Back and forth!
Back and forth, back and forth—
my one point of rest
is the orange and black
oriole's swinging nest!

Florence

(FOR MARY MCCARTHY)

I long for the black ink,
cuttlefish, April, Communists
and brothels of Florence—
everything, even the British
fairies who haunted the hills,
even the chills and fever
that came once a month
and forced me to think.
The apple was more human there than here,
but it took a long time for the blinding
golden rind to mellow.

How vulnerable the horseshoe crabs
dredging the bottom like flat-irons
in their antique armor,
with their swordgrass blackbone tails,
made for a child to grab
and throw strangling ashore!

Oh Florence, Florence, patroness
of the lovely tyrannicides!
Where the tower of the Old Palace
pierces the sky
like a hypodermic needle,
Perseus, David and Judith,
lords and ladies of the Blood,
Greek demi-gods of the Cross,
rise sword in hand
above the unshaven,
formless decapitation
of the monsters, tubs of guts,
mortifying chunks for the pack.
Pity the monsters!
Pity the monsters!

Perhaps, one always took the wrong side—
Ah, to have known, to have loved
too many Davids and Judiths!
My heart bleeds black blood for the monster.
I have seen the Gorgon.
The erotic terror
of her helpless, big bosomed body
lay like slop.
Wall-eyed, staring the despot to stone,
her severed head swung
like a lantern in the victor's hand.

Eye and Tooth

My whole eye was sunset red,
the old cut cornea throbbed,
I saw things darkly,
as through an unwashed goldfish globe.

I lay all day on my bed.
I chain-smoked through the night,
learning to flinch
at the flash of the matchlight.

Outside, the summer rain,
a simmer of rot and renewal,
fell in pinpricks.
Even new life is fuel.

My eyes throb.
Nothing can dislodge
the house with my first tooth
noosed in a knot to the doorknob.

Nothing can dislodge
the triangular blotch
of rot on the red roof,
a cedar hedge, or the shade of a hedge.

No ease from the eye
of the sharp-shinned hawk in the birdbook there,
with reddish brown buffalo hair
on its shanks, one ascetic talon

clasping the abstract imperial sky.
It says:
an eye for an eye,
a tooth for a tooth.

No ease for the boy at the keyhole,
his telescope,
when the women's white bodies flashed
in the bathroom. Young, my eyes began to fail.

Nothing! No oil
for the eye, nothing to pour
on those waters or flames.
I am tired. Everyone's tired of my turmoil.

Alfred Corning Clark

(1916–1961)

You read the *New York Times*
every day at recess,
but in its dry
obituary, a list
of your wives, nothing is news,
except the ninety-five
thousand dollar engagement ring
you gave the sixth.
Poor rich boy,
you were unreasonably adult
at taking your time,
and died at forty-five.
Poor Al Clark,
behind your enlarged,
hardly recognizable photograph,
I feel the pain.
You were alive. You are dead.
You wore bow-ties and dark
blue coats, and sucked
wintergreen or cinnamon lifesavers
to sweeten your breath.
There must be something—
some one to praise
your triumphant diffidence,
your refusal of exertion,
the intelligence
that pulsed in the sensitive,
pale concavities of your forehead.
You never worked,
and were third in the form.
I owe you something—
I was befogged,
and you were too bored,
quick and cool to laugh.

You are dear to me, Alfred;
our reluctant souls united
in our unconventional
illegal games of chess
on the St. Mark's quadrangle.
You usually won—
motionless
as a lizard in the sun.

Child's Song

My cheap toy lamp
gives little light
all night, all night,
when my muscles cramp.

Sometimes I touch your hand
across my cot,
and our fingers knot,
but there's no hand

to take me home—
no Caribbean
island, where even
the shark is at home.

It must be heaven.
There on that island
the white sand shines
like a birchwood fire.

Help, saw me in two,
put me on the shelf!
Sometimes the little muddler
can't stand itself!

The Public Garden

Burnished, burned-out, still burning as the year
you lead me to our stamping ground.
The city and its cruising cars surround
the Public Garden. All's alive—
the children crowding home from school at five,
punting a football in the bricky air,
the sailors and their pick-ups under trees
with Latin labels. And the jaded flock
of swanboats paddles to its dock.
The park is drying.
Dead leaves thicken to a ball
inside the basin of a fountain, where
the heads of four stone lions stare
and suck on empty faucets. Night
deepens. From the arched bridge, we see
the shedding park-bound mallards, how they keep
circling and diving in the lanternlight,
searching for something hidden in the muck.
And now the moon, earth's friend, that cared so much
for us, and cared so little, comes again—
always a stranger! As we walk,
it lies like chalk
over the waters. Everything's aground.
Remember summer? Bubbles filled
the fountain, and we splashed. We drowned
in Eden, while Jehovah's grass-green lyre
was rustling all about us in the leaves
that gurgled by us, turning upside down . . .
The fountain's failing waters flash around
the garden. Nothing catches fire.

Going to and fro

It's authentic perhaps
to have been there, if now
you could loll on the ledge for a moment,
sunning like a couple,
and look down at the gaps—
if you could for a moment . . .

One step, two steps, three steps:
the hot-dog and coca-cola bar,
the Versailles steps,
the Puritan statue—
if you could get through the Central Park
by counting . . .

But the intestines shiver,
the ferry saloon thugs with your pain
across the river—pain,
suffering without purgation,
the back-track of the screw.
But you had instants,

to give the devil his due—
he and you
once dug it all out of the dark
unconscious bowels of the nerves:
pure gold, the root of evil,
sunshine that gave the day a scheme.

And now? Ah Lucifer!
how often you wanted your fling
with those French girls, Mediterranean
luminaries, Mary, Myrtho, Isis—
as far out as the sphinx!
The love that moves the stars

moved you!
It set you going to and fro
and up and down—
If you could get loose
from the earth by counting
your steps to the noose . . .

Myopia: a Night

Bed, glasses off, and all's
ramshackle, streaky, weird
for the near-sighted, just
a foot away.
                    The light's
still on an instant. Here
are the blurred titles, here
the books are blue hills, browns,
greens, fields, or color.
                              This
is the departure strip,
the dream-road. Whoever built it
left numbers, words and arrows.
He had to leave in a hurry.

I see
a dull and alien room,
my cell of learning,
white, brightened by white pipes,
ramrods of steam . . . I hear
the lonely metal breathe
and gurgle like the sick.
And yet my eyes avoid
that room. No need to see.
No need to know I hoped
its blank, foregoing whiteness
would burn away the blur,
as my five senses clenched
their teeth, thought stitched to thought,
as through a needle's eye . . .

I see the morning star . . .

Think of him in the Garden,
that seed of wisdom, Eve's
seducer, stuffed with man's
corruption, stuffed with triumph:
Satan triumphant in
the Garden! In a moment,
all that blinding brightness
changed into a serpent,
lay grovelling on its gut.

What has disturbed this household?
Only a foot away,
the familiar faces blur.
At fifty we're so fragile,
a feather . . .

The things of the eye are done.
On the illuminated black dial,
green ciphers of a new moon—
one, two, three, four, five, six!
I breathe and cannot sleep.
Then morning comes,
saying, "This was a night."

The Drinker

The man is killing time—there's nothing else.
No help now from the fifth of Bourbon
chucked helter-skelter into the river,
even its cork sucked under.

Stubbed before-breakfast cigarettes
burn bull's-eyes on the bedside table;
a plastic tumbler of alka seltzer
champagnes in the bathroom.

No help from his body, the whale's
warm-hearted blubber, foundering down
leagues of ocean, gasping whiteness.
The barbed hooks fester. The lines snap tight.

When he looks for neighbors, their names blur in the window,
his distracted eye sees only glass sky.
His despair has the galvanized color
of the mop and water in the galvanized bucket.

Once she was close to him
as water to the dead metal.

He looks at her engagements inked on her calendar.
A list of indictments.
At the numbers in her thumbed black telephone book.
A quiver full of arrows.

Her absence hisses like steam,
the pipes sing . . .
even corroded metal somehow functions.
He snores in his iron lung,

and hears the voice of Eve,
beseeching freedom from the Garden's
perfect and ponderous bubble. No voice
outsings the serpent's flawed, euphoric hiss.

The cheese wilts in the rat-trap,
the milk turns to junket in the cornflakes bowl,
car keys and razor blades
shine in an ashtray.

Is he killing time? Out on the street,
two cops on horseback clop through the April rain
to check the parking meter violations—
their oilskins yellow as forsythia.

Hawthorne

Follow its lazy main street lounging
from the alms house to Gallows Hill
along a flat, unvaried surface
covered with wooden houses
aged by yellow drain
like the unhealthy hair of an old dog.
You'll walk to no purpose
in Hawthorne's Salem.

I cannot resilver the smudged plate.

I drop to Hawthorne, the customs officer,
measuring coal and mostly trying to keep warm—
to the stunted black schooner,
the dismal South-end dock,
the wharf-piles with their fungus of ice.
On State Street
a steeple with a glowing dial-clock
measures the weary hours,
the merciless march of professional feet.

Even this shy distrustful ego
sometimes walked on top of the blazing roof,
and felt those flashes
that char the discharged cells of the brain.

Look at the faces—
Longfellow, Lowell, Holmes and Whittier!
Study the grizzled silver of their beards.
Hawthorne's picture,
however, has a blond mustache
and golden General Custer scalp.
He looks like a Civil War officer.

He shines in the firelight. His hard
survivor's smile is touched with fire.
Leave him alone for a moment or two,
and you'll see him with his head
bent down, brooding, brooding,
eyes fixed on some chip,
some stone, some common plant,
the commonest thing,
as if it were the clue.
The disturbed eyes rise,
furtive, foiled, dissatisfied
from meditation on the true
and insignificant.

Jonathan Edwards in Western Massachusetts

Edwards' great millstone and rock
of hope has crumbled, but the square
white houses of his flock
stand in the open air,

out in the cold,
like sheep outside the fold.
Hope lives in doubt.
Faith is trying to do without

faith. In western Massachusetts,
I could almost feel the frontier
crack and disappear.
Edwards thought the world would end there.

We know how the world will end,
but where is paradise, each day farther
from the Pilgrim's blues for England
and the Promised Land.

Was it some country house
that seemed as if it were
Whitehall, if the Lord were there?
so nobly did he live.

Gardens designed
that the breath of flowers in the wind,
or crushed underfoot,
came and went like warbling music?

Bacon's great oak grove
he refused to sell,
when he fell,
saying, "Why should I sell my feathers?"

Ah paradise! Edwards,
I would be afraid
to meet you there as a shade.
We move in different circles.

As a boy, you built a booth
in a swamp for prayer;
lying on your back,
you saw the spiders fly,

basking at their ease,
swimming from tree to tree—
so high, they seemed tacked to the sky.
You knew they would die.

Poor country Berkeley at Yale,
you saw the world was soul,
the soul of God! The soul
of Sarah Pierrepont!

So filled with delight in the Great Being,
she hardly cared for anything—
walking the fields, sweetly singing,
conversing with some one invisible.

Then God's love shone in sun, moon and stars,
on earth, in the waters,
in the air, in the loose winds,
which used to greatly fix your mind.

Often she saw you come home from a ride
or a walk, your coat dotted with thoughts
you had pinned there
on slips of paper.

You gave
her Pompey, a Negro slave,
and eleven children.
Yet people were spiders

in your moment of glory,
at the Great Awakening—"Alas, how many
in this very meeting house are more than likely
to remember my discourse in hell!"

The meeting house remembered!
You stood on stilts in the air,
but you fell from your parish.
"All rising is by a winding stair."

On my pilgrimage to Northampton,
I found no relic,
except the round slice of an oak
you are said to have planted.

It was flesh-colored, new,
and a common piece of kindling,
only fit for burning.
You too must have been green once.

White wig and black coat,
all cut from one cloth,
and designed
like your mind!

I love you faded,
old, exiled and afraid
to leave your last flock, a dozen
Housatonic Indian children;

afraid to leave
all your writing, writing, writing,
denying the Freedom of the Will.
You were afraid to be president

of Princeton, and wrote:
"My deffects are well known;
I have a constitution
peculiarly unhappy:

flaccid solids,
vapid, sizzy, scarse fluids,
causing a childish weakness,
a low tide of spirits.

I am contemptible,
stiff and dull.

Why should I leave behind
my delight and entertainment,
those studies
that have swallowed up my mind?"

Tenth Muse

Tenth Muse, Oh my heart-felt Sloth,
how often now you come to my bed,
thin as a canvas in your white and red
check dresses like a table cloth,
my Dearest, settling like my shroud!

Yes, yes, I ought to remember Moses
jogging down on his mule from the Mount
with the old law, the old mistake,
safe in his saddlebags, and chiselled
on the stones we cannot bear or break.

Here waiting, here waiting for an answer
from this malignant surf of unopened letters,
always reaching land too late,
as fact and abstraction accumulate,
and the signature fades from the paper—

I like to imagine it must have been simpler
in the days of Lot,
or when Greek and Roman picturebook
gods sat combing their golden beards,
each on his private hill or mountain.

But I suppose even God was born
too late to trust the old religion—
all those settings out
that never left the ground,
beginning in wisdom, dying in doubt.

The Neo-Classical Urn

I rub my head and find a turtle shell
stuck on a pole,
each hair electrical
with charges, and the juice alive
with ferment. Bubbles drive
the motor, always purposeful . . .
Poor head!
How its skinny shell once hummed,
as I sprinted down the colonnade
of bleaching pines, cylindrical
clipped trunks without a twig between them. Rest!
I could not rest. At full run on the curve,
I left the cast stone statue of a nymph,
her soaring armpits and her one bare breast,
gray from the rain and graying in the shade,
as on, on, in sun, the pathway now a dyke,
I swerved between two water bogs,
two seines of moss, and stooped to snatch
the painted turtles on dead logs.
In that season of joy,
my turtle catch
was thirty-three,
dropped splashing in our garden urn,
like money in the bank,
the plop and splash
of turtle on turtle,
fed raw gobs of hash . . .

Oh neo-classical white urn, Oh nymph,
Oh lute! The boy was pitiless who strummed
their elegy,
for as the month wore on,
the turtles rose,
and popped up dead on the stale scummed

surface—limp wrinkled heads and legs withdrawn
in pain. What pain? A turtle's nothing. No
grace, no cerebration, less free will
than the mosquito I must kill—
nothings! Turtles! I rub my skull,
that turtle shell,
and breathe their dying smell,
still watch their crippled last survivors pass,
and hobble humpbacked through the grizzled grass.

Caligula

My namesake, Little Boots, Caligula,
you disappoint me. Tell me what I saw
to make me like you when we met at school?
I took your name—poor odd-ball, poor spoiled fool,
my prince, young innocent and bowdlerized!
Your true face sneers at me, mean, thin, agonized,
the rusty Roman medal where I see
my lowest depths of possibility.

What can be salvaged from your life? A pain
that gently darkens over heart and brain,
a fairy's touch, a cobweb's weight of pain,
now makes me tremble at your right to live.
I live your last night. Sleepless fugitive,
your purple bedclothes and imperial eagle
grow so familiar they are home. Your regal
hand accepts my hand. You bend my wrist,
and tear the tendons with your strangler's twist . . .
You stare down hallways, mile on stoney mile,
where statues of the gods return your smile.
Why did you smash their heads and give them yours?
You hear your household panting on all fours,
and itemize your features—sleep's old aide!
Item: your body hairy, badly made,
head hairless, smoother than your marble head;
Item: eyes hollow, hollow temples, red
cheeks rough with rouge, legs spindly, hands that leave
a clammy snail's trail on your soggy sleeve . . .
a hand no hand will hold . . . nose thin, thin neck—
you wish the Romans had a single neck!

Small thing, where are you? Child, you sucked your thumb,
and could not sleep unless you hugged the numb
and wooly-witted toys of your small zoo.

There was some reason then to fondle you
before you found the death-mask for your play.
Lie very still, sleep with clasped hands, and pray
for nothing, Child! Think, even at the end,
good dreams were faithful. You betray no friend
now that no animal will share your bed.
Don't think! . . . And yet the God Adonis bled
and lay beside you, forcing you to strip.
You felt his gored thigh spurting on your hip.
Your mind burned, you were God, a thousand plans
ran zig-zag, zig-zag. You began to dance
for joy, and called your menials to arrange
deaths for the gods. You worshipped your great change,
took a cold bath, and rolled your genitals
until they shrank to marbles . . .

              Animals
fattened for your arena suffered less
than you in dying—yours the lawlessness
of something simple that has lost its law,
my namesake, and the last Caligula.

July in Washington

The stiff spokes of this wheel
touch the sore spots of the earth.

On the Potomac, swan-white
power launches keep breasting the sulphurous wave.

Otters slide and dive and slick back their hair,
raccoons clean their meat in the creek.

On the circles, green statues ride like South American
liberators above the breeding vegetation—

prongs and spearheads of some equatorial
backland that will inherit the globe.

The elect, the elected . . . they come here bright as dimes,
and die dishevelled and soft.

We cannot name their names, or number their dates—
circle on circle, like rings on a tree—

but we wish the river had another shore,
some further range of delectable mountains,

distant hills powdered blue as a girl's eyelid.
It seems the least little shove would land us there,

that only the slightest repugnance of our bodies
we no longer control could drag us back.

Buenos Aires

In my room at the Hotel Continentál
a thousand miles from nowhere,
I heard
the bulky, beefy breathing of the herds.

Cattle furnished my new clothes:
my coat of limp, chestnut-colored suede,
my sharp shoes
that hurt my toes.

A false fin de siècle decorum
snored over Buenos Aires
lost in the pampas
and run by the barracks.

All day I read about newspaper coups d'état
of the leaden, internecine generals—
lumps of dough on the chessboard—and never saw
their countermarching tanks.

Along the sunlit cypress walks
of the Republican martyrs' graveyard,
hundreds of one-room Roman temples
hugged their neo-classical catafalques.

Literal commemorative busts
preserved the frogged coats
and fussy, furrowed foreheads
of those soldier bureaucrats.

By their brazen doors
a hundred marble goddesses
wept like willows. I found rest
by cupping a soft palm to each hard breast.

I was the worse for wear,
and my breath whitened the winter air
next morning, when Buenos Aires filled
with frowning, starch-collared crowds.

Soft Wood

(FOR HARRIET WINSLOW)

Sometimes I have supposed seals
must live as long as the Scholar Gypsy.
Even in their barred pond at the zoo they are happy,
and no sunflower turns
more delicately to the sun
without a wincing of the will.

Here too in Maine things bend to the wind forever.
After two years away, one must get used
to the painted soft wood staying bright and clean,
to the air blasting an all-white wall whiter,
as it blows through curtain and screen
touched with salt and evergreen.

The green juniper berry spills crystal-clear gin,
and even the hot water in the bathtub
is more than water,
and rich with the scouring effervescence
of something healing,
the illimitable salt.

Things last, but sometimes for days here
only children seem fit to handle children,
and there is no utility or inspiration
in the wind smashing without direction.
The fresh paint
on the captains' houses hides softer wood.

Their square-riggers used to whiten
the four corners of the globe,
but it's no consolation to know
the possessors seldom outlast the possessions,
once warped and mothered by their touch.
Shed skin will never fit another wearer.

Yet the seal pack will bark past my window
summer after summer.
This is the season
when our friends may and will die daily.
Surely the lives of the old
are briefer than the young.

Harriet Winslow, who owned this house,
was more to me than my mother.
I think of you far off in Washington,
breathing in the heat wave
and air-conditioning, knowing
each drug that numbs alerts another nerve to pain.

New York 1962: Fragment

(FOR E.H.L.)

This might be nature—twenty stories high,
two water tanks, tanned shingle, corseted
by stapled pasture wire, while bed to bed,
we two, one cell here, lie
gazing into the ether's crystal ball,
sky and a sky, and sky, and sky, till death—
my heart stops . . .
This might be heaven. Years ago,
we aimed for less and settled for
a picture, out of style then and now in,
of seven daffodils. We watched them blow:
buttercup yellow were the flowers, and green
the stems as fresh paint, over them the wind,
the blousy wooden branches of the elms,
high summer in the breath that overwhelms
the termites digging in the underpinning . . .
Still over us, still in parenthesis,
this sack of hornets sopping up the flame,
still over us our breath,
sawing and pumping to the terminal,
and down below, we two, two in one waterdrop
vitalized by a needle drop of blood,
up, up, up, up and up,
soon shot, soon slugged into the overflow
that sets the wooden workhorse working here below.

The Flaw

A seal swims like a poodle through the sheet
of blinding salt. A country graveyard, here
and there a rock, and here and there a pine,
throbs on the essence of the gasoline.
Some mote, some eye-flaw, wobbles in the heat,
hair-thin, hair-dark, the fragment of a hair—

a noose, a question? All is possible;
if there's free will, it's something like this hair,
inside my eye, outside my eye, yet free,
airless as grace, if the good God . . . I see.
Our bodies quiver. In this rustling air,
all's possible, all's unpredictable.

Old wives and husbands! Look, their gravestones wait
in couples with the names and half the date—
one future and one freedom. In a flash,
I see us whiten into skeletons,
our eager, sharpened cries, a pair of stones,
cutting like shark-fins through the boundless wash.

Two walking cobwebs, almost bodiless,
crossed paths here once, kept house, and lay in beds.
Your fingertips once touched my fingertips
and set us tingling through a thousand threads.
Poor pulsing *Fête Champêtre!* The summer slips
between our fingers into nothingness.

We too lean forward, as the heat waves roll
over our bodies, grown insensible,
ready to dwindle off into the soul,
two motes or eye-flaws, the invisible . . .

Hope of the hopeless launched and cast adrift
on the great flaw that gives the final gift.

Dear Figure curving like a questionmark,
how will you hear my answer in the dark?

Night Sweat

Work-table, litter, books and standing lamp,
plain things, my stalled equipment, the old broom—
but I am living in a tidied room,
for ten nights now I've felt the creeping damp
float over my pajamas' wilted white . . .
Sweet salt embalms me and my head is wet,
everything streams and tells me this is right;
my life's fever is soaking in night sweat—
one life, one writing! But the downward glide
and bias of existing wrings us dry—
always inside me is the child who died,
always inside me is his will to die—
one universe, one body . . . in this urn
the animal night sweats of the spirit burn.

Behind me! You! Again I feel the light
lighten my leaded eyelids, while the gray
skulled horses whinny for the soot of night.
I dabble in the dapple of the day,
a heap of wet clothes, seamy, shivering,
I see my flesh and bedding washed with light,
my child exploding into dynamite,
my wife . . . your lightness alters everything,
and tears the black web from the spider's sack,
as your heart hops and flutters like a hare.
Poor turtle, tortoise, if I cannot clear
the surface of these troubled waters here,
absolve me, help me, Dear Heart, as you bear
this world's dead weight and cycle on your back.

For the Union Dead

"Relinquunt Omnia Servare Rem Publicam."

The old South Boston Aquarium stands
in a Sahara of snow now. Its broken windows are boarded.
The bronze weathervane cod has lost half its scales.
The airy tanks are dry.

Once my nose crawled like a snail on the glass;
my hand tingled
to burst the bubbles
drifting from the noses of the cowed, compliant fish.

My hand draws back. I often sigh still
for the dark downward and vegetating kingdom
of the fish and reptile. One morning last March,
I pressed against the new barbed and galvanized

fence on the Boston Common. Behind their cage,
yellow dinosaur steamshovels were grunting
as they cropped up tons of mush and grass
to gouge their underworld garage.

Parking spaces luxuriate like civic
sandpiles in the heart of Boston.
A girdle of orange, Puritan-pumpkin colored girders
braces the tingling Statehouse,

shaking over the excavations, as it faces Colonel Shaw
and his bell-cheeked Negro infantry
on St. Gaudens' shaking Civil War relief,
propped by a plank splint against the garage's earthquake.

Two months after marching through Boston,
half the regiment was dead;
at the dedication,
William James could almost hear the bronze Negroes breathe.

Their monument sticks like a fishbone
in the city's throat.
Its Colonel is as lean
as a compass-needle.

He has an angry wrenlike vigilance,
a greyhound's gentle tautness;
he seems to wince at pleasure,
and suffocate for privacy.

He is out of bounds now. He rejoices in man's lovely,
peculiar power to choose life and die—
when he leads his black soldiers to death,
he cannot bend his back.

On a thousand small town New England greens,
the old white churches hold their air
of sparse, sincere rebellion; frayed flags
quilt the graveyards of the Grand Army of the Republic.

The stone statues of the abstract Union Soldier
grow slimmer and younger each year—
wasp-waisted, they doze over muskets
and muse through their sideburns . . .

Shaw's father wanted no monument
except the ditch,
where his son's body was thrown
and lost with his "niggers."

The ditch is nearer.
There are no statues for the last war here;
on Boylston Street, a commercial photograph
shows Hiroshima boiling

over a Mosler Safe, the "Rock of Ages"
that survived the blast. Space is nearer.
When I crouch to my television set,
the drained faces of Negro school-children rise like balloons.

Colonel Shaw
is riding on his bubble,
he waits
for the blessèd break.

The Aquarium is gone. Everywhere,
giant finned cars nose forward like fish;
a savage servility
slides by on grease.

Near the Ocean
(1967)

Near the Ocean

1. Waking Early Sunday Morning

O to break loose, like the chinook
salmon jumping and falling back,
nosing up to the impossible
stone and bone-crushing waterfall—
raw-jawed, weak-fleshed there, stopped by ten
steps of the roaring ladder, and then
to clear the top on the last try,
alive enough to spawn and die.

Stop, back off. The salmon breaks
water, and now my body wakes
to feel the unpolluted joy
and criminal leisure of a boy—
no rainbow smashing a dry fly
in the white run is free as I,
here squatting like a dragon on
time's hoard before the day's begun!

Vermin run for their unstopped holes;
in some dark nook a fieldmouse rolls
a marble, hours on end, then stops;
the termite in the woodwork sleeps—
listen, the creatures of the night
obsessive, casual, sure of foot,
go on grinding, while the sun's
daily remorseful blackout dawns.

Fierce, fireless mind, running downhill.
Look up and see the harbor fill:
business as usual in eclipse
goes down to the sea in ships—
wake of refuse, dacron rope,
bound for Bermuda or Good Hope,

all bright before the morning watch
the wine-dark hulls of yawl and ketch.

I watch a glass of water wet
with a fine fuzz of icy sweat,
silvery colors touched with sky,
serene in their neutrality—
yet if I shift, or change my mood,
I see some object made of wood,
background behind it of brown grain,
to darken it, but not to stain.

O that the spirit could remain
tinged but untarnished by its strain!
Better dressed and stacking birch,
or lost with the Faithful at Church—
anywhere, but somewhere else!
And now the new electric bells,
clearly chiming, "Faith of our fathers,"
and now the congregation gathers.

O Bible chopped and crucified
in hymns we hear but do not read,
none of the milder subtleties
of grace or art will sweeten these
stiff quatrains shovelled out four-square—
they sing of peace, and preach despair;
yet they gave darkness some control,
and left a loophole for the soul.

No, put old clothes on, and explore
the corners of the woodshed for
its dregs and dreck: tools with no handle,
ten candle-ends not worth a candle,
old lumber banished from the Temple,
damned by Paul's precept and example,
cast from the kingdom, banned in Israel,
the wordless sign, the tinkling cymbal.

When will we see Him face to face?
Each day, He shines through darker glass.
In this small town where everything
is known, I see His vanishing
emblems, His white spire and flag-
pole sticking out above the fog,
like old white china doorknobs, sad,
slight, useless things to calm the mad.

Hammering military splendor,
top-heavy Goliath in full armor—
little redemption in the mass
liquidations of their brass,
elephant and phalanx moving
with the times and still improving,
when that kingdom hit the crash:
a million foreskins stacked like trash . . .

Sing softer! But what if a new
diminuendo brings no true
tenderness, only restlessness,
excess, the hunger for success,
sanity of self-deception
fixed and kicked by reckless caution,
while we listen to the bells—
anywhere, but somewhere else!

O to break loose. All life's grandeur
is something with a girl in summer . . .
elated as the President
girdled by his establishment
this Sunday morning, free to chaff
his own thoughts with his bear-cuffed staff,
swimming nude, unbuttoned, sick
of his ghost-written rhetoric!

No weekends for the gods now. Wars
flicker, earth licks its open sores,
fresh breakage, fresh promotions, chance
assassinations, no advance.
Only man thinning out his kind
sounds through the Sabbath noon, the blind
swipe of the pruner and his knife
busy about the tree of life . . .

Pity the planet, all joy gone
from this sweet volcanic cone;
peace to our children when they fall
in small war on the heels of small
war—until the end of time
to police the earth, a ghost
orbiting forever lost
in our monotonous sublime.

2. Fourth of July in Maine

(FOR HARRIET WINSLOW)

Another summer! Our Independence
Day Parade, all innocence
of children's costumes, helps resist
the communist and socialist.
Five nations: Dutch, French, Englishmen,
Indians, and we, who held Castine,
rise from their graves in combat gear—
world-losers elsewhere, conquerors here!

Civil Rights clergy face again
the scions of the good old strain,
the poor who always must remain
poor and Republicans in Maine,
upholders of the American Dream,
who will not sink and cannot swim—
Emersonian self-reliance,
lethargy of Russian peasants!

High noon. Each child has won his blue,
red, yellow ribbon, and our statue,
a dandyish Union Soldier, sees
his fields reclaimed by views and spruce—
he seems a convert to old age,
small, callous, elbowed off the stage,
while the canned martial music fades
from scene and green—no more parades!

Blue twinges of mortality
remind us the theocracy
drove in its stakes here to command
the infinite, and gave this land
a ministry that would have made
short work of Christ, the Son of God,
and then exchanged His crucifix,
hardly our sign, for politics.

This white Colonial frame house,
willed downward, Dear, from you to us,
still matters—the Americas'
best artifact produced en masse.
The founders' faith was in decay,
and yet their building seems to say:
"Every time I take a breath,
my God you are the air I breathe."

New England, everywhere I look,
old letters crumble from the Book,
China trade rubble, one more line
unravelling from the dark design
spun by God and Cotton Mather—
our *bell'età dell'oro*, another
bright thing thinner than a cobweb,
caught in Calvinism's ebb.

Dear Cousin, life is much the same,
though only fossils know your name
here since you left this solitude,
gone, as the Christians say, for good.
Your house, still outwardly in form
lasts, though no emissary come
to watch the garden running down,
or photograph the propped-up barn.

If memory is genius, you
had Homer's, enough gossip to
repeople Trollope's Barchester,
nurses, Negro, diplomat, down-easter,
cousins kept up with, nipped, corrected,
kindly, majorfully directed,
though family furniture, decor,
and rooms redone meant almost more.

How often when the telephone
brought you to us from Washington,
we had to look around the room

to find the objects you would name—
lying there, ten years paralyzed,
half blind, no voice unrecognized,
not trusting in the afterlife,
teasing us for a carving knife.

High New England summer, warm
and fortified against the storm
by nightly nips you once adored,
though never going overboard,
Harriet, when you used to play
your chosen Nadia Boulanger
Monteverdi, Purcell, and Bach's
precursors on the Magnavox.

Blue-ribboned, blue-jeaned, named for you,
our daughter cartwheels on the blue—
may your proportion strengthen her
to live through the millennial year
Two Thousand, and like you possess
friends, independence, and a house,
herself God's plenty, mistress of
your tireless sedentary love.

Her two angora guinea pigs
are nibbling seed, the news, and twigs—
untroubled, petrified, atremble,
a mother and her daughter, so humble,
giving, idle and sensitive,
few animals will let them live,
and only a vegetarian God
could look on them and call them good.

Man's poorest cousins, harmonies
of lust and appetite and ease,
little pacific things, who graze
the grass about their box, they praise
whatever stupor gave them breath
to multiply before their death—

Evolution's snails, by birth,
outrunning man who runs the earth.

And now the frosted summer night-dew
brightens, the north wind rushes through
your ailing cedars, finds the gaps;
thumbtacks rattle from the white maps,
food's lost sight of, dinner waits,
in the cold oven, icy plates—
repeating and repeating, one
Joan Baez on the gramophone.

And here in your converted barn,
we burn our hands a moment, borne
by energies that never tire
of piling fuel on the fire;
monologue that will not hear,
logic turning its deaf ear,
wild spirits and old sores in league
with inexhaustible fatigue.

Far off that time of gentleness,
when man, still licensed to increase,
unfallen and unmated, heard
only the uncreated Word—
when God the Logos still had wit
to hide his bloody hands, and sit
in silence, while his peace was sung.
Then the universe was young.

We watch the logs fall. Fire once gone,
we're done for: we escape the sun,
rising and setting, a red coal,
until it cinders like the soul.
Great ash and sun of freedom, give
us this day the warmth to live,
and face the household fire. We turn
our backs, and feel the whiskey burn.

3. The Opposite House

All day the opposite house,
an abandoned police stable,
just an opposite house,
is square enough—six floors,
six windows to a floor,
pigeons ganging through
broken windows and cooing
like gangs of children tooting
empty bottles.

Tonight, though, I see it shine
in the Azores of my open window.
Its manly, old-fashioned lines
are gorgeously rectilinear.
It's like some firework to be fired
at the end of the garden party,
some Spanish *casa*, luminous
with heraldry and murder,
marooned in New York.

A stringy policeman is crooked
in the doorway, one hand on his revolver.
He counts his bullets like beads.
Two on horseback sidle
the crowd to the curb. A red light
whirls on the roof of an armed car,
plodding slower than a turtle.
Deterrent terror!
Viva la muerte!

4. Central Park

Scaling small rocks, exhaling smog,
gasping at game-scents like a dog,
now light as pollen, now as white
and winded as a grounded kite—
I watched the lovers occupy
every inch of earth and sky:
one figure of geometry,
multiplied to infinity,
straps down, and sunning openly . . .
each precious, public, pubic tangle
an equilateral triangle,
lost in the park, half covered by
the shade of some low stone or tree.
The stain of fear and poverty
spread through each trapped anatomy,
and darkened every mote of dust.
All wished to leave this drying crust,
borne on the delicate wings of lust
like bees, and cast their fertile drop
into the overwhelming cup.

Drugged and humbled by the smell
of zoo-straw mixed with animal,
the lion prowled his slummy cell,
serving his life-term in jail—
glaring, grinding, on his heel,
with tingling step and testicle . . .

Behind a dripping rock, I found
a one-day kitten on the ground—
deprived, weak, ignorant and blind,
squeaking, tubular, left behind—
dying with its deserter's rich
Welfare lying out of reach:

milk cartons, kidney heaped to spoil,
two plates sheathed with silver foil.

Shadows had stained the afternoon;
high in an elm, a snagged balloon
wooed the attraction of the moon.
Scurrying from the mouth of night,
a single, fluttery, paper kite
grazed Cleopatra's Needle, and sailed
where the light of the sun had failed.
Then night, the night—the jungle hour,
the rich in his slit-windowed tower . . .
Old Pharaohs starving in your foxholes,
with painted banquets on the walls,
fists knotted in your captives' hair,
tyrants with little food to spare—
all your embalming left you mortal,
glazed, black, and hideously eternal,
all your plunder and gold leaf
only served to draw the thief . . .

We beg delinquents for our life.
Behind each bush, perhaps a knife;
each landscaped crag, each flowering shrub,
hides a policeman with a club.

5. Near the Ocean

(FOR E.H.L.)

The house is filled. The last heartthrob
thrills through her flesh. The hero stands,
stunned by the applauding hands,
and lifts her once head to please the mob . . .
No, young and starry-eyed, the brother
and sister wait before their mother,
old iron-bruises, powder, "Child,
these breasts . . ." He knows. And if she's killed

his treadmill heart will never rest—
his wet mouth pressed to some slack breast,
or shifting over on his back . . .
The severed radiance filters back,
athirst for nightlife—gorgon head,
fished up from the Aegean dead,
with all its stranded snakes uncoiled,
here beheaded and despoiled.

We hear the ocean. Older seas
and deserts give asylum, peace
to each abortion and mistake.
Lost in the Near Eastern dreck,
the tyrant and tyrannicide
lie like the bridegroom and the bride;
the battering ram, abandoned, prone,
beside the apeman's phallic stone.

Betrayals! Was it the first night?
They stood against a black and white
inland New England backdrop. No dogs
there, horse or hunter, only frogs
chirring from the dark trees and swamps.
Elms watching like extinguished lamps.
Knee-high hedges of black sheep
encircling them at every step.

Some subway-green coldwater flat,
its walls tattooed with neon light,
then high delirious squalor, food
burned down with vodka . . . menstrual blood
caking the covers, when they woke
to the dry, childless Sunday walk,
saw cars on Brooklyn Bridge descend
through steel and coal dust to land's end.

Was it years later when they met,
and summer's coarse last-quarter drought
had dried the hardveined elms to bark—
lying like people out of work,
dead sober, cured, recovered, on
the downslope of some gritty green,
all access barred with broken glass;
and dehydration browned the grass?

Is it this shore? Their eyes worn white
as moons from hitting bottom? Night,
the sandfleas scissoring their feet,
the sandbed cooling to concrete,
one borrowed blanket, lights of cars
shining down at them like stars? . . .
Sand built the lost Atlantis . . . sand,
Atlantic Ocean, condoms, sand.

Sleep, sleep. The ocean, grinding stones,
can only speak the present tense;
nothing will age, nothing will last,
or take corruption from the past.
A hand, your hand then! I'm afraid
to touch the crisp hair on your head—
Monster loved for what you are,
till time, that buries us, lay bare.

from

History

(1973)

History

History has to live with what was here,
clutching and close to fumbling all we had—
it is so dull and gruesome how we die,
unlike writing, life never finishes.
Abel was finished; death is not remote,
a flash-in-the-pan electrifies the skeptic,
his cows crowding like skulls against high-voltage wire,
his baby crying all night like a new machine.
As in our Bibles, white-faced, predatory,
the beautiful, mist-drunken hunter's moon ascends—
a child could give it a face: two holes, two holes,
my eyes, my mouth, between them a skull's no-nose—
O there's a terrifying innocence in my face
drenched with the silver salvage of the mornfrost.

Man and Woman

The sheep start galloping in moon-blind wheels
shedding a dozen ewes—is it faulty vision?
Will we get them back . . . and everything,
marriage and departure, departure and marriage,
village to family, family to village—
all the sheep's parents in geometric progression?
It's too much heart-ache to go back to that—
not life-enhancing like the hour a student
first discovers the authentic Mother
on the Tuscan hills of Berenson,
or of Galileo, his great glass eye
admiring the spots on the erroneous moon. . . .
I watch this night out grateful to be alone
with my wife—your slow pulse, my outrageous eye.

Alexander

His sweet moist eye missed nothing—the vague guerilla,
new ground, new tactics, the time for his hell-fire drive,
Demosthenes knotting his nets of dialectic—
phalanxes oiled ten weeks before their trial,
engines on oxen for the fall of Tyre—
Achilles . . . in Aristotle's annotated copy—
health burning like the dewdrop on his flesh
hit in a hundred calculated sallies
to give the Persians the cup of love, of brothers—
the wine-bowl of the Macedonian drinking bout . . .
drinking out of friendship, then meeting Medius,
then drinking, then bathing, then sleeping, then meeting Medius,
then drinking, then bathing . . . dead at thirty-two—
in this life only is our hope in Christ.

Death of Alexander

The young man's numinous eye is like the sun,
for three days the Macedonian soldiers pass;
speechless, he knows them as if they were his sheep.
Shall Alexander be carried in the temple
to pray there, and perhaps, recover? But
the god forbids it, "It's a better thing
if the king stay where he is." He soon dies,
this after all, perhaps, the "better thing.". . .
No one was like him. Terrible were his crimes—
but if you wish to blackguard the Great King,
think how mean, obscure and dull you are,
your labors lowly and your merits less—
we know this, of all the kings of old,
he alone had the greatness of heart to repent.

Hannibal 1. Roman Disaster at the Trebia

The dawn of an ill day whitens the heights.
The camp wakes. Below, the river grumbles and rolls,
and light Numidian horsemen water their horses;
everywhere, sharp clear blasts of the trumpeters.
Though warned by Scipio, and the lying augurs,
the Trebia in flood, the blowing rain,
the Consul Sempronius, proud of his new glory,
has raised the axe for battle, he marches his lictors.
A gloomy flamboyance reddens the dull sky,
Gallic villages smoulder on the horizon.
Far off, the hysterical squeal of an elephant. . . .
Down there, below a bridge, his back on the arch,
Hannibal listens, thoughtful, glorying,
to the dead tramp of the advancing Roman legions.

Marcus Cato 234–149 B.C.

My live telephone swings crippled to solitude
two feet from my ear; as so often and so often,
I hold your dialogue away to breathe—
still this is love, Old Cato forgoing his wife,
then jumping her in thunderstorms like *Juppiter Tonans*;
his forthrightness gave him long days of solitude,
then deafness changed his gifts for rule to genius.
Cato knew from the Greeks that empire is hurry,
and dominion never goes to the phlegmatic—
it was hard to be Demosthenes in his stone-deaf Senate:
"Carthage must die," he roared . . . and Carthage died.
He knew a blindman looking for gold
in a heap of dust must take the dust with the gold,
Rome, if built at all, must be built in a day.

Marcus Cato 95–46 B.C.

As a boy he was brought to Sulla's villa, The Tombs,
saw people come in as men, and leave as heads.
"Why hasn't someone killed him?" he asked. They answered,
"Men fear Sulla even more than they hate him."
He asked for a sword, and wasn't invited back. . . .
He drowned Plato in wine all night with his friends,
gambled his life in the forum, was stoned like Paul,
and went on talking till soldiers saved the State,
saved Caesar. . . . At the last cast of his lost Republic,
he bloodied his hand on the slave who hid his sword;
he fell in a small sleep, heard the dawn birds chirping,
but couldn't use his hand well . . . when they tried to put
his bowels back, he tore them. . . . He's where he would be:
one Roman who died, perhaps, for Rome.

Cicero, the Sacrificial Killing

It's somewhere, somewhere, thought beats stupidly—
a scarlet patch of Tacitus or the Bible,
Pound's Cantos lost in the rockslide of history?
The great man flees his greatness, fugitive husk
of Cicero or Marius without a toga,
old sheep sent out to bite the frosty stubble.
The Republic froze and fattened its high ranks,
the Empire was too much brass for what we are;
who asks for legions to bring the baby milk?
Cicero bold, garrulous in his den
chatting as host on his sofa of magazines;
a squad of state doctors stands by him winking . . .
he minds his hands shaking, and they keep shaking;
if infirmity has a color, it isn't yellow.

Nunc est bibendum, Cleopatra's Death

Nunc est bibendum, nunc pede liberum
the time to drink and dance the earth in rhythm.
Before this it was infamous to banquet,
while Cleopatra plotted to enthrone
her depravity naked in the Capitol—
impotent, yet drunk on fortune's favors!
Caesar has tamed your soul, you see with a
now sober eye the scowling truth of terror—
O Cleopatra scarcely escaping with a single ship
Caesar, three decks of oars—O scarcely escaping
when the sparrowhawk falls on the soft-textured dove. . . .
You found a more magnanimous way to die,
not walking on foot in triumphant Caesar's triumph,
no queen now, but a private woman much humbled.

Juvenal's Prayer

What's best, what serves us . . . leave it to the gods.
We're dearer to the gods than to ourselves.
Harassed by impulse and diseased desire,
we ask for wives, and children by those wives—
what wives and children heaven only knows.
Still if you will ask for something, pray for
a healthy body and a healthy soul,
a mind that is not terrified of death,
thinks length of days the least of nature's gifts—
courage that drives out anger and longing . . . our hero,
Hercules, and the pain of his great labor. . . .
Success is worshipped as a god; it's we
who set her up in palace and cathedral.
I give you simply what you have already.

Attila, Hitler

Hitler had fingertips of apprehension,
"Who knows how long I'll live? Let us have war.
We *are* the barbarians, the world is near the end."
Attila mounted on raw meat and greens
galloped to massacre in his single fieldmouse suit,
he never left a house that wasn't burning,
could only sleep on horseback, sinking deep
in his rural dream. Would he have found himself
in this coarsest, cruelest, least magnanimous,
most systematic, most philosophical . . .
a nomad stay-at-home: *He who has, has*;
a barbarian wondering why the old world collapsed,
who also left his festering fume of refuse,
old tins, dead vermin, ashes, eggshells, youth?

Mohammed

Like Henry VIII, Mohammed got religion
in the dangerous years, and smashed the celibates,
haters of life, though never takers of it—
changed their monasteries to foundries,
reset their non-activist Buddhistic rote
to the *schrecklichkeit* and warsongs of his tribe.
The Pope still twangs his harp for chastity—
the boys of the jihad on a string of unwitting camels
rush paradise, halls stocked with adolescent
beauties, both sexes for simple nomad tastes—
how warmly they sleep in tile-abstraction alcoves;
love is resurrection, and her war a rose:
woman wants man, man woman, as naturally
as the thirsty frog desires the rain.

Death of Count Roland

King Marsilius of Saragossa
does not love God, he is carried to the shade of the orchard,
and sits reclining on his bench of blue tile,
with more than twenty thousand men about him;
his speech is only the one all kings must make,
it did to spark the Franco-Moorish War. . . .
At war's end Roland's brains seeped from his ears;
he called for the Angel Michael, his ivory horn,
prayed for his peers, and scythed his sword, Durendal—
farther away than a man might shoot a crossbow,
toward Saragossa, there is a grassy place,
Roland went to it, climbed the little mound:
a beautiful tree there, four great stones of marble—
on the green grass, he has fallen back, has fainted.

Joinville and Louis IX

"Given my pilgrim's scarf and staff, I left
the village of Joinville on foot, barefoot, in my shirt,
never turning my eyes for fear my heart would melt
at leaving my mortgaged castle, my two fair children—
a Crusader? Some of us were, and lived to be ransomed.
Bishops, nobles, and Brothers of the King
strolled free in Acre, and begged the King to sail home,
and leave the meaner folk. Sore of heart then,
I went to a barred window, and passed my arms through the bars
of the window, and someone came, and leant on my shoulders,
and placed his two hands on my forehead—Philip de Nemours?
I screamed, 'Leave me in peace!' His hand dropped by chance,
and I knew the King by the emerald on his finger:
'If I should leave Jerusalem, who will remain?' "

Dante 3. Buonconte

"No one prays for me . . . Giovanna or the others."
What took you so far from Campaldino
we never found your body? "Where the Archiano
at the base of the Casentino loses its name
and becomes the Arno, I stopped running,
the war lost, and wounded in the throat—
flying on foot and splashing the field with blood.
There I lost sight and speech, and died saying *Maria*. . . .
I'll tell you the truth, tell it to the living,
an angel and devil fought with claws for my soul:
You angel, why do you rob me for his last word?
The rain fell, then the hail, my body froze,
until the raging Archiano snatched me,
and loosened my arms I'd folded like the cross."

Dames du Temps Jadis

Say in what country, where
is Flora, the Roman,
Archipaida or Thais
far lovelier,
or Echo whose voice would answer
across the land or river—
her beauty more than human.
Where is our wise Eloise
and Peter Abelard
gelded at Saint Denis
for love of her—
Jehanne the good maid of Lorraine
the English burned at Rouen?
Where, mother of God, is last year's snow?

Coleridge and Richard II

Coleridge wasn't flatter-blinded by
his kinship with Richard II . . . a *feminine friendism*,
the constant overflow of imagination
proportioned to his dwindling will to act.
Richard unkinged saw shipwreck in the mirror,
not the King; womanlike, he feared
he must see himself more frequently to exist,
the white glittering inertia of the iceberg.
Coleridge had the cheering fancy only blacks
would cherish slavery for two thousand years;
though most negroes in 1800 London were
onwardlooking and further exiled
from the jungle of dead kings than Coleridge,
the one poet who blamed his failure on himself.

Bosworth Field

In a minute, two inches of rain stream through my dry
garden stones, clear as crystal, without trout—
we have gone down and down, gone the wrong brook.
Robespierre and Stalin mostly killed people they knew,
Richard the Third was Dickon, Duke of Gloucester,
long arm of the realm, goddam blood royal,
terrible underpinning of what he let breathe.
No wonder, we have dug him up past proof,
still fighting drunk on mortal wounds,
ready to gallop down his own apologist.
What does he care for Thomas More and Shakespeare
pointing fingers at his polio'd body;
for the moment, he is king; he is the king
saying: *it's better to have lived, than live.*

Sir Thomas More

Holbein's More, my patron saint as a convert,
the gold chain of *S*'s, the golden rose,
the plush cap, the brow's damp feathertips of hair,
the good eyes' stern, facetious twinkle, ready
to turn from executioner to martyr—
or saunter with the great King's bluff arm on your neck,
feeling that friend-slaying, terror-dazzled heart
ballooning off into its awful dream—
a noble saying, "How the King must love you!"
And you, "If it were a question of my head,
or losing his meanest village in France . . ."
then by the scaffold and the headsman's axe—
"Friend, give me your hand for the first step,
as for coming down, I'll shift for myself."

Anne Boleyn

The cows of Potter and Albert Cuyp are timeless;
in the depths of Europe, scrawly pastures
and scrawlier hamlets unwatered by paint or Hegel,
the cow is king. None of our rear-guard painters,
lovers of nature and haters of abstraction,
make an art of farming. With a bull's moist eye,
dewlap and misty phallus, Cuyp caught the farthest glisten,
tonnage and rumination of the sod. . . .
There was a whiteness to Anne Boleyn's throat,
shiver of heresy, *raison d'état,*
the windfall abandon of a Giorgione,
Renaissance high hand with nature—only the lovely,
the good, the wealthy serve the Venetian, whose art
knows nothing yet of husbandry and cattle.

Death of Anne Boleyn

Summer hail flings crystals on the window—
they wrapped the Lady Anne's head in a white handkerchief. . . .
To Wolsey, *the nightcrow*, but to Anthony Froude,
stoic virtue spoke from her stubborn lips and chin—
five adulteries in three years of marriage;
the game was hotly charged. "I hear say I'll
not die till noon; I am very sorry therefore,
I thought to be dead this hour and past my pain."
Her jailer told her that beheading was no pain—
"It is subtle." "I have a little neck,"
she said, and put her hands about it laughing.
They guessed she had much pleasure and joy in death—
no foreigners admitted. By the King's abundance
the scene was open to any Englishman.

Charles V by Titian

But we cannot go back to Charles V
barreled in armor, more gold fleece than king;
he haws on the gristle of a Flemish word,
his upper and lower Hapsburg jaws won't meet.
The sunset he tilts at is big Venetian stuff,
the true Charles, done by Titian, never lived.
The battle he rides offstage to is offstage.
No St. Francis, he did what Francis shied at,
gave up office, one of twenty monarchs
since Saturn who willingly made the grand refusal.
In his burgherish monastery, he learned he couldn't
put together a clock with missing parts.
He had dreamed of a democracy of Europe,
and carried enemies with him in a cage.

Marlowe

Vain surety of man's mind so near to death,
twenty-nine years with hopes to total fifty—
one blurred, hurried, still undecoded month
hurled Marlowe from England to his companion shades.
His mighty line denies his shady murder:
"How uncontrollably sweet and swift my life
with two London hits and riding my high tide,
drinking out May in Deptford with three friends,
one or all four perhaps in Secret Service.
Christ was a bastard, His Testament's filthily Greeked—
I died sweating, stabbed with friends who knew me—
was it the bar-check? . . . Tragedy is to die . . .
for that vacant parsonage, Posterity;
my plays are stamped in bronze, my life in tabloid."

Mary Stuart

They ran for their lives up nightslope, gained the car,
the girl's maxi-coat, Tsar officer's, dragged the snow,
she and he killed her husband, they stained the snow.
Romance of the snowflakes! Men swam up the night,
grass pike in overalls with scythe and pitchfork;
shouting, "Take the car, we'll smash the girl."
Once kings were on firstname terms with the poor,
a car was a castle, and money belonged to the rich. . . .
They roared off hell-wheel and scattered the weak mob;
happily only one man splashed the windshield,
they dared not pluck him, it was hard at night
to hold to the road with a carcass on the windshield—
at nightmare's end, the bedroom, dark night of marriage,
the bloodiest hands were joined and took no blood.

Rembrandt

His faces crack . . . if mine could crack and breathe!
His Jewish Bridegroom, hand spread on the Jewish Bride's
bashful, tapestried, level bosom, is faithful;
the fair girl, poor background, gives soul to his flayed steer.
Her breasts, the snowdrops, have lasted out the storm.
Often the Dutch were sacks, their women sacks,
the obstinate, undefeated hull of an old scow;
but Bathsheba's ample stomach, her heavy, practical feet,
are reverently dried by the faithful servant,
his eyes dwell lovingly on each fulfilled sag;
her unfortunate body is the privilege of service,
is radiant with an homage void of possession. . . .
We see, if we see at all, through a copper mist
the strange new idol for the marketplace.

The Worst Sinner, Jonathan Edwards' God

The earliest sportsman in the earliest dawn,
waking to what redness, waking a killer,
saw the red cane was sweet in his red grip;
the blood of the shepherd matched the blood of the wolf.
But Jonathan Edwards prayed to think himself
worse than any man that ever breathed;
he was a good man, and he prayed with reason—
which of us hasn't thought his same thought worse?
Each night I lie me down to heal in sleep;
two or three mornings a week, I wake to my sin—
sins, not sin; not two or three mornings, seven.
God himself cannot wake five years younger,
and drink away the venom in the chalice—
the best man in the best world possible.

Watchmaker God

Say life is the one-way trip, the one-way flight,
say this without hysterical undertones—
then you could say you stood in the cold light of science,
seeing as you are seen, espoused to fact.
Strange, life is both the fire and fuel; and we,
the animals and objects, must be here
without striking a spark of evidence
that anything that ever stopped living
ever falls back to living when life stops.
There's a pale romance to the watchmaker God
of Descartes and Paley; He drafted and installed
us in the Apparatus. He loved to tinker;
but having perfected what He had to do,
stood off shrouded in his loneliness.

Robespierre and Mozart as Stage

Robespierre could live with himself: "The republic
of Virtue without *la terreur* is a disaster.
Loot the châteaux, give bread to Saint Antoine."
He found the guillotine was not an idler
hearing *mort à Robespierre* from the Convention floor,
the high harsh laughter of the innocents,
the Revolution returning to grand tragedy—
is life the place where we find happiness,
or not at all? . . . Ask the voyeur
what blue movie is worth a seat at the keyhole. . . .
Even the prompted Louis Seize was living theater,
sternly and lovingly judged by his critics, who knew
a Mozart's insolent slash at folk could never
cut the gold thread of the suffocating curtain.

Saint-Just 1767–93

Saint-Just: his name seems stolen from the Missal. . . .
His chamois coat, the dandy's vast cravat
knotted with pretentious negligence;
he carried his head like the Holy Sacrament.
He thought only the laconic fit to rule
the austerity of his hideous cardboard Sparta.
"I shall move with the stone footsteps of the sun—
faction plagues the ebb of revolution,
as reptiles follow the dry bed of a torrent.
I am young and therefore close to nature.
Happiness is a new idea in Europe;
we bronzed liberty with the guillotine.
I'm still twenty, I've done badly, I'll do better."
He did, the scaffold, "Je sais où je vais."

Napoleon

Boston's used bookshops, anachronisms from London,
are gone; it's hard to guess now why I spent
my vacations lugging home his third-hand *Lives*—
shaking the dust from that stationary stock:
cheap deluxe lithographs and gilt-edged pulp
on a man . . . not bloodthirsty, not sparing of blood,
with an eye and *sang-froid* to manage everything;
his iron hand no mere appendage of his mind
for improbable contingencies . . .
for uprooting races, lineages, Jacobins—
the price was paltry . . . three million soldiers dead,
grand opera fixed like morphine in their veins.
Dare we say, he had no moral center?
All gone like the smoke of his own artillery?

Waterloo

A thundercloud hung on the mantel of our summer
cottage by the owners, Miss Barnard and Mrs. Curtis:
a sad picture, half life-scale, removed and no doubt
scrapped as too English Empire for our taste:
Waterloo, Waterloo! You could choose sides then:
the engraving made the blue French uniforms black,
the British Redcoats gray; those running were French—
an aide-de-camp, Napoleon's perhaps,
wore a cascade of overstated braid,
there sabered, dying, his standard wrenched from weak hands;
his killer, a bonneted fog-gray dragoon—
six centuries, this field of their encounter,
death-round of French sex against the English *no* . . .
La Gloire fading to *sauve qui peut* and *merde*.

Beethoven

Our cookbook is bound like Whitman's *Leaves of Grass*—
gold title on green. I have escaped its death,
take two eggs with butter, drink and smoke;
I live past prudence, not possibility—
who can banquet on the shifting cloud,
lie to friends and tell the truth in print,
be Othello offstage, or Lincoln retired from office?
The vogue of the vague, what can it teach an artist?
Beethoven was a Romantic, but too good;
did kings, republics or Napoleon teach him?
He was his own Napoleon. Did even deafness?
Does the painted soldier in the painting bleed?
Is the captive chorus of *Fidelio* bound?
For a good voice hearing is a torture.

Coleridge

Coleridge stands, he flamed for the one friend. . . .
This shower is warm, I almost breathe-in the rain
horseclopping from fire escape to skylight
down to a dungeon courtyard. In April, New York
has a smell and taste of life. For whom . . . what?
A newer younger generation faces
the firing squad, then their blood is wiped from the pavement. . . .
Coleridge's laudanum and brandy,
his alderman's stroll to positive negation—
his passive courage is paralysis,
standing him upright like tenpins for the strike,
only kept standing by a hundred scared habits . . .
a large soft-textured plant with pith within,
power without strength, an involuntary imposter.

The Lost Tune

As I grow older, I must admit with terror:
I have been there, the works of the masters lose,
songs with a mind, philosophy that danced.
Their *vivace* clogs, I am too tired, or wise.
I have read in books that even woman dies;
a figure cracks up sooner than a landscape—
your subject was Maine, a black and white engraving,
able to enlarge the formal luxury of
foliage rendered by a microscope,
a thousand blueberry bushes marching up
the flank of a hill; the artist, a lady, shoots
her lover panting like a stag at bay;
not very true, yet art—had Schubert scored it,
and his singer left the greenroom with her voice.

Margaret Fuller Drowned

You had everything to rattle the men who wrote.
The first American woman? Margaret Fuller . . .
in a white nightgown, your hair fallen long
at the foot of the foremast, you just forty,
your husband Angelo thirty, your Angelino one—
all drowned with brief anguish together. . . . Your fire-call,
your voice, was like thorns crackling under a pot,
you knew the Church burdens and infects as all dead forms,
however gallant and lovely in their life;
progress is not by renunciation.
"Myself," you wrote, "is all I know of heaven.
With my intellect, I always can
and always shall make out, but that's not half—
the life, the life, O my God, will life never be sweet?"

Abraham Lincoln

All day I bang and bang at you in thought,
as if I had the license of your wife. . . .
If War is the continuation of politics—
is politics the discontinuation of murder?
You may have loved underdogs and even mankind,
this one thing made you different from your equals . . .
you, our one genius in politics . . . who followed
the bull to the altar . . . to death in unity.
J'accuse, j'accuse, j'accuse, j'accuse, j'accuse!
Say it in American. Who shot the deserters?
Winter blows sparks in the face of the new God,
who breathes-in fire and dies with cooling faith,
as the firebrand turns black in the black hand,
and the squealing pig darts sidewise from his foot.

Verdun

I bow down to the great goiter of Verdun,
I know what's buried there, ivory telephone,
ribs, hips bleached to parchment, a pale machinegun—
they lie fatigued from too much punishment,
cling by a string to friends they knew firsthand,
to the God of our fathers still twenty like themselves.
Their medals and rosettes have kept in bloom,
they stay young, only living makes us age.
I know the sort of town they came from, straight brownstone,
each house cooled by a rectilinear private garden,
a formal greeting and a slice of life.
The city says, "I am the finest city"—
landmass held by half a million bodies
for Berlin and Paris, twin cities saved at Verdun.

Dream of Fair Ladies

Those maidens' high waists, languid steel and wedding cake,
fell, as waists must, and the white, white bust, to heel—
these once, the new wave; mostly they were many,
and would not let the children speak. They spoke
making a virtue of lost innocence.
They were never sober after ten
because life hit them, as it must by forty;
whenever they smoothed a dead cheek, it bled.
High-waisted maidens, languid steel and wedding cake . . .
they lost us on the road from chapel to graveyard.
Pace, pace, they asked for no man's seeding. . . .
Meeting them here is like ten years back home,
when hurting others was as necessary as breathing,
hurting myself more necessary than breathing.

Serpent

"When I was changed from a feeble cosmopolite
to a fanatical antisemite,
I didn't let you chew my time with chatter,
bury my one day's reasonable explanations
in your equal verisimilitude the next. . . .
But I got to the schools, their hysterical faith
in the spoken word, hypnotic hammer blows,
indelible, ineradicable,
the politician wedded to a mind—
I come once in a blue moon. . . . I my age,
its magical interpretation of the world,
enslaved to will and not intelligence. . . .
Soon it was obvious I didn't enjoy my war.
I'd no time for concerts, theater, to go to movies."

Words

Christ's first portrait was a donkey's head,
the simple truth is in his simple word,
lies buried in a random, haggard sentence,
cutting ten ways to nothing clearly carried. . . .
In our time, God is an entirely lost person—
there were two: Benito Mussolini and Hitler,
blind mouths shouting people into things.
After their Chicago deaths with girls and Lügers,
we know they gave a plot to what they planned.
No league against the ephemeral Enemy lasts;
not even the aristocracy of the Commune
curing the seven plagues of economics,
to wither daily in favor of the state,
a covenant of swords without the word.

Sunrise

There is always enough daylight in hell to blind;
the flower of what was left grew sweeter for them,
two done people conversing with bamboo fans
as if to brush the firefall from the air—
Admiral Onishi, still a cult to his juniors,
the father of the Kamikazes . . . he became a fish-hawk
flying our armadas down like game;
his young pilots loved him to annihilation.
He chats in his garden, the sky is zigzag fire.
One butchery is left, his wife keeps nagging him to do it.
Husband and wife taste cup after cup of Scotch;
how garrulously they patter about their grandchildren—
when his knife goes home, it goes home wrong. . . .
For eighteen hours you died with your hand in hers.

Randall Jarrell 1. October 1965

Sixty, seventy, eighty: I would see you mellow,
unchanging grasshopper, whistling down the grass-fires;
the same hair, snow-touched, and wrist for tennis; soon doubles
not singles. . . . Who dares go with you to your deadfall,
see the years wrinkling up the reservoir,
watch the ivy turning a wash of blood
on your infirmary wall? Thirty years ago,
as students waiting for Europe and spring term to end—
we saw below us, golden, small, stockstill,
the college polo field, cornfields, the feudal airdrome,
the McKinley Trust; behind, above us, the tower,
the dorms, the fieldhouse, the Bishop's palace and chapel—
Randall, the scene still plunges at the windshield,
apples redden to ripeness on the whiplash bough.

Randall Jarrell 2

I grizzle the embers of our onetime life,
our first intoxicating disenchantments,
dipping our hands once, not twice in the newness . . .
coming back to Kenyon on the Ohio local—
the view, middle distance, back and foreground, shifts,
silos shifting squares like chessmen—a wheel
turned by the water buffalo through the blue
of true space before the dawn of days. . . .
Then the night of the caged squirrel on his wheel,
lights, eyes, peering at you from the overpass;
black-gloved, black-coated, you plod out stubbornly
as if in lockstep to grasp your blank not-I
at the foot of the tunnel . . . as if asleep, Child Randall,
greeting the cars, and approving—your harsh luminosity.

Randall Jarrell 3

The dream went like a rake of sliced bamboo,
slats of dust distracted by a downdraw;
I woke and knew I held a cigarette;
I looked, there was none, could have been none;
I slept off years before I woke again,
palming the floor, shaking the sheets. I saw
nothing was burning. I awoke, I saw
I was holding two lighted cigarettes. . . .
They come this path, old friends, old buffs of death.
Tonight it's Randall, his spark still fire though humble,
his gnawed wrist cradled like *Kitten.* "What kept you so long,
racing the cooling grindstone of your ambition?
You didn't write, you *rewrote.* . . . But tell me,
Cal, why did we live? Why do we die?"

T. S. Eliot

Caught between two streams of traffic, in the gloom
of Memorial Hall and Harvard's war-dead. . . . And he:
"Don't you loathe to be compared with your relatives?
I do. I've just found two of mine reviewed by Poe.
He wiped the floor with them . . . and I was *delighted*."
Then on with warden's pace across the Yard,
talking of Pound, "It's balls to say he only
pretends to be Ezra. . . . He's better though. This year,
he no longer wants to rebuild the Temple at Jerusalem.
Yes, he's better. '*You* speak,' he said, when he'd talked two hours.
By then I had absolutely nothing to *say*."
Ah Tom, one muse, one music, had one your luck—
lost in the dark night of the brilliant talkers,
humor and honor from the everlasting dross!

Ezra Pound

Horizontal on a deckchair in the ward
of the criminal mad. . . . A man without shoestrings clawing
the Social Credit broadside from your table, you saying,
". . . here with a black suit and black briefcase; in the brief,
an abomination, Possum's *hommage* to Milton."
Then sprung; Rapallo, and the decade gone;
and three years later, Eliot dead, you saying,
"Who's left alive to understand my jokes?
My old Brother in the arts . . . besides, he was a smash of a poet."
You showed me your blotched, bent hands, saying, "Worms.
When I talked that nonsense about Jews on the Rome
wireless, Olga knew it was shit, and still loved me."
And I, "Who else has been in Purgatory?"
You, "I began with a swelled head and end with swelled feet."

William Carlos Williams

Who loved more? William Carlos Williams,
in collegiate black slacks, gabardine coat,
and loafers polished like rosewood on yachts,
straying stonefoot through his town-end garden,
man and flower seedy with three autumn strokes,
his brown, horned eyes enlarged, an ant's, through glasses;
his Mother, stonedeaf, her face a wizened talon,
her hair the burnt-out ash of lush Puerto Rican grass;
her black, blind, bituminous eye inquisitorial.
"Mama," he says, "which would you rather see here,
me or two blondes?" Then later, "The old bitch
is over a hundred, I'll kick off tomorrow."
He said, "I am sixty-seven, and more
attractive to girls than when I was seventeen."

Robert Frost

Robert Frost at midnight, the audience gone
to vapor, the great act laid on the shelf in mothballs,
his voice is musical and raw—he writes in the flyleaf:
For Robert from Robert, his friend in the art.
"Sometimes I feel too full of myself," I say.
And he, misunderstanding, "When I am low,
I stray away. My son wasn't your kind. The night
we told him Merrill Moore would come to treat him,
he said, 'I'll kill him first.' One of my daughters thought things,
thought every male she met was out to make her;
the way she dressed, she couldn't make a whorehouse."
And I, "Sometimes I'm so happy I can't stand myself."
And he, "When I am too full of joy, I think
how little good my health did anyone near me."

Stalin

Winds on the stems make them creak like things of man;
a hedge of vines and bushes—three or four
kinds, grape-leaf, elephant-ear and alder,
an arabesque, imperfect and alive,
a hundred hues of green, the darkest shades
fall short of black, the whitest leaf-back short of white.
The state, if we could see behind the wall,
is woven of perishable vegetation.
Stalin? What shot him clawing up the tree of power—
millions plowed under with the crops they grew,
his intimates dying like the spider-bridegroom?
The large stomach could only chew success. What raised him
was an unusual lust to break the icon,
joke cruelly, seriously, and be himself.

Caracas 1

Through another of our cities without a center,
Los Angeles, and with as many cars
per foot, and past the 20-foot neon sign
for *Coppertone* on the cathedral, past the envied,
$700 per capita a year
in jerry skyscraper living slabs—to the White House
of El Presidente Leoni, his small men with 18-
inch repeating pistols, firing 45 bullets a minute,
two armed guards frozen beside us, and our champagne . . .
someone bugging the President: "Where are the girls?"
And the enclosed leader, quite a fellow, saying,
"I don't know where yours are, I know where to find mine". . . .
This house, this pioneer democracy, built
on foundations, not of rock, but blood as hard as rock.

The March 1

(FOR DWIGHT MACDONALD)

Under the too white marmoreal Lincoln Memorial,
the too tall marmoreal Washington Obelisk,
gazing into the too long reflecting pool,
the reddish trees, the withering autumn sky,
the remorseless, amplified harangues for peace—
lovely to lock arms, to march absurdly locked
(unlocking to keep my wet glasses from slipping)
to see the cigarette match quaking in my fingers,
then to step off like green Union Army recruits
for the first Bull Run, sped by photographers,
the notables, the girls . . . fear, glory, chaos, rout . . .
our green army staggered out on the miles-long green fields,
met by the other army, the Martian, the ape, the hero,
his new-fangled rifle, his green new steel helmet.

The March 2

Where two or three were flung together, or fifty,
mostly white-haired, or bald, or women . . . sadly
unfit to follow their dream, I sat in the sunset
shade of our Bastille, the Pentagon,
nursing leg- and arch-cramps, my cowardly,
foolhardy heart; and heard, alas, more speeches,
though the words took heart now to show how weak
we were, and right. An MP sergeant kept
repeating, "March slowly through them. Don't even brush
anyone sitting down." They tiptoed through us
in single file, and then their second wave
trampled us flat and back. Health to those who held,
health to the green steel head . . . to your kind hands
that helped me stagger to my feet, and flee.

Worse Times

In college, we harangued our platitudes,
and hit democracy with Plato's corkscrew—
we demanded art as disciplined
and dark as Marx or Calvin's *Institutes*—
there was precedent for this argument:
flames from the open hearth of Thor and Saul,
beef frescoed on the vaults of cave and clan,
fleshpots, firewater, slung chunks of awk and man—
the missiles no dialectician's hand could turn.
Children have called the anthropoid, father;
he'd stay home Sunday, and they walked on coals. . . .
The passage from lower to upper middle age
is quicker than the sigh of a match in the water—
we too were students, and betrayed our hand.

Ulysses

Shakespeare stand-ins, same string hair, gay, dirty . . .
there's a new poetry in the air, it's youth's
patent, lust coolly led on by innocence—
late-flowering Garden, far from Eden fallen,
and still fair! None chooses as his model
Ulysses landhugging from port to port for girls . . .
his marriage a cover for the underworld,
dark harbor of suctions and the second chance.
He won Nausicaa twenty years too late. . . .
Scarred husband and wife sit naked, one Greek smile,
thinking *we were bound to fall in love*
if only we stayed married long enough—
because our ships are burned and all friends lost.
How we wish we were friends with half our friends!

Fever

Desultory, sour commercial September
lies like a mustard plaster on the back—
Pavlov's dogs, when tortured, turned neurotics. . . .
If I see something unbelievable in the city,
it is the woman shopper out in war-paint—
the druggist smiles etherealized in glass. . . .
Sometimes, my mind is a rocked and dangerous bell;
I climb the spiral stairs to my own music,
each step more poignantly oracular,
something inhuman always rising in me—
a friend drops in the street and no one stirs.
Even if I should indiscreetly write
the perfect sentence, it isn't English—
I go to bed Lord Byron, and wake up bald.

Two Walls
(1968, Martin Luther King's Murder)

Somewhere a white wall faces a white wall,
one wakes the other, the other wakes the first,
each burning with the other's borrowed splendor—
the walls, awake, are forced to go on talking,
their color looks much alike, two shadings of white,
each living in the shadow of the other.
How fine our distinctions when we cannot choose!
Don Giovanni can't stick his sword through stone,
two contracting, white stone walls—their pursuit
of happiness and his, coincident. . . .
At this point of civilization, this point of the world,
the only satisfactory companion we
can imagine is death—this morning, skin lumping in my throat,
I lie here, heavily breathing, the soul of New York.

For Robert Kennedy 1925–68

Here in my workroom, in its listlessness
of Vacancy, like the old townhouse we shut for summer,
airtight and sheeted from the sun and smog,
far from the hornet yatter of his gang—
is loneliness, a thin smoke thread of vital
air. But what will anyone teach you now?
Doom was woven in your nerves, your shirt,
woven in the great clan; they too were loyal,
and you too were loyal to them, to death.
For them like a prince, you daily left your tower
to walk through dirt in your best cloth. Untouched,
alone in my Plutarchan bubble, I miss
you, you out of Plutarch, made by hand—
forever approaching your maturity.

For Eugene McCarthy
(July 1968)

I love you so. . . . Gone? Who will swear you wouldn't
have done good to the country, that fulfillment wouldn't
have done good to you—the father, as Freud says:
you? We've so little faith that anyone
ever makes anything better . . . the same and less—
ambition only makes the ambitious great.
The state lifts us, we cannot raise the state. . . . All
was yours though, lining down the balls for hours,
freedom of the hollow bowling-alley,
the thundered strikes, the boys. . . . Picking a quarrel
with you is like picking the petals of the daisy—
the game, the passing crowds, the rapid young
still brand your hand with sunflecks . . . coldly willing
to smash the ball past those who bought the park.

Publication Day

"Dear Robert: I wish you were not a complete stranger,
I wish I knew something more about your mercy,
could total your minimum capacity
for empathy—this varies so much from genius.
Can you fellow-suffer for a turned-down book?
Can you see through your tragic vision, and
have patience with one isolated heart?
Do you only suffer for other famous people,
and socially comforting non-entities?
Has the thistle of failure a place in your affection?
It's important to know these things; in your equestrian
portrait by Mailer, I don't find these things. . . .
I write as a woman flung from a sinking ship—
one raft in the distance . . . you represent that raft."

Lévi-Strauss in London

Lévi-Strauss, seeing two green plants in a cleft
of a cliff choosing diverse ammonites,
imagined a crevasse of millennia spanned—
when he told me this in English, our hostess spoke French;
I left the party with a severed head.
Since France gave the English their tongue, most civilized
Englishmen can muck along in French. . . .
I was so tired of camp and decoration,
so dog-tired of wanting social hope—
is *structuralism* the bridge from Marx to death?
Cézanne left his spine sticking in the landscape,
his slow brush sucked the resin from the pines;
Picasso's bullfighter's wrist for foil and flare—
they cannot fill the crack in everything God made.

The Nihilist as Hero

"All our French poets can turn an inspired line;
who has written six passable in sequence?"
said Valéry. That was a happy day for Satan. . . .
I want words meat-hooked from the living steer,
but a cold flame of tinfoil licks the metal log,
beautiful unchanging fire of childhood
betraying a monotony of vision. . . .
Life by definition breeds on change,
each season we scrap new cars and wars and women.
But sometimes when I am ill or delicate,
the pinched flame of my match turns unchanging green,
a cornstalk in green tails and seeded tassel. . . .
A nihilist wants to live in the world as is,
and yet gaze the everlasting hills to rubble.

Reading Myself

Like thousands, I took just pride and more than just,
struck matches that brought my blood to a boil;
I memorized the tricks to set the river on fire—
somehow never wrote something to go back to.
Can I suppose I am finished with wax flowers
and have earned my grass on the minor slopes of Parnassus. . . .
No honeycomb is built without a bee
adding circle to circle, cell to cell,
the wax and honey of a mausoleum—
this round dome proves its maker is alive;
the corpse of the insect lives embalmed in honey,
prays that its perishable work live long
enough for the sweet-tooth bear to desecrate—
this open book . . . my open coffin.

For Elizabeth Bishop 4

The new painting must live on iron rations,
rushed brushstrokes, indestructible paint-mix,
fluorescent lofts instead of French *plein air.*
Albert Ryder let his crackled amber moonscapes
ripen in sunlight. His painting was repainting,
his tiniest work weighs heavy in the hand.
Who is killed if the horseman never cry halt?
Have you seen an inchworm crawl on a leaf,
cling to the very end, revolve in air,
feeling for something to reach to something? Do
you still hang your words in air, ten years
unfinished, glued to your notice board, with gaps
or empties for the unimaginable phrase—
unerring Muse who makes the casual perfect?

Death and the Bridge
(From a Landscape by Frank Parker)

Death gallops on a bridge of red rail-ties and girder,
a onetime view of Boston humps the saltmarsh;
it is handpainted: this the eternal, provincial
city Dante saw as Florence and hell. . . .
On weekends even, the local TV station's
garbage disposer starts to sing at daybreak:
keep Sunday clean. We owe the Lord that much;
from the first, God squared His socialistic conscience,
gave universal capital punishment.
The red scaffolding relaxes and almost breathes:
no man is ever too good to die. . . .
We will follow our skeletons on the girder,
out of life and Boston, singing with Freud:
"God's ways are dark and very seldom pleasant."

Ice

Iced over soon; it's nothing; we're used to sickness;
too little perspiration in the bucket—
in the beginning, polio once a summer. Not now;
each day the cork more sweetly leaves the bottle,
except a sudden falseness in the breath. . . .
Sooner or later the chalk wears out the smile,
and angrily we skate on blacker ice,
playthings of the current and cold fish—
the naught is no longer asset or disadvantage,
our life too long for comfort and too brief
for perfection—Cro-Magnon, dinosaur . . .
the neverness of meeting nightly like surgeons'
apprentices studying their own skeletons,
old friends and mammoth flesh preserved in ice.

End of a Year

These conquered kings pass furiously away;
gods die in flesh and spirit and live in print,
each library a misquoted tyrant's home.
A year runs out in the movies, must be written
in bad, straightforward, unscanning sentences—
stamped, trampled, branded on backs of carbons,
lines, words, letters nailed to letters, words, lines—
the typescript looks like a Rosetta Stone. . . .
One more annus mirabilis, its hero *hero demens*,
ill-starred of men and crossed by his fixed stars,
running his ship past sound-spar on the rocks. . . .
The slush-ice on the east bank of the Hudson
is rose-heather in the New Year sunset;
bright sky, bright sky, carbon scarred with ciphers.

from

For Lizzie and Harriet
(1973)

Part One

Harriet
(Born January 4, 1957)

Half a year, then a year and a half, then
ten and a half—the pathos of a child's fractions, turn-
ing up each summer. Her God a seaslug, God a queen
with forty servants, God—you gave up . . . things whirl
in the chainsaw bite of whatever squares
the universe by name and number. For
the hundredth time, we slice the fog, and round
the village with our headlights on the ground,
like the first philosopher Thales who thought all things water,
and fell in a well . . . trying to find a car
key. . . . It can't be here, and so it must be there
behind the next crook in the road or growth
of fog—there blinded by our feeble beams,
a face, clock-white, still friendly to the earth.

Harriet

A repeating fly, blueblack, thumbthick—so gross,
it seems apocalyptic in our house—
whams back and forth across the nursery bed
manned by a madhouse of stuffed animals,
not one a fighter. It is like a plane
dusting apple orchards or Arabs on the screen—
one of the mighty . . . one of the helpless. It
bumbles and bumps its brow on this and that,
making a short, unhealthy life the shorter.
I kill it, and another instant's added
to the horrifying mortmain of
ephemera: keys, drift, sea-urchin shells,
you packrat off with joy . . . a dead fly swept
under the carpet, wrinkling to fulfillment.

Elizabeth

An unaccustomed ripeness in the wood;
move but an inch and moldy splinters fall
in sawdust from the walls' aluminum-paint,
once loud and fresh, now aged to weathered wood.
Squalls of the seagull's exaggerated outcry
dim out in the fog. . . . *Pace, pace.* All day our words
were rusty fish-hooks—wormwood . . . Dear Heart's-Ease,
we rest from all discussion, drinking, smoking,
pills for high blood, three pairs of glasses—soaking
in the sweat of our hard-earned supremacy,
offering a child our leathery love. We're fifty,
and free! Young, tottering on the dizzying brink
of discretion once, you wanted nothing,
but to be old, do nothing, type and think.

These Winds (Harriet)

I see these winds, these are the tops of trees,
these are no heavier than green alder bushes;
touched by a light wind, they begin to mingle
and race for instability—too high placed
to stoop to the strife of the brush, these are the winds. . . .
Downstairs, you correct notes at the upright piano,
twice upright this midday Sunday torn from the whole
green cloth of summer; your room was once the laundry,
the loose tap beats time, you hammer the formidable
chords of *The Nocturne*, your second composition.
Since you first began to bawl and crawl
from the unbreakable lawn to this sheltered room, how often
winds have crossed the wind of inspiration—
in these too, the unreliable touch of the all.

Harriet

Spring moved to summer—the rude cold rain
hurries the ambitious, flowers and youth;
our flash-tones crackle for an hour, and then
we too follow nature, imperceptibly
change our mouse-brown to white lion's mane,
thin white fading to a freckled, knuckled skull,
bronzed by decay, by many, many suns. . . .
Child of ten, three-quarters animal,
three years from Juliet, half Juliet,
already ripened for the night on stage—
beautiful petals, what shall we hope for,
knowing one choice not two is all you're given,
health beyond the measure, dangerous
to yourself, more dangerous to others?

Part Two

Snake

One of God's creatures, just as much as you,
or God; what other bends its back in crooks
and curves so gracefully, to yield a point;
brews a more scalding venom from cold blood;
or flings a spine-string noosed about their throats:
hysterical bird, wild pig, or screaming rabbit?
Often I see it sunning on bright, brisk days,
when the heat has ebbed from its beloved rocks;
it is seamless, scaled-down to its integrity,
coiled for indiscriminate malevolence.
Lately, its valor pushed it past man's patience;
stoned, raw-fleshed, it finds its hole—sentenced
to hibernate fifty years. . . . It will thaw, then kill—
my little whip of wisdom, lamb in wolf-skin.

Christmas Tree

Twenty or more big cloth roses, pale rose or scarlet,
coil in the branches—a winning combination
for you, who have gathered them eight years or more:
bosom-blossoms from Caribbean steambath forests,
changeless, though changed from tree to tree, from Boston to here—
transplants like you. . . . Twenty small birds or more
nip the needles; a quail, a golden warbler—
the rest not great, except for those minnowy
green things, no known species, made of woven straw:
small dangling wicker hampers to tease a cat.
A fine thing, built with love; too unconventional
for our child to buy . . . the modesty
and righteousness of a woman's ego stripped naked:
"Because I lacked ambition, men thought me mad."

Dear Sorrow

We never see him now, except at dinner,
then you quarrel, and he goes upstairs. . . .
The old playground hasn't improved its asphalt base:
no growth, two broken swings, one OK—as was!
Our half century fought to stay in place.
But my eye lies, the precinct has turned hard,
hard more like a person than a thing.
Time that mends an object lets men go,
no doctor does the work of the carpenter.
It's our nerve and ideologies die first—
then we, so thumbed, worn out, used, got by heart.
Each new day I cherish a juster perspective,
doing all for the best, and therefore doing nothing,
fired by my second alcohol, remorse.

Harriet's Dream

"The broom trees twirped by our rosewood bungalow,
not wildlife, these were tropical and straw;
the Gulf fell like a shower on the fiber-sand;
it wasn't the country like our coast of Maine—
on ice for summer. We met a couple, not people,
squares asking Father if he was his name—
none ever said that I was Harriet. . . .
They were laying beach-fires with scarlet sticks and hatchets,
our little bungalow was burning—it
had burned, I was in it. I couldn't laugh,
I was afraid when the ceiling crashed in scarlet;
the shots were boom, the fire was fizz. . . . While sleeping
I scrubbed away my scars and blisters, unable
to answer if I had ever hurt."

Left Out of Vacation

"Some fathers may have some consideration,
but he is so wonderfully eccentric,
drinking buttermilk and wearing red socks.
It was OK—not having him in Florida;
Florence is different, Mother—big deal, two girls
eating alone in the Italian restaurant!" . . .
Only God could destroy the wonders He makes,
and shelve you too among them, Charles Sumner Lowell,
shiny horsechestnut-colored Burmese Cat,
waggling your literary haunches like Turgenev,
our animal whose only friends are persons—
now boarded with cats in a cathouse, moved at random
by the universal Love that moves the stars
forever rehearsing for the perfect comeback.

Das Ewig Weibliche

Birds have a finer body and tinier brain—
who asks the swallows to do drudgery,
clean, cook, pick up a peck of dust per diem?
If we knock on their homes, they wince uptight with fear,
farting about all morning past their young,
small as wasps fuming in their ash-leaf ball.
Nature lives off the life that comes to hand—
if we could feel and softly touch their being,
wasp, bee and swallow might live with us like cats.
The boiling yellow-jacket in her sack
of felon-stripe cut short above the knee
sings home . . . nerve-wrung creatures, wasp, bee and bird,
guerillas by day then keepers of the cell,
my wife in her wooden crib of seed and feed. . . .

Our Twentieth Wedding Anniversary   (Elizabeth)

Leaves espaliered jade on our barn's loft window,
sky stretched on a two-pane sash . . . it doesn't open:
stab of roofdrip, this leaf, that leaf twings,
an assault the heartless leaf rejects.
The picture is too perfect for our lives:
in Chardin's stills, the paint bleeds, juice is moving.
We have weathered the wet of twenty years.
Many cripples have won their place in the race;
Immanuel Kant remained unmarried and sane,
no one could Byronize his walk to class.
Often the player outdistances the game. . . .
This week is our first this summer to go unfretted;
we smell as green as the weeds that bruise the flower—
a house eats up the wood that made it.

The Hard Way   (Harriet)

Don't hate your parents, or your children will hire
unknown men to bury you at your own cost.
Child, forty years younger, will we live to see
your destiny written by our hands rewritten,
your adolescence snap the feathered barb,
the phosphorescence of your wake?
Under the stars, one sleeps, is free from household,
tufts of grass and dust and tufts of grass—
night oriented to the star of youth.
I only learn from error; till lately I trusted
in the practice of my hand. In backward Maine,
ice goes in season to the tropical,
then the mash freezes back to ice, and then
the ice is broken by another wave.

Words for Muffin, a Guinea-Pig

"Of late they leave the light on in my entry,
so I won't scare, though I never scare in the dark;
I bless this arrow that flies from wall to window . . .
five years and a nightlight given me to breathe—
Heidegger said spare time is ecstasy. . . .
I am not scared, although my life was short;
my sickly breathing sounded like dry leather.
Mrs. Muffin! It clicks. I had my day.
You'll paint me like Cromwell with all my warts:
small mop with a tumor and eyes too popped for thought.
I was a rhinoceros when jumped by my sons.
I ate and bred, and then I only ate,
my life zenithed in the Lyndon Johnson 'sixties . . .
this short pound God threw on the scales, found wanting."

End of Camp Alamoosook   (Harriet)

Less than a score, the dregs of the last day,
counselors and campers squat waiting for the ferry—
the unexpected, the exotic, the early
morning sunlight is more like premature twilight:
last day of the day, foreclosure of the camp.
Glare on the amber squatters, fire of fool's-gold—
like bits of colored glass, they cannot burn.
The Acadians must have gathered in such arcs;
a Winslow, our cousin, shipped them from Nova Scotia—
no malice, merely pushing his line of work,
herding guerillas in some Morality.
The campers suspect us, and harden in their shyness,
their gruff, faint voices hardly say hello,
singing, "Do we love it? *We love it.*"

Bringing a Turtle Home

On the road to Bangor, we spotted a domed stone,
a painted turtle petrified by fear.
I picked it up. The turtle had come a long walk,
200 millennia understudy to dinosaurs,
then their survivor. A god for the out-of-power. . . .
Faster gods come to Castine, flush yachtsmen who see
hell as a city very much like New York,
these gods give a bad past and worse future to men
who never bother to set a spinnaker;
culture without cash isn't worth their spit.
The laughter on Mount Olympus was always breezy. . . .
Goodnight, little Boy, little Soldier, live,
a toy to your friend, a stone of stumbling to God—
sandpaper Turtle, scratching your pail for water.

Returning Turtle

Weeks hitting the road, one fasting in the bathtub,
raw hamburger mossing in the watery stoppage,
the room drenched with musk like kerosene—
no one shaved, and only the turtle washed.
He was so beautiful when we flipped him over:
greens, reds, yellows, fringe of the faded savage,
the last Sioux, old and worn, saying with weariness,
"Why doesn't the Great White Father put his red
children on wheels, and move us as he will?"
We drove to the Orland River, and watched the turtle
rush for water like rushing into marriage,
swimming in uncontaminated joy,
lovely the flies that fed that sleazy surface,
a turtle looking back at us, and blinking.

Growth   (Harriet)

"I'm talking the whole idea of life, and boys,
with Mother; and then the heartache, when we're fifty. . . .
You've got to call your *Notebook, Book of the Century*,
but it will take you a century to write,
then I will have to revise it, when you die."
Latin, Spanish, swimming half a mile,
writing a saga with a churl named Eric,
Spanish, Spanish, math and rollerskates;
a love of party dresses, but not boys;
composing something with the bells of *Boris*:
"UNTITLED, would have to be the name of it. . . ."
You grow apace, you grow too fast apace,
too soon adult; no, not adult, like us. . . .
On the telephone, they say, "We're tired, aren't you?"

The Graduate   (Elizabeth)

"Transylvania's Greek Revival Chapel
is one of the best Greek Revival things in the South;
the College's most distinguished graduate
was a naturalist, he had a French name like Audubon.
My sister Margaret, a two-bounce basketball
player and all-Southern Center, came home
crying each night because of 'Happy' Chandler,
the coach, and later Governor of Kentucky.
Our great big tall hillbilly idiots keep
Kentucky pre-eminent in basketball.
And how! Still, if you are somewhat ill-born,
you feel your soul is not quite first-class. . . ."
Never such shimmering of intelligence,
though your wind was short, and you stopped smoking.

Long Summer

At dawn, the crisp goodbye of friends; at night,
enemies reunited, who tread, unmoving,
like circus poodles dancing on a ball—
something inhuman always rising on us,
punching you with embraces, holding out
a hesitant hand, unbending as a broom;
heaping the bright logs brighter, till we sweat
and shine as if anointed with hot oil:
straight alcohol, bright drops, dime-size and silver. . . .
Each day more poignantly resolved to stay,
each day more brutal, oracular and rooted,
dehydrated, and smiling in the fire,
unbandaging his tender, blood-baked foot,
hurt when he kicked aside the last dead bottle.

No Hearing

Belief in God is an inclination to listen,
but as we grow older and our freedom hardens,
we hardly even want to hear ourselves . . .
the silent universe our auditor—
I am to myself, and my trouble sings.
The Penobscot silvers to Bangor, the annual V
of geese beats above the moonborne bay—
their flight is too certain. Dante found this path
even before his first young leaves turned green;
exile gave seniority to his youth. . . .
White clapboards, black window, white clapboards, black window, white
    clapboards—
my house is empty. In our yard, the grass straggles. . . .
I stand face to face with lost Love—my breath
is life, the rough, the smooth, the bright, the drear.

No Hearing

Discovering, discovering trees light up green at night,
braking headlights-down, ransacking the roadsides
for someone strolling, fleeing to her wide goal;
passing blanks, the white Unitarian Church,
my barn on its bulwark, two allday padlocked shacks,
the town pool drained, the old lighthouse unplugged—
I watch the muddy breakers bleach to beerfroth,
our steamer, THE STATE OF MAINE, an iceberg at drydock.
Your question, my questioner? It is for you—
crouched in the gelid drip of the pine in our garden,
invisible almost when found, till I toss a white raincoat
over your sky-black, blood-trim quilted stormcoat—
you saying *I would prefer not*, like Bartleby:
small deer trembly and steel in your wet nest!

Outlivers   (Harriet and Elizabeth)

"If we could reverse the world to what it changed
a hundred years ago, or even fifty,
scrupulous drudgery, sailpower, hand-made wars;
God might give us His right to live forever
despite the eroding miracle of science. . . ."
"Was everything that much grander than it is?"
"Nothing seems admirable until it fails;
but it's only people we should miss.
The Goth, retarded epochs like crab and clam,
wept, as we do, for his dead child." We talk
like roommates bleeding night to dawn. You say,
"I hope, of course, you both will outlive me,
but you and Harriet are perhaps like countries
not yet ripe for self-determination."

My Heavenly Shiner   (Elizabeth)

The world atop Maine and our heads is north,
zeroes through Newfoundland to Hudson Bay:
entremets chinois et canadiens.
A world like ours will tumble on our heads,
my heavenly Shiner, think of it curving on?
You quiver on my finger like a small
minnow swimming in a crystal ball,
flittering radiance on my flittering finger.
The fish, the shining fish, they go in circles,
not one of them will make it to the Pole—
this isn't the point though, this is not the point;
think of it going on without a life—
in you, God knows, I've had the earthly life—
we were kind of religious, we thought in images.

It Did   (Elizabeth)

Luck, we've had it; our character the public's—
and yet we will ripen, ripen, know we once
did most things better, not just physical
but moral—turning in too high for love,
living twenty-four hours in one shirt or skirt,
breathless gossip, the breathless singles' service.
We could have done much worse. I hope we did
a hundred thousand things much worse! Poor *X's*,
chance went this way, that way with us here:
gain counted as loss, and loss as gain: our tideluck.
It did to live with, but finally all men worsen:
drones die of stud, the saint by staying virgin . . .
old jaw only smiles to bite the feeder;
corruption serenades the wilting tissue.

Seals

If we must live again, not us; we might
go into seals, we'd handle ourselves better:
able to dawdle, able to torpedo,
all too at home in our three elements,
ledge, water and heaven—if man could restrain his hand. . . .
We flipper the harbor, blots and patches and oilslick,
so much bluer than water, we think it sky.
Creature could face creator in this suit,
fishers of fish not men. Some other August,
the easy seal might say, "I could not sleep
last night; suddenly I could write my name. . . ."
Then all seals, preternatural like us,
would take direction, head north—their haven
green ice in a greenland never grass.

Obit

Our love will not come back on fortune's wheel—

in the end it gets us, though a man know what he'd have:
old cars, old money, old undebased pre-Lyndon
silver, no copper rubbing through . . . old wives;
I could live such a too long time with mine.
In the end, every hypochondriac is his own prophet.
Before the final coming to rest, comes the rest
of all transcendence in a mode of being, hushing
all becoming. I'm for and with myself in my otherness,
in the eternal return of earth's fairer children,
the lily, the rose, the sun on brick at dusk,
the loved, the lover, and their fear of life,
their unconquered flux, insensate oneness, painful "It was. . . ."
After loving you so much, can I forget
you for eternity, and have no other choice?

from

The Dolphin

(1973)

Fishnet

Any clear thing that blinds us with surprise,
your wandering silences and bright trouvailles,
dolphin let loose to catch the flashing fish . . .
saying too little, then too much.
Poets die adolescents, their beat embalms them,
the archetypal voices sing offkey;
the old actor cannot read his friends,
and nevertheless he reads himself aloud,
genius hums the auditorium dead.
The line must terminate.
Yet my heart rises, I know I've gladdened a lifetime
knotting, undoing a fishnet of tarred rope;
the net will hang on the wall when the fish are eaten,
nailed like illegible bronze on the futureless future.

Window

Tops of the midnight trees move helter-skelter
to ruin, if passion can hurt the classical
in the limited window of the easel painter—
love escapes our hands. We open the curtains:
a square of white-faced houses swerving, foaming,
the swagger of the world and chalk of London.
At each turn the houses wall the path of meeting,
and yet we meet, stand taking in the storm.
Even in provincial capitals,
storms will rarely enter a human house,
the crude and homeless wet is windowed out.
We stand and hear the pummeling unpurged,
almost uneducated by the world—
the tops of the moving trees move helter-skelter.

The Serpent

In my dream, my belly is yellow, panels
of mellowing ivory, splendid and still young,
though slightly ragged from defending me.
My tan and green backscales are cool to touch.
For one who has always loved snakes, it is no loss
to change nature. My fall was elsewhere—
how often I made the woman bathe in her waters.
With daylight, I turn small, a small snake
on the river path, arrowing up the jags.
Like this, like this, as the great clock clangs round,
and the green hunter leaps from turn to turn,
a new brass bugle slung on his invisible baldric;
he is groping for trout in the private river,
wherever it opens, wherever it happens to open.

Symptoms

I fear my conscience because it makes me lie.
A dog seems to lap water from the pipes,
life-enhancing water brims my bath—
(the bag of waters or the lake of the grave . . . ?)
from the palms of my feet to my wet neck—
I have no mother to lift me in her arms.
I feel my old infection, it comes once yearly:
lowered good humor, then an ominous
rise of irritable enthusiasm. . . .
Three dolphins bear our little toilet-stand,
the grin of the eyes rebukes the scowl of the lips,
they are crazy with the thirst. I soak,
examining and then examining
what I really have against myself.

Voices

"What a record year, even for us—
last March, I knew you'd manage by yourself,
you were the true you; now finally
your clowning makes visitors want to call a taxi,
you tease the patients as if they were your friends,
your real friends who want to save your image
from this genteel, disgraceful hospital.
Your trousers are worn to a mirror. . . . That new creature,
when I hear her name, I have to laugh.
You left two houses and two thousand books,
a workbarn by the ocean, and two slaves
to kneel and wait upon you hand and foot—
tell us why in the name of Jesus." Why
am I clinging here so foolishly alone?

Old Snapshot from Venice 1952

From the salt age, yes from the salt age,
courtesans, Christians fill the churchyard close;
that silly swelled tree is a spook with a twig for a head.
Carpaccio's Venice is as wide as the world,
Jerome and his lion lope to work unfeared. . . .
In Torcello, the stone lion I snapped behind you,
venti anni fa, still keeps his poodled hair—
wherever I move this snapshot, you have moved—
it's twenty years. The courtesans and lions
swim in Carpaccio's brewing tealeaf color.
Was he the first in the trade of painting to tell tales? . . .
You are making Boston in the sulfury a.m.,
dropping Harriet at camp, Old Love,
Eternity, You . . . a future told by tealeaves.

Fall Weekend at *Milgate*

1.

The day says nothing, and lacks for nothing . . . God;
but it's moonshine trying to gold-cap my life,
asking fees from the things I lived and loved,
pilgrim on this hard-edge Roman road.
Your portrait is fair-faced with your honesty,
the painter, your first husband, made girls stare.
Your wall mirror, a mat of plateglass sapphire,
mirror scrolls and claspleaves, shows this face,
huge eyes and dawn-gaze, rumination unruffled,
unlearning apparently, since 1952. . . .
I watch a feverish huddle of shivering cows;
you sit making a fishspine from a chestnut leaf.
We are at our crossroads, we are astigmatic
and stop uncomfortable, we are humanly low.

2.

The soaking leaves, green yellow, hold like rubber,
longer than our eyes glued to the window can take;
none tumble in the inundating air. . . .
A weak eye sees a miracle of birth.
I'm counterclockwise . . . did we meet
last April in London, late fifties in New York?
Autumn sops on our windshield with huge green leaves;
the seasons race engines in America
burying old lumber without truce—
leaf-blight and street dye and the discard girl . . .
the lover sops gin all day to solve his puzzle.
Nature, like philosophers, has one plot,
only good for repeating what it does well:
life emerges from wood and life from life.

3.
Milgate kept standing for four centuries,
good landlord alternating with derelict.
Most fell between. We're landlords for the weekend,
and watch October go balmy. Midday heat
draws poison from the Jacobean brick,
and invites the wilderness to our doorstep:
moles, nettles, last Sunday news, last summer's toys,
bread, cheeses, jars of honey, a felled elm
stacked like construction in the kitchen garden.
The warm day brings out wasps to share our luck,
suckers for sweets, pilots of evolution;
dozens drop in the beercans, clamber, buzz,
debating like us whether to stay and drown,
or, by losing legs and wings, take flight.

Records

". . . I was playing records on Sunday,
arranging all my records, and I came
on some of your voice, and started to suggest
that Harriet listen: then immediately
we both shook our heads. It was like hearing
the voice of the beloved who had died.
All this is a new feeling . . . I got the letter
this morning, the letter you wrote me Saturday.
I thought my heart would break a thousand times,
but I would rather have read it a thousand times
than the detached unreal ones you wrote before—
you doomed to know what I have known with you,
lying with someone fighting unreality—
love vanquished by his mysterious carelessness."

Mermaid

1.

I have learned what I wanted from the mermaid
and her singeing conjunction of tail and grace.
Deficiency served her. What else could she do?
Failure keeps snapping up transcendence,
bubble and bullfrog boating on the surface,
belly lustily lagging three inches lowered—
the insatiable fiction of desire.
None swims with her and breathes the air.
A mermaid flattens soles and picks a trout,
knife and fork in chainsong at the spine,
weeps white rum undetectable from tears.
She kills more bottles than the ocean sinks,
and serves her winded lovers' bones in brine,
nibbled at recess in the marathon.

3.

Our meetings are no longer like a screening;
I see the nose on my face is just a nose,
your *bel occhi grandi* are just eyes
in the photo of you arranged as figurehead
or mermaid on the prow of a Roman dory,
bright as the morning star or a blond starlet.
Our twin black and tin Ronson butane lighters
knock on the sheet, are what they are,
too many, and burned too many cigarettes. . . .
Night darkens without your necessary call,
it's time to turn your pictures to the wall;
your moon-eyes water and your nervous throat
gruffs my directive, *"You must go now go."*
Contralto mermaid, and stone-deaf at will.

4.

I see you as a baby killer whale,
free to walk the seven seas for game,
warmhearted with an undercoat of ice,
a nerve-wrung back . . . all muscle, youth, intention,
and skill expended on a lunge or puncture—
hoisted now from conquests and salt sea
to flipper-flapper in a public tank,
big deal for Sunday children. . . . My blind love—
on the Via Veneto, a girl
counting windows in a glass cafe,
now frowning at her menu, now counting out
neanderthals flashed like shorebait on the walk. . . .
Your stamina as *inside-right* at school
spilled the topheavy boys, and keeps you pure.

5.

One wondered who would see and date you next,
and grapple for the danger of your hand.
Will money drown you? Poverty, though now
in fashion, debases women as much as wealth.
You use no scent, dab brow and lash with shoeblack,
willing to face the world without more face.
I've searched the rough black ocean for you,
and saw the turbulence drop dead for you,
always lovely, even for those who had you,
Rough Slitherer in your grotto of haphazard.
I lack manhood to finish the fishing trip.
Glad to escape beguilement and the storm,
I thank the ocean that hides the fearful mermaid—
like God, I almost doubt if you exist.

In the Mail

"Your student wrote me, if he took a plane
past Harvard, at any angle, at any height,
he'd see a missing person, *Mr. Robert Lowell*.
You insist on treating Harriet as if she
were thirty or a wrestler—she is only thirteen.
She is normal and good because she had normal and good
parents. She is threatened of necessity. . . .
I love you, darling, there's a black void,
as black as night without you. I long to see
your face and hear your voice, and take your hand—
I'm watching a scruffy, seal-colored woodchuck graze
on weeds, then lift his greedy snout and listen;
then back to speedy feeding. He weighs a ton,
and has your familiar human aspect munching."

Flounder

In a day we pass from the Northern Lights
to doomsday dawns. Crowds crush to work at eight,
and walk with less cohesion than the mist;
the sky, without malice, is acid, Christmas lights
are needed to reveal the Thames. God sees—
wash me as white as the sole I ate last night,
acre of whiteness, back of Folkestone sand,
cooked and skinned and white—the heart appeased.
Soles live in depth, see not, spend not . . . eat;
their souls are camouflaged to die in dishes,
flat on their backs, the posture of forgiveness—
squinch-eyes, bubbles of bloodshot worldliness,
unable ever to turn the other cheek—
at sea, they bite like fleas whatever we toss.

Exorcism

This morning, as if I were home in Boston, snow,
the pure witchery-bitchery of kindergarten winters;
my window whitens like a movie screen,
glaring, specked, excluding rival outlook—
I can throw what I want on this blank screen,
but only the show already chosen shows:
Melodrama with her stiletto heel
dancing bullet wounds in the parquet.
My words are English, but the plot is hexed:
one man, two women, the common novel plot . . .
what you love you are. . . .
You can't carry your talent with you like a suitcase.
Don't you dare mail us the love your life denies;
do you really know *what you have done?*

Plotted

Planes arc like arrows through the highest sky,
ducks *V* the ducklings across a puckered pond;
Providence turns animals to things.
I roam from bookstore to bookstore browsing books,
I too maneuvered on a guiding string
as I execute my written plot.
I feel how Hamlet, stuck with the Revenge Play
his father wrote him, went scatological
under this clotted London sky.
Catlike on a paper parapet,
he declaimed the words his prompter fed him,
knowing convention called him forth to murder,
loss of free will and license of the stage.
Death's not an event in life, it's not lived through.

The Couple

"Twice in the past two weeks I think I met
Lizzie in the recurrent dream.
We were out walking. *What sort of street*, you ask,
fair or London? It was our own street.
What did you hear and say? We heard ourselves.
The sidewalk was two feet wide. We, arm in arm,
walked, squelching the five-point oakleaves under heel—
happily, they melted under heel.
Our manner had some intimacy in my dream.
What were you doing on this honeymoon?
Our conversation had a simple plot,
a story of a woman and a man
versifying her tragedy—
we were talking like sisters . . . you did not exist."

Artist's Model

"*If it were done, 'twere well it were done quickly*—
to quote a bromide, your vacillation
is acne." And we totter off the strewn stage,
knowing tomorrow's migraine will remind us
how drink heightened the brutal flow of elocution. . . .
We follow our script as timorously as actors,
divorced from making a choice by our need to act.
"If you woke and found an egg in your shoe,
would you feel you'd lost this argument?"
It's over, my clothes fly into your borrowed suitcase,
the good day is gone, the broken champagne glass
crashes in the ashcan . . . private whims, and illusions,
too messy for our character to survive.
I come on walking off-stage backwards.

Mermaid Emerging

The institutions of society
seldom look at a particular—
Degas's snubnosed dancer swings on high,
legging the toplights, never leaving stage,
enchanting lovers of art, discerning none.
Law fit for all fits no one like a glove. . . .
Mermaid, why are you another species?
"Because, you, I, everyone is unique."
Does anyone ever make you do anything?
"Do this, do that, do nothing; you're not chained.
I am a woman or I am a dolphin,
the only animal man really loves,
I spout the smarting waters of joy in your face—
rough-weather fish, who cuts your nets and chains."

Angling

Withdrawn to a third your size, and frowning doubts,
you stare in silence through the afterdinner,
when wine takes our liberty and loosens tongues—
fair-face, ball-eyes, profile of a child,
except your eyelashes are always blacked,
each hair colored and quickened like tying a fly.
If a word amuses you, the room includes your voice,
you are audible; none can catch you out,
your flights are covered by a laughing croak—
a flowered dress lost in the flowered wall.
I am waiting like an angler with practice and courage;
the time to cast is now, and the mouth open,
the huge smile, head and shoulders of the dolphin—
I am swallowed up alive . . . I am.

Leaf-Lace Dress

Leaf-lace, a simple intricate design—
if you were not inside it, nothing much,
bits of glinting silver on crinkled lace—
you fall perhaps metallic and as good.
Hard to work out the fact that makes you good,
whole spirit wrought from toys and nondescript,
though nothing less than the best woman in the world.
Cold the green shadows, iron the seldom sun,
harvest has worn her swelling shirt to dirt.
Agony says we cannot live in one house,
or under a common name. This was the sentence—
I have lost everything. I feel a strength,
I have walked five miles, and still desire to throw
my feet off, be asleep with you . . . asleep and young.

Late Summer at *Milgate*

An air of lateness blows through the redone bedroom,
a sweetish smell of shavings, wax and oil;
the sun in heaven enflames a sanded floor.
Age is our reconciliation with dullness,
my varnish complaining, *I will never die.*
I still remember more things than I forgo:
once it was the equivalent of everlasting
to stay loyal to my other person loved—
in the fallen apple lurked a breath of spirits,
the uninhabitable granite shone
in Maine, each rock our common gravestone. . . .
I sit with my staring wife, children . . . the dour Kent sky
a smudge of mushroom. In temperate years the grass
stays green through New Year—I, my wife, our children.

Robert Sheridan Lowell

Your midnight ambulances, the first knife-saw
of the child, feet-first, a string of tobacco tied
to your throat that won't go down, your window heaped
with brown paper bags leaking peaches and avocados,
your meals tasting like Kleenex . . . too much blood is seeping . . .
after twelve hours of labor to come out right,
in less than thirty seconds swimming the blood-flood:
Little Gingersnap Man, homoform,
flat and sore and alcoholic red,
only like us in owning to middle-age.
"If you touch him, he'll burn your fingers."
"It's his health, not fever. Why are the other babies so pallid?
His navy-blue eyes tip with his head. . . . Darling,
we have escaped our death-struggle with our lives."

Careless Night

So country-alone, and O so very friendly,
our heaviness lifted from us by the night . . .
we dance out into its diamond suburbia,
and see the hill-crown's unrestricted lights—
all day these encroaching neighbors are out of sight.
Huge smudge sheep in burden becloud the grass,
they swell on moonlight and weigh two hundred pounds—
hulky as you in your white sheep-coat, as nervous to gallop. . . .
The Christ-Child's drifter shepherds have left this field,
gone the shepherd's breezy too predictable pipe.
Nothing's out of earshot in this daylong night;
nothing can be human without man.
What is worse than hearing the late-born child crying—
and each morning waking up glad we wake?

Wildrose

A mongrel image for all summer, our scene at breakfast:
a bent iron fence of straggly wildrose glowing
below the sausage-rolls of new-mown hay—
Sheridan splashing in his blue balloon tire:
whatever he touches he's told not to touch
and whatever he reaches tips over on him.
Things have gone on and changed, the next oldest
daughter bleaching her hair three shades lighter with beer—
but if you're not a blonde, it doesn't work. . . .
Sleeping, the always finding you there with day,
the endless days revising our revisions—
everyone's wildrose? . . . And our golden summer
as much as such people can. When most happiest
how do I know I can keep any of us alive?

Ivana

Small-soul-pleasing, loved with condescension,
even through the cro-magnon tirades of six,
the last madness of child-gaiety
before the trouble of the world shall hit.
Being chased upstairs is still instant-heaven,
not yet your sisters' weekends of voluntary scales,
accompanying on a recorder carols
rescored by the Sisters of the Sacred Heart in Kent.
Though burned, you are hopeful, accident cannot tell you
experience is what you do not want to experience.
Is the teenager the dominant of ache?
Or flirting seniles, their conversation three noises,
their life-expectancy shorter than the martyrs?
How all ages hate another age,

and lifelong wonder what was the perfect age!

Lost Fish

My heavy step is treacherous in the shallows—
once squinting in the sugared eelgrass for game,
I saw the glass torpedo of a big fish,
power strayed from unilluminating depth,
roaming through the shallows worn to bone.
I was seven, and fished without a hook.
Luckily, Mother was still omnipotent—
a battered sky, a more denuded lake,
my heavy rapier trolling rod bent *L*,
drowned stumps, muskrat huts, my record fish,
its endless waddling outpull like a turtle. . . .
The line snapped, or my knots pulled—I am free
to reach the end of the marriage on my knees.
The mud we stirred sinks in the lap of plenty.

Sick

I wake now to find myself this long alone,
the sun struggling to renounce ascendency—
two elephants are hauling at my head.
It might have been redemptive not to have lived—
in sickness, mind and body might make a marriage
if by depression I might find perspective—
a patient almost earns the beautiful,
a castle, two cars, old polished heirloom servants,
Alka-Seltzer on his breakfast tray—
the fish for the table bunching in the fishpond.
None of us can or wants to tell the truth,
pay fees for the over-limit we caught, while floating
the lonely river to senility
to the open ending. Sometimes in sickness,

we are weak enough to enter heaven.

Plane-Ticket

A virus and its hash of knobby aches—
more than ever flying seems too lofty,
the season unlucky for visiting New York,
for telephoning kisses transatlantic. . . .
The London damp comes in, its smell so fertile
trees grow in my room. I read Ford's *Saddest Story*,
his *triangle* I read as his student in Nashville.
Things that change us only change a fraction,
twenty-five years of marriage, a book of life—
a choice of endings? I have my round-trip ticket. . . .
After fifty so much joy has come,
I hardly want to hide my nakedness—
the shine and stiffness of a new suit, a feeling,
not wholly happy, of having been reborn.

Christmas

All too often now your voice is too bright;
I always hear you . . . commonsense and tension . . .
waking me to myself: truth, the truth, until
things are just as if they had never been.
I can't tell the things we planned for you this Christmas.
I've written my family not to phone today,
we had to put away your photographs.
We had to. We have no choice—we, I, they? . . .
Our Christmas tree seems fallen out with nature,
shedding to a naked cone of triggered wiring.
This worst time is not unhappy, green sap
still floods the arid rind, the thorny needles
catch the drafts, as if alive—I too,
because I waver, am counted with the living.

Christmas

The tedium and déjà-vu of home
make me love it; bluer days will come
and acclimatize the Christmas gifts:
redwood bear, lemon-egg shampoo, home-movie-
projector, a fat book, sunrise-red, inscribed
to me by Lizzie, "Why don't you lose yourself
and write a play about the fall of Japan?"
Slight spirits of birds, light burdens, no grave duty
to seem universally sociable
and polite. . . . We are at home and warm,
as if we had escaped the gaping jaws—
underneath us like a submarine,
nuclear and protective like a mother,
swims the true shark, the shadow of departure.

Dolphin

My Dolphin, you only guide me by surprise,
captive as Racine, the man of craft,
drawn through his maze of iron composition
by the incomparable wandering voice of Phèdre.
When I was troubled in mind, you made for my body
caught in its hangman's-knot of sinking lines,
the glassy bowing and scraping of my will. . . .
I have sat and listened to too many
words of the collaborating muse,
and plotted perhaps too freely with my life,
not avoiding injury to others,
not avoiding injury to myself—
to ask compassion . . . this book, half fiction,
an eelnet made by man for the eel fighting—

my eyes have seen what my hand did.

from

Selected Poems

(1976)

NINETEEN THIRTIES

First Things

Worse things could happen, life is insecure,
child's fears mostly a fallacious dream;
days one like the other let you live:
up at seven-five, to bed at nine,
the absolving repetitions, the three meals,
the nutritive, unimaginative dayschool meal,
laughing like breathing, one night's sleep a day—
solitude is the reward for sickness:
leafless, dusty February trees,
the field fretted in your window, all one cloth—
your mother harrowed by child gaiety. . . .
I remember that first desertion with fear;
something made so much of me lose ground,
the irregular and certain flight to art.

First Love

Two grades above me, though two inches shorter,
Leon Straus, sixthgrade fullback, his reindeer shirt—
passion put a motor in my heart.
I pretended he lived in the house across the street.
In first love a choice is seldom and blinding:
acres of whitecaps strew that muddy swell,
old crap and white plastic jugs lodge on shore.
Later, we learn better places to cast
our saffron sperm, and grasp what wisdom fears,
breasts stacked like hawknests in her boy friend's shirt,
things a deft hand tips on its back with a stick. . . .
Is it refusal of error breaks our life—
the supreme artist, Flaubert, was a boy before
the mania for phrases enlarged his heart.

1930's

The vaporish closeness of this two-month fog;
forty summers back, my brightest summer:
the rounds of Dealer's Choice, the housebound girls,
fog, the nightlife. Then, as now, the late curfew
boom of an unknown nightbird, local hemlock
gone black as Roman cypress, the barn-garage
below the tilted Dipper lighthouse-white,
a single misanthropic frog complaining
from the water hazard on the shortest hole;
till morning! Long dreams, short nights; their faces flash
like burning shavings, scattered bait and ptomaine
caught by the gulls with groans like straining rope;
windjammer pilgrims cowled in yellow hoods,
gone like the summer in their yellow bus.

Searching

I look back to you, and cherish what I wanted:
your flashing superiority to failure,
hair of yellow oak leaves, the arrogant
tanned brunt in the snow-starch of a loosened shirt—
your bullying half-erotic rollicking. . . .
The white bluffs rise above the old rock piers,
wrecked past insuring by two hurricanes.
As a boy I climbed those scattered blocks and left
the sultry Sunday seaside crowd behind,
seeking landsend, with my bending fishing rod
a small thread slighter than the dark arc of your eyebrow. . . .
Back at school, alone and wanting you,
I scratched my four initials, R.T.S.L.
like a dirty word across my bare, blond desk.

1930's

Shake of the electric fan above our village;
oil truck, refrigerator, or just men,
nightly reloading of the village flesh—
plotting worse things than marriage. They found dates
wherever summer is, the nights of the swallow
clashing in heat, storm-signal to stay home.
At night the lit blacktop fussing like a bosom;
Court Street, Dyer Lane, School, Green, Main Street
dropping through shade-trees to the shadeless haven—
young girls are white as ever. I only know
their mothers, sweatshirts gorged with tennis balls,
still air expiring from the tilting bubble—
I too wore armor, strode riveted in cloth,
stiff, a broken clamshell labeled man.

1930's

The boys come, each year more gallant, playing chicken,
then braking to a standstill for a girl—
like bullets hitting bottles, spars and gulls,
echoing and ricocheting across the bay . . .
hardy perennials! Kneedeep in the cowpond,
far from this cockfight, cattle stop to watch us,
and having had their fill, go back to lapping
soiled water indistinguishable from heaven.
Cattle get through living, but to *live*:
Kokoschka at eighty, saying, "If you last,
you'll see your reputation die three times,
or even three cultures; young girls are always here."
They *were* there . . . two fray-winged dragonflies,
clinging to a thistle, too clean to mate.

1930's

My legs hinge on my foreshortened bathtub
small enough for Napoleon's marching tub. . . .
The sun sallows a tired swath of balsam needles,
the color soothes, and yet the scene confines;
sun falls on so many, many other things:
Custer, leaping with his wind-gold scalplock,
half a furlong or less from the Sioux front line,
and Sitting Bull, who sent our rough riders under—
both now dead drops in the decamping mass. . . .
This wizened balsam, the sea-haze of blue gauze,
the distance plighting a tree-lip of land to the islands—
who can cash a check on solitude,
or is more loved for being distant . . . love-longing
mists my windshield, soothes the eye with milk.

Bobby Delano

The labor to breathe that younger, rawer air:
St. Mark's last football game with Groton lost on the ice-crust,
the sunlight gilding the golden polo coats
of boys with country seats on the Upper Hudson.
Why does that stale light stay? First Form hazing,
first day being sent on errands by an oldboy,
Bobby Delano, cousin of Franklin Delano Roosevelt—
deported soused off the Presidential yacht
baritoning *You're the cream in my coffee* . . .
his football, hockey, baseball letter at 15;
at 15, expelled. He dug my ass with a compass,
forced me to say "My mother is a whore."
My freshman year, he shot himself in Rio,
odious, unknowable, inspired as Ajax.

Humble in victory, chivalrous in defeat,
almost, almost. . . . I bow and watch the ashes
blush, crash, reflect: an age less privileged,
though burdened with its nobles, serfs and Faith.
The possessors. The fires men build live after them,
this night, this night, I elfin, I stonefoot,
walking the wildfire wildrose of those lawns,
filling this cottage window with the same
alluring emptiness, hearing the simmer
of the moon's mildew on the same pile of shells,
fruits of the banquet . . . boiled a brittle lobster-
shell-red, the hollow foreclaw, cracked, sucked dry,
flung on the ash-heap of a soggy carton—
two burnt-out, pinhead, black and popping eyes.

Long Summers

Months of it, and the inarticulate mist so thick
we turned invisible to one another
across the room; the floor, aslant, shot hulling
through thunderheads, gun-cotton dipped in pitch,
salmon, when lighted, as the early moon,
snuffed by the malodorous and frosted murk—
not now! Earth's solid and the sky is light,
yet even on the steadiest day, dead noon,
the sun stockstill like Joshua's in midfield,
I have to brace my hand against a wall
to keep myself from swaying—swaying wall,
straitjacket, hypodermic, helmeted
doctors, one crowd, white-smocked, in panic, hit,
stop, bury the runner on the cleated field.

Long Summers

Two in the afternoon. The restlessness.
Greek Islands. Maine. I have counted the catalogue
of ships down half its length: the blistered canvas,
the metal bowsprits, once pricking up above
the Asian outworks like a wedge of geese,
the migrant yachtsmen, and the fleet in irons. . . .
The iron bell is rocking like a baby,
the high tide's turning on its back exhausted,
the colored, dreaming, silken spinnakers
shove through the patches in the island pine,
as if vegetating millennia of lizards fed
on fern and cropped the treetops . . . a nation of gazelles,
straw-chewers in the African siesta. . . .
I never thought scorn of things; struck fear in no man.

Long Summers

Up north here, in my own country, and free—
look on it with a jaundiced eye, you'll see
the manhood of the sallowing south, *noblesse*
oblige turned redneck, and the fellaheen;
yet sometimes the Nile is wet; life's lived as painted:
those couples, one in love and profit, swaying
their children and their slaves the height of children,
supple and gentle as giraffes or newts;
the waist still willowy, and the paint still fresh;
decorum without hardness; no harness on
the woman, and no armor on the husband,
the red clay Master with his feet of clay,
catwalking lightly through his conquests, leaving
one model, dynasties of faithless copies.

1930's

The circular moon saw-wheels through the oak-grove;
below it, clouds . . . permanence of the clouds,
many as have drowned in the Atlantic.
It makes one larger to sleep with the sublime;
the Great Mother shivers under the dead oak—
such cures the bygone Reichian prophets swore to,
such did as gospel for their virgin time—
two elements were truants: man and nature.
By sunrise, the sky is nearer. Strings of fog,
such as we haven't seen in fifteen months,
catch shyly over stopping lobster boats—
smoke-dust the Chinese draftsman made eternal.
His brushwork wears; the hand decayed. A hand does—
we can have faith, at least, the hand decayed.

1930's

"After my marriage, I found myself in constant
companionship with this almost stranger I found
neither agreeable, interesting, nor admirable,
though he was always kind and irresponsible.
The first years after our one child was born,
his daddy was out at sea; that helped, I could bask
on the couch of inspiration and my dreams.
Our courtship was rough, his disembarkation
unwisely abrupt. I was animal,
healthy, easily tired; I adored luxury,
and should have been an extrovert; I usually
managed to make myself pretty comfortable. . . .
Well," she laughed, "we both were glad to dazzle.
A genius temperament should be handled with care."

Anne Dick 1. 1936

Father's letter to your father said
stiffly and much too tersely he'd been told
you visited my college rooms alone—
I can still crackle that slight note in my hand.
I see your pink father—you, the outraged daughter.
That morning nursing my dark, quiet fire
on the empty steps of the Harvard Fieldhouse in
vacation . . . saying the start of *Lycidas* to myself
fevering my mind and cooling my hot nerves—
we were nomad quicksilver and drove to Boston;
I knocked my father down. He sat on the carpet—
my mother calling from the top of the carpeted stairs,
their glass door locking behind me, no cover; you
idling in the station wagon, no retreat.

Anne Dick 2. 1936

Longer ago than I had lived till then . . .
before the *Anschluss*, the ten or twenty million
war-dead . . . but who knows now off-hand how many?
I wanted to marry you, we gazed through your narrow
bay window at the hideous concrete dome
of M.I.T., its last blanched, hectic glow
sunsetted on the bay of the Esplanade:
like the classical seaport done by Claude,
an artist more out of fashion now than Nero,
his heaven-vaulting aqueducts, swords forged from plowshares,
the fresh green knife of his unloved mother's death. . . .
The blood of our spirit dries in veins of brickdust—
Christ lost, our only king without a sword,
turning the word *forgiveness* to a sword.

Father

There was rebellion, Father, and the door was slammed.
Front doors were safe with glass then . . . you fell backward
on your heirloom-clock, the phases of the moon,
the highboy quaking to its toes. My Father . . .
I haven't lost heart to say *I knocked you down*. . . .
I have breathed the seclusion of the life-tight den,
card laid on card until the pack is used,
old Helios turning the houseplants to blondes,
moondust blowing in the prowling eye—
a parental sentence on each step misplaced. . . .
You were further from Death than I am now—
that Student ageless in her green cloud of hash,
her bed a mattress half a foot off floor . . .
as far from us as her young breasts will stretch.

Mother and Father 1

If the clock had stopped in 1936
for them, or again in '50 and '54—
they are not dead, and not until death parts us,
will I stop sucking my blood from their hurt.
They say, "I had my life when I was young."
They must have . . . dying young in middle-age;
yet often the old grow still more beautiful,
watering out the hours, biting back their tears,
as the white of the moon streams in on them unshaded;
and women too, the tanning rose, their ebb,
neither a medical, nor agricultural problem.
I struck my father; later my apology
hardly scratched the surface of his invisible
coronary . . . never to be effaced.

Mother and Father 2

This glorious oversleeping half through Sunday,
the sickroom's crimeless mortuary calm,
reprieved from leafing through the Sunday papers,
my need as a reader to think celebrities
are made for suffering, and suffer well. . . .
I remember flunking all courses but Roman history—
a kind of color-blindness made the world gray,
though a third of the globe was painted red for Britain. . . .
I think of all the ill I do and will;
love hits like the *infantile* of pre-Salk days.
I always went too far—few children can love,
or even bear their bearers, the never-forgotten
my father, *my* mother . . . these names, this function, given
by them once, given existence now by me.

Returning

If, Mother and Daddy, you were to visit us
still seeing you as beings, you'd not be welcome,
as you sat here groping the scars of the house,
spangling reminiscence with reproach,
cutting us to shades you used to skim from Freud—
that first draft lost and never to be rewritten.
No one like one's mother and father ever lived;
when I see my children, I see them only
as children, only-children like myself.
Mother and Father, I try to receive you
as if you were I, as if I were you,
trying to laugh at my old nervewracking jokes . . .
a young, unlettered couple who want to leave—
childhood, closer to me than what I love.

Mother, 1972

More than once taking both roads one night
to shake the inescapable hold of New York—
now more than before fearing everything I do
is only (only) a mix of mother and father,
no matter how unlike they were, they are—
it's not what you were or thought, but you . . .
the choked oblique joke, the weighty luxurious stretch.
Mother, we are our true selves in the bath—
a cold splash each morning, the long hot evening loll.
O dying of your cerebral hemorrhage,
lost at Rapallo, dabbing your brow a week,
bruised from stumbling to your unceasing baths,
as if you hoped to drown your killer wound—
to keep me safe a generation after your death.

Father in a Dream

We were at the faculty dining table,
Freudianizing gossip . . . not of our world;
you wore your Sunday white ducks and blue coat
seeming more in character than life.
At our end of the table, I spattered gossip,
shook salt on my wine-spill; soon we were alone,
suddenly I was talking to you alone.
Your hair, grown heavier, was peacocked out in bangs;
"I do it," you said, "to be myself . . . or younger.
I'll have to make a penny for our classes:
calc and Kipling, and catching small-mouth bass."
Age had joined us at last in the same study.
"I have never loved you so much in all my life."
You answered, "Doesn't love begin at the beginning?"

To Daddy

I think, though I don't believe it, you were my airhole,
and resigned perhaps from the Navy to be an airhole—
that Mother not warn me to put my socks on before my shoes.

Will Not Come Back
(After Bécquer)

Dark swallows will doubtless come back killing
the injudicious nightflies with a clack of the beak;
but these that stopped full flight to see your beauty
and my good fortune . . . as if they knew our names—
they'll not come back. The thick lemony honeysuckle,
climbing from the earthroot to your window,
will open more beautiful blossoms to the evening;
but these . . . like dewdrops, trembling, shining, falling,
the tears of day—they'll not come back. . . .
Some other love will sound his fireword for you
and wake your heart, perhaps, from its cool sleep;
but silent, absorbed, and on his knees,
as men adore God at the altar, as I love you—
don't blind yourself, you'll not be loved like that.

MEXICO

Mexico

1.

The difficulties, the impossibilities . . .
I, fifty, humbled with the years' gold garbage,
dead laurel grizzling my back . . . like spines of hay;
you, some sweet, uncertain age, say twenty-seven,
untempted, unseared by honors or deception.
What help then? Not the sun, the scarlet blossom,
and the high fever of this seventh day,
the predestined diarrhea of the pilgrim,
the multiple mosquito spots, round as pesos.
Hope not for God here, or even for the gods;
the Aztecs knew the sun, the source of life,
will die, unless we feed it human blood—
we two are clocks, and only count in time . . .
the hand a knife-edge pressed against the future.

3.

The lizard rusty as a leaf rubbed rough
does nothing for days but puff his throat
for oxygen . . . and tongue up passing flies,
loves only identical rusty lizards panting:
harems worthy this lord of the universe—
each thing he does generic, and not the best.
We sit on a cliff like curs, chins pressed to thumbs—
how fragrantly our cold hands warm to the live coal!
The Toltec temples pass to dust in the dusk—
the clock dial of the rising moon, dust out of time—
two clocks set back to Montezuma's fate . . .
as if we still wished to pull teeth with firetongs—
when they took a city, they murdered everything,
till the Spaniards, by reflex, finished them.

4.

South of Boston, south of Washington,
south of any bearing . . . I walk the glazed moonlight:
dew on the grass and nobody about,
drawn on by my unlimited desire,
like a bull with a ring in his nose, a chain in the ring. . . .
We moved far, bull and cow, could one imagine
cattle obliviously pairing six long days:
up road and down, then up again passing the same
brick garden wall, stiff spines of hay stuck in my hide;
and always in full sight of everyone,
from the full sun to silhouetting sunset,
pinned by undimming lights of hurried cars. . . .
You're gone; I am learning to live in history.
What is history? What you cannot touch.

5.

Midwinter in Cuernavaca, tall red flowers
stand up on many trees; the rock is in leaf.
The sun bakes the wallbrick large as loaves of bread—
somewhere I must have met this feverish pink
and knew its message; or is it that I've walked
you past them twenty times, and now walk back?
This stream will not flow back, not once, not twice.
I've waited, I think, a lifetime for this walk.
The white powder slides out beneath our feet,
the sterile white salt of purity; even
your puffed lace blouse is salt. The red brick glides;
bread baked for a dinner never to be served. . . .
When you left, I thought of you each hour of the day,
each minute of the hour, each second of the minute.

6.

As if we chewed dry twigs and salt grasses,
filling our mouths with dust and bits of adobe,
lizards, rats and worms, we walk downhill,
love demanding we be calm, not lawful,
for laws imprison as much as they protect.
Six stone lions, allday drinkers, sit like frogs,
guarding the fountain; the three rusty arc-lights sweat;
four stone inkfish, too much sat on, bear the fountain—
no star for the guidebook . . . this city of the plain,
where the water rusts as if it bled,
and thirteen girls sit at the barroom tables,
then none, then only twenty coupled men,
homicidal with morality and lust—
devotion hikes uphill in iron shoes.

7.

We're knotted together in innocence and guile;
yet we are not equal, I have lived without
sense so long the loss no longer hurts,
reflex and the ways of the world will float me free—
you, God help you, must will each breath you take . . .
The lavatory breathes sweet shocking perfume.
In Cuernavaca the night's illusory houselights
watch everyone, not just the girls, in houses
like boxes on streets where buses eat the sidewalk.
It's New Year's midnight; we three drink beer in the market
from cans garnished with salt and lime—one woman, Aztec,
sings adultery ballads, and weeps because
her husband has left her for three women—
to face the poverty all men must face at the hour of death.

8.

Three pillows, end on end, rolled in a daybed
blanket—elastic, round, untroubled. For a second,
by some hallucination of my hand
I imagined I was unwrapping you. . . .
Two immovable nuns, out of habit, too fat to leave
the dormitory, have lived ten days on tea,
bouillon cubes and cookies brought from Boston.
You curl in your metal bunk-bed like my child,
I sprawl on an elbow troubled by the floor—
nuns packing, nuns ringing the circular iron stair,
nuns in pajamas scalloped through their wrappers,
nuns boiling bouillon, tea or cookies, nuns
brewing and blanketing reproval . . .
the soul groans and laughs at its lack of stature.

9.

No artist perhaps, you go beyond their phrases;
you were too simple to lose yourself in words . . .
Take our last day baking on the marble veranda,
the roasting brown rock, the smoking grass, the breath
of the world risen like the ripe smoke of chestnuts,
a cleavage dropping miles to the valley's body;
and the following sick and thoughtful day,
the red flower, the hills, the valley, the Volcano—
this not the greatest thing, though great; the hours
of shivering, ache and burning, when we charged
so far beyond our courage—altitude . . .
then falling back on honest speech;
infirmity's a food the flesh must swallow,
feeding our minds . . . the mind which is also flesh.

10.

Poor Child, you were kissed so much you thought you were walked on;
yet you wait in my doorway with bluebells in your hair.
Those other me's, you think, *are they meaningless in toto,*
hills coarsely eyed for a later breathless conquest,
leaving no juice in the flaw, mind lodged in mind?
A girl's not quite mortal, she asks everything. . . .
If you want to make the frozen serpent dance,
you must sing it the music of its mouth:
Sleep wastes the day lifelong behind our eyes,
night shivers at noonday in the boughs of the fir. . . .
Our conversation moved from lust to love,
asking only coolness, stillness, intercourse—
then days, days, days, days . . . how can I love you more,
short of turning into a criminal?

Eight Months Later

The flower I took away and wither and fear—
to clasp, not grasp the life, the light and fragile. . . .
It's certain we burned the grass, the grass still fumes,
the girl stands in the doorway, the red flower on the trees
where once the intermeshing limbs of Lucifer
sank to sleep on the tumuli of Lilith—
did anyone ever sleep with anyone
without thinking a split second he was God? . . .
Midsummer Manhattan—we are burnt black chips.
The worst of New York is everything is stacked,
ten buildings dance in the hat of one . . . half Europe
in half a mile. I wish we were elsewhere:
Mexico . . . Mexico? Where is Mexico?
Who will live the year back, cat on the ladder?

2. DIE GOLD-ORANGEN

I see the country where the lemon blossoms,
and the pig-gold orange glows on its dark branch,
and the south wind stutters from the blue hustings;
I see it; it's behind us, love, behind us—
the bluebell is brown, the cypress points too straight—
do you see the house, the porch on marble pillars?
The sideboard is silver, and the candles blaze;
the statue stands naked to stare at you.
What have I done with us, and what was done?
And the mountain, El Volcan, a climber of clouds?
The mule-man lost his footing in the cloud,
seed of the dragon coupled in that cave. . . .
The cliff drops; over it, the water drops,
and steams out the footprints that led us on.

from

Day by Day

(1977)

Ulysses and Circe

I.

Ten years before Troy, ten years before Circe—
things changed to the names he gave them,
then lost their names:
Myrmidons, Spartans, soldier of dire Ulysses . . .
Why should I renew his infamous sorrow?
He had his part, he thought of building
the wooden horse as big as a house
and ended the ten years' war.
"By force of fraud," he says, "I did
what neither Diomedes, nor Achilles son of Thetis,
nor the Greeks with their thousand ships . . .
I destroyed Troy."

II.

What is more uxorious than waking at five
with the sun and three hours free?
He sees the familiar bluish-brown river
dangle down her flat young forearm,
then crisscross. The sun rises,
a red bonfire,
weakly rattling in the lower branches—
that eats like a locust and leaves the tree entire.
In ten minutes perhaps,
or whenever he next wakes up,
the sun is white as it mostly is,
dull changer of night to day,
itself unchanged, in war or peace.
The blinds give
bars of sunlight, bars of shade,
but the latter predominate
over the sincerity of her sybaritic bed.
She lies beside him,

a delicious, somnolent log. She says,
"Such wonderful things are being said to me—
I'm such an old sleeper, I can't respond."

III.
O that morning might come without the day—
he lies awake and fears the servants,
the civilities
of their savage, assiduous voices.
It's out of hand . . . her exotic palace
spun in circles no sober Greek can navigate.
He is afraid the whining, greasy animals
who bury chewed meat beneath his window
are only human, and will claim
his place of honor on the couch.
His heart is swallowed in his throat;
it is only an ache of the mind,
the twilight of early morning . . .
"Why am I my own fugitive,
because her beauty
made me feel as other men?"

IV.
She stands, her hair
intricate and winding as her heart.
They talk like two guests
waiting for the other
to leave the house—
her mongrel harmony
of the irreconcilable.
Here his derelict choice
changes to necessity;
compassion is terror,
no schism can split
the ruthless openness
of her yielding character.
Her eyes well,

and hypnotize
his followers,
the retarded animals.
They cannot stay awake,
and keep their own hours,
like degenerates
drinking the day in,
sweating it out in hysterical submission.

Young,
he made strategic choices;
in middle age he accepts
his unlikely life to come;
he will die like others as the gods will,
drowning his last crew
in uncharted ocean,
seeking the unpeopled world beyond the sun,
lost in the uproarious rudeness of a great wind.

On Circe's small island,
he grew from narrowness—
by pettiness,
he ennobled himself to fit the house.
He dislikes everything
in his impoverished life of myth.

The lotus brings a nostalgia
for the no-quarter duels he hated;
but she is only where she is.
Her speech is spiced with the faded slang
of a generation younger than his—
now the patois of the island.
Her great season goes with her;
the gorgeous girls she knew
are still her best friends,
their reputations lost like Helen's,
saved by her grace.

She is a snipper-off'er—
her discards lie about the floors,
the unused, the misused,
seacoats and insignia,
the beheaded beast.

She wants her house askew—
kept keys to lost locks,
unidentifiable portraits, dead things
wrapped in paper the color of dust . . .

the surge of the wine before the quarrel.

Slight pleasantries leave lasting burns—
the air in the high hall simmers
in the cracked beams with a thousand bugs;
though this is mid-autumn,
the moment when insects die
instantly as one would ask of a friend.

On his walk to the ship,
a solitary tree suddenly
drops half its leaves;
they stay green on the ground.
Other trees hold. In a day or two,
their leaves also will fall,
like his followers,
stained by their hesitation
prematurely brown.

V.
"Long awash and often touching bottom
by the sea's great green go-light
I found my exhaustion
the light of the world.

Earth isn't earth
if my eyes are on the moon,
her likeness caught
in the split-second of vacancy—

duplicitous,
open to all men, unfaithful.

After so many millennia,
Circe,
are you tired
of turning swine to swine?

How can I please you,
if I am not a man?

I have grown bleak-boned with survival—
I who hoped to leave the earth
younger than I came.

Age is the bilge
we cannot shake from the mop.

Age walks on our faces—
at the tunnel's end,
if faith can be believed,
our flesh will grow lighter."

VI.
Penelope

Ulysses circles—
neither his son's weakness,
nor passion for his wife,
which might have helped her, held him.
She sees no feat
in his flight or his flight back—

ten years to and ten years fro.
On foot and visible,
he walks from Long Wharf home.
Nobody in Ithaca knows him,
and yet he is too much remarked.
His knees run quicker than his feet,
his held-in mouth is puffy,
his eye is a traveled welcomer.
He looks for his lighthouse,
once so aggressively white—
a landmark, now a marina.
How white faced and unlucky-looking
he was twenty years ago,
even on the eve of his embarkation
and carnival of glory,
when he enticed Penelope
to dance herself to coma in his arms.
Risk was his métier.
His dusty, noontime road is home now;
he imagines her dashing to him
in the eager sacklike shift
she wore her last month pregnant.
Her then unspectacled eyes were stars—
a cornered rabbit . . . Today his house
is more convivial and condescending;
she is at home,
well furnished with her entourage,
her son, her son's friends, her lovers—
the usual chaos of living well,
health and wealth in clashing outfits—
only infirmity could justify
the deformity . . .
He has seen the known world,
the meanness and beacons of men;
the full heat of his pilgrimage
assumes the weight
and gravity of being alive.
He enters the house,
eyes shut, mouth loose.

The conjugal bed is just a step;
he mistakes
a daughter for her mother.
It is not surprising.
The men move him away—
a foolish but evil animal.
He is outdoors;
his uninvited hands are raw, they say
I love you through the locked window.
At forty, she is still
the best bosom in the room.
He looks at her,
she looks at him admiring her,
then turns to the suitors—knowing
the lying art of the divine Minerva
will not make him
invincible as he was,
her life ago, or young . . .
Volte-face—
he circles as a shark circles
visibly behind the window—
flesh-proud, sore-eyed, scar-proud,
a vocational killer
in the machismo of senility,
foretasting the apogee of mayhem—
breaking water to destroy his wake.
He is oversize. To her suitors,
he is Tom, Dick, or Harry—
his gills are pleated and aligned—
unnatural ventilation-vents
closed by a single lever
like cells in a jail—
ten years fro and ten years to.

Our Afterlife 1

(FOR PETER TAYLOR)

Southbound—
a couple in passage,
two Tennessee cardinals
in green December outside the window
dart and tag and mate—
young as they want to be.
We're not.
Since my second fatherhood
and stay in England,
I am a generation older.
We are dangerously happy—
our book-bled faces
streak like red birds,
dart unstably,
ears cocked to catch
the first shy whisper of deafness.
This year killed
Pound, Wilson, Auden . . .
promise has lost its bloom,
the inheritor reddens
like a false rose—
nodding, nodding, nodding.
Peter, in our boyish years,
30 to 40,
when Cupid was still the Christ of love's religion,
time stood on its hands.

Sleight of hand.

We drink in the central heat
to keep the cold wave out.
The stifled telephone that rings in my ear
doesn't exist.
After fifty,

the clock can't stop,
each saving breath
takes something. This is riches:
the eminence not to be envied,
the account
accumulating layer and angle,
face and profile,
50 years of snapshots,
the ladder of ripening likeness.

We are things thrown in the air
alive in flight . . .
our rust the color of the chameleon.

For John Berryman

(After reading his last *Dream Song*)

The last years we only met
when you were on the road,
and lit up for reading
your battering *Dream*—
audible, deaf . . .
in another world then as now.
I used to want to live
to avoid your elegy.
Yet really we had the same life,
the generic one
our generation offered
(*Les Maudits*—the compliment
each American generation
pays itself in passing):
first students, then with our own,
our galaxy of grands maîtres,
our fifties' fellowships
to Paris, Rome and Florence,
veterans of the Cold War not the War—
all the best of life . . .
then daydreaming to drink at six,
waiting for the iced fire,
even the feel of the frosted glass,
like waiting for a girl . . .
if you had waited.
We asked to be obsessed with writing,
and we were.

Do you wake dazed like me,
and find your lost glasses in a shoe?

Something so heavy lies on my heart—
there, still here, the good days
when we sat by a cold lake in Maine,

talking about the *Winter's Tale*,
Leontes' jealousy
in Shakespeare's broken syntax.
You got there first.
Just the other day,
I discovered how we differ—humor . . .
even in this last *Dream Song*,
to mock your catlike flight
from home and classes—
to leap from the bridge.

Girls will not frighten the frost from the grave.

To my surprise, John,
I pray *to* not for you,
think of you not myself,
smile and fall asleep.

Square of Black

On this book, large enough to write on,
is a sad, black, actual photograph
of Abraham Lincoln and Tad in 1861,
father and son,
their almost matching silver watchchains,
as they stare into the blank ledger,
its murders and failures . . . they.
Old Abe, and old at 52—
in life, in office, no lurking illusion,
clad for the moment in robes of splendor,
passed him unchallenged . . .
Only in a dream was he able to hear
his voice in the East Room of the White House
saying over his own dead body:
"Lincoln is dead."

Dreams, they've had their vogue,
so alike in their modernist invention,
so dangerously distracted by commonplace,
their literal insistence on the letter,
trivia indistinguishable from tragedy—
his monstrous melodrama terminating
at a playhouse . . . dreaming, overhearing
his own voice,
the colloquial sibilance of the circuit-court,
once freedom, the law and home to Lincoln—
shot while sleeping through the final act.

Fortunately
I only dream inconsequence.
Last night I saw a little
flapping square of pure black cloth.
It flew to the corners of my bedroom,
hugging, fluttering there coquettishly—

a bat, if wing and pelt could be one-color black.
It was a mouse. (So my dream explained.)
It taught me to feed and tame it
with nagging love . . . only existing
in my short dream's immeasurable leisure.

In the Ward

Ten years older in an hour—

I see your face smile,
your mouth is stepped on without bruising.
You are very frightened by the ward,
your companions were chosen for age;
you are the youngest
and sham-flirt with the nurse—
your chief thought is scheming
the elaborate surprise of your escape.

Being old in good times is worse
than being young in the worst.

Five days
on this grill, this mattress
over nothing—
the wisdom of this sickness
is piously physical,
ripping up memory
to find your future—
old beauties, old masters
who lost their friends before they lost their minds.

Your days are dark,
and night is light—
here the child says:
heaven is a big house
with lots of water and flowers—
you go in in a trunk.

Your feet are wired above your head—

If you could hear the glaring lightbulb
sing

your old modernist classics . . .
They are for a lost audience.

Last year
in buoyant unrest,
you gathered two or three young friends
in the *champagne room*
of your coldwater flat
to explore the pedantry
and daimonic lawlessness
of Arnold Schoenberg
born when music was still imperfect science—
his ever-retreating borderlands of being
that could not console.

If you keep cutting your losses,
you have no loss to cut.

Nothing you see now
can mean anything;
your will is fixed on the lightbulb,
its blinding impassivity
withholding disquiet—
the art of the possible
that art abhors.

It's an illusion death or technique
can wring the truth from us like water.

What helpless paperishness,
if vocation
is only shouting what we will.

Somewhere your spirit
led the highest life;
all places matched
with that place
come to nothing.

Day by Day

from Part I

The Day

It's amazing
the day is still here
like lightning on an open field,
terra firma and transient
swimming in variation,
fresh as when man first broke
like the crocus all over the earth.

From a train, we saw cows
strung out on a hill
at differing heights,
one sex, one herd,
replicas in hierarchy—
the sun had turned
them noonday bright.

They were child's daubs in a book
I read before I could read.

They fly by like a train window:
flash-in-the-pan moments
of the Great Day,
the *dies illa*,
when we lived momently
together forever
in love with our nature—

as if in the end,
in the marriage with nothingness,
we could ever escape
being absolutely safe.

Domesday Book

Let nothing be done twice—

When Harold fell
with an arrow in his eye at Hastings,
the bastard Conqueror taxed
everything in his Domesday Book:
ox, cow, swine,
the villages and hundreds
his French clerks tore to shreds
and fed
to berserk hawk and baron.
His calculated devastation,
never improvidently
merciful to the helpless,
made anarchy anachronism
and English a speech for serfs.

England/Scotland/Ireland
had better days—
now the elephantiasis of the great house
is smothered in the beauty of its English garden
changed already to a feathery, fertile waste,
lawns drenched with the gold-red sorrel.
The hectic, seeded rose
climbs a neglected gravel drive
cratered to save the children from delivery vans.
The beef-red bricks and sky-gray stones
are buried in the jungle leaf of June—
wildflowers take root in the kitchen garden.

The dower house goes with the house,
the dowager with her pale, white cup of tea
she inspired with brandy.

Lathom House, Middleton Manor,
New Hall, Silverton,
Brickling with its crinkled windows
and rose-pink gables
are converted to surgeries, polytechnics,
cells of the understaffed asylum
crumbling on the heads of the mad.

The country houses that rolled
like railways are now
more stationary than anthills—
their service gone. Will they fall
under the ax of penal taxes
they first existed to enact . . .
too grand for any gallery?
Will the house for pleasure
predecease its predecessor,
the cathedral,
once outshone in art and cost?

Cold chimneystacks and greening statuary
outlive the living garden
parceled to irreversible wilderness
by one untended year—
from something to nothing . . .
like King Charles who lost his head
and shared the luck and strange
fibered Puritan violence
of his antagonist, the Protector,
whose carcass
they drew on a hurdle to Tyburn,
hanged and buried under the gallows.

If they have you by the neck, a rope will be found.

Nulle terre sans seigneur.

The old follies, as usual, never return—
the houses still burn

in the golden lowtide steam of Turner.
Only when we start to go,
do we notice the outrageous phallic flare
of the splash flowers that fascinated children.

The reign of the kingfisher was short.

Marriage

I.
We were middle-class and verismo
enough to suit Van Eyck,
when we crowded together in Maidstone,
patriarch and young wife
with our three small girls
to pose in Sunday-best.
The shapeless comfort of your flowered frock
was transparent against the light,
but the formal family photograph in color
shows only a rousing brawn of shoulder
to tell us you were pregnant.

Even there, Sheridan, though unborn,
was a center of symmetry;
even then he was growing in hiding
toward gaucheness and muscle—
to be a war-
chronicler of vast inaccurate memory.
Later, his weird humor
made him elf and dustman,
like him, early risers.
This summer, he is a soldier—
unlike father or mother,
or anyone he knows,
he can choose both sides:
Redcoat, Minuteman, or George the Third . . .
the ambivalence of the Revolution that made him
half-British, half-American.

II.

I turn to the *Arnolfini Marriage*,
and see
Van Eyck's young Italian merchant
was neither soldier nor priest.
In an age of Faith,
he is not abashed to stand weaponless,
long-faced and dwindling
in his bridal bedroom.
Half-Jewish, perhaps,
he is freshly married,
and exiled for his profit to Bruges.
His wife's with child;
he lifts a hand,
thin and white as his face
held up like a candle to bless her . . .
smiling, swelling, blossoming . . .

Giovanni and Giovanna—
even in an age of costumes,
they seem to flash their fineness . . .
better dressed than kings.

The picture is too much like their life—
a crisscross, too many petty facts,
this bedroom
with one candle still burning in the candelabrum,
and peaches blushing on the windowsill,
Giovanni's high-heeled raw wooden slippers
thrown on the floor by her smaller ones . . .
dyed *sang de boeuf*
to match the restless marital canopy.

They are rivals in homeliness and love;
her hand lies like china in his,
her other hand
is in touch with the head of her unborn child.
They wait and pray,
as if the airs of heaven

that blew on them when they married
were now a common visitation,
not a miracle of lighting
for the photographer's sacramental instant.

Giovanni and Giovanna,
who will outlive him by 20 years . . .

from Part II

Robert T. S. Lowell

Son

I futilely wished
to meet you at my age;
the date never came off.
It would take two lifetimes
to pick the crust
and uncover the face
under our two menacing,
iconoclastic masks.

Father

You had your chance to meet me.
My father died before I was born.
I was half orphaned . . . such a son
as the stork seldom flings to ambition.

I lay
in the lee of my terrible elders;
the age had a largeness I lacked,
an appetite that forgave everything . . .
our Spanish War's oversubscribed,
battle-bright decks.

At fourteen
I enlisted at Annapolis.

At twenty-seven
I proposed in uniform
and married your mother—
a service I served with even wistfulness,
enslaved by the fire I courted.

I only wished idly
with dilated eyes
to relive my life.

Your game-leg beagle would tiptoe to my room,
if she heard you were asleep—
loneliness to loneliness!

You think that having
your two children on the same floor this fall,
one questioning, one climbing and breaking,
is like living on a drum
or a warship—it can't be that,
it's your life, and dated like mine.

For Sheridan

We only live between
before we are and what we were.

In the lost negative
you exist,
a smile, a cypher,
an old-fashioned face
in an old-fashioned hat.

Three ages in a flash:
the same child in the same picture,
he, I, you,
chockablock, one stamp
like mother's wedding silver—

gnome, fish, brute cherubic force.

We could see clearly
and all the same things
before the glass was hurt.

Past fifty, we learn with surprise and a sense
of suicidal absolution
that what we intended and failed
could never have happened—
and must be done better.

Grass Fires

In the realistic memory
the memorable must be forgone;
it never matters,
except in front of our eyes.

I made it a warning,
a cure, that stabilized nothing.
We cannot recast the faulty drama,
play the child,
unable to align
his toppling, elephantine script,
the hieroglyphic letters
he sent home.

I hold big kitchen matches to flaps of frozen grass
to smoke a rabbit from its hole—
then the wind bites them, then they catch,
the grass catches, fire everywhere,
everywhere
inextinguishable roots,
the tree grandfather planted for his shade,
combusting, towering
over the house he anachronized with stone.

I can't tell you how much larger
and more important it was than I,
how many summers before conscience
I enjoyed it.

My grandfather towered above me,
"You damned little fool,"
nothing to quote, but for him original.
The fire-engines deployed with stage bravado,
yet it was I put out the fire,

who slapped it to death with my scarred leather jacket.
I snuffed out the inextinguishable root,
I—
really I can do little,
as little now as then,
about the infernal fires—
I cannot blow out a match.

St. Mark's, 1933

The fourth form dining-table
was twenty feet by four,
six boys to a side;
at one end, Mr. Prendie the Woodchuck,
dead to the world, off picking daisies;
at the other end, another boy.
Mid-meal, they began
to pull me apart.
"Why is he always grubbing in his nose?"
"Because his nose is always snotty."
"He likes to wipe his thumb in it."
"Cal's a creep of the first water."
"He had a hard-on for his first shower."
"He only presses his trousers once a term."
"Every other term." "No term."
Over the years I've lost
the surprise and sparkle of that slang
our abuse made perfect.
"Dimbulb." "Fogbound." "Droopydrawers."
"The man from the Middle West."
"Cal is a slurp."
"A slurp farts in the bathtub."
"So he can bite the bubbles."
How did they say my face
was pearl-gray like toe-jam—
that I was foul
as the gymsocks I wore a week?
A boy next to me breathed my shoes,
and lay choking on the bench.

"Cal doesn't like everyone."
"Everyone doesn't like Cal."
"Cal,
who is your best friend at this table?"

"Low-ell, Low-ell"
(to the tune of *Noël, Noël*).

This was it, though I bowdlerize . . .
All term I had singled out classmates,
and made them listen to and remember
the imperfections of their friends.
I broke one on the other—
but who could break them,
they were so many,
rich, smooth and loved?

I was fifteen;
they made me cry in public.
Chicken?

Perhaps they had reason . . .
even now
my callous unconscious drives me
to torture my closest friend.

Huic ergo parce, Deus.

Suburban Surf
(After Caroline's Return)

You lie in my insomniac arms,
as if you drank sleep like coffee.

Then,
like a bear tipping a hive for honey,
you shake the pillow for French cigarettes.

No conversation—
then suddenly as always cars
helter-skelter for feed like cows—

suburban surf come alive,

diamond-faceted like your eyes,
glassy, staring lights
lighting the way they cannot see—

friction, constriction etc.
the racket killing
gas like alcohol.

Long, unequal whooshing waves
break in volume,
always very loud enough to hear—

méchants, mechanical—

soothe, delay, divert
the crescendo always surprisingly attained
in a panic of breathlessness—

too much assertion and skipping
of the heart to greet the day . . .
the truce with uncertain heaven.

A false calm is the best calm.

In noonday light,
the cars are tin, stereotype and bright,
a farce
of their former selves at night—
invisible as exhaust,
personal as animals.

Gone
the sweet agitation of the breath of Pan.

from Part III

Ten Minutes

The single sheet keeps shifting on the double bed,
the more I kick it smooth, the less it covers;
it is the bed I made.
Others have destinations, my train is aimless.
I know I will fall off into the siding and thistle—
imagining the truth will hide my lies.

Mother under one of her five-minute spells
had a flair for total recall,
and told me, item by item, person by person,
how my relentless, unpredictable selfishness
had disappointed and removed
anyone who tried to help—
but I cannot correct the delicate compass-needle
so easily set ajar.

I am companionless;
occasionally, I see a late, suicidal headlight
burn on the highway and vanish.
Now the haunted vacancy fills with friends—
they are waspishly familiar and aggrieved,
a rattling makeshift of mislaid faces,
a whiplash of voices. They cry,
"Can you love me, can you love me?
Oh hidden in your bubble and protected by your wife,
and luxuriously nourished without hands,
you wished us dead,
but vampires are too irreplaceable to die."

They stop, as cars that have the greenlight
stop, and let a pedestrian go . . .
Though I work nightshift,
there's no truth in this processing of words—
the dull, instinctive glow inside me

refuels itself, and only blackens
such bits of paper brought to feed it . . .

My frightened arms
anxiously hang out before me like bent L's,
as if I feared I was a laughingstock,
and wished to catch and ward you off . . .
This is becoming a formula:
after the long, dark passage,
I offer you my huddle of flesh and dismay.
"This time it was all night," I say.
You answer, "Poseur,
why, you haven't been awake ten minutes."

•   •   •

I grow too merry,
when I stand in my nakedness to dress.

Notice

The resident doctor said,
"We are not deep in ideas, imagination or enthusiasm—
how can we help you?"
I asked,
"These days of only poems and depression—
what can I do with them?
Will they help me to notice
what I cannot bear to look at?"

The doctor is forgotten now
like a friend's wife's maiden-name.
I am free
to ride elbow to elbow on the rush-hour train
and copy on the back of a letter,
as if alone:
"When the trees close branches and redden,
their winter skeletons are hard to find—"
to know after long rest
and twenty miles of outlying city
that the much-heralded spring is here,
and say,
"Is this what you would call a blossom?"
Then home—I can walk it blindfold.
But we must notice—
we are designed for the moment.

Shifting Colors

I fish until the clouds turn blue,
weary of self-torture, ready to paint
lilacs or confuse a thousand leaves,
as landscapists must.

My eye returns to my double,
an ageless big white horse,
slightly discolored by dirt
cropping the green shelf diagonal
to the artificial troutpond—
unmoving, it shifts as I move,
and works the whole field in the course of the day.

Poor measured, neurotic man—
animals are more instinctive virtuosi.

Ducks splash deceptively like fish;
fish break water with the wings of a bird to escape.

A hissing goose sways in stationary anger;
purple bluebells rise in ledges on the lake.

A single cuckoo gifted with a pregnant word
shifts like the sun from wood to wood.

All day my miscast troutfly buzzes about my ears
and empty mind.

But nature is sundrunk with sex—
how could a man fail to notice, man
the one pornographer among the animals?
I seek leave unimpassioned by my body,
I am too weak to strain to remember, or give
recollection the eye of a microscope. I see

horse and meadow, duck and pond,
universal consolatory
description without significance,
transcribed verbatim by my eye.

This is not the directness that catches
everything on the run and then expires—
I would write only in response to the gods,
like Mallarmé who had the good fortune
to find a style that made writing impossible.

Unwanted

Too late, all shops closed—
I alone here tonight on *Antabuse,*
surrounded only by iced white wine and beer,
like a sailor dying of thirst on the Atlantic—
one sip of alcohol might be death,
death for joy.
Yet in this tempting leisure,
good thoughts drive out bad;
causes for my misadventure, considered
for forty years too obvious to name,
come jumbling out
to give my simple autobiography a plot.

I read an article on a friend,
as if recognizing my obituary:
"Though his mother loved her son consumingly,
she lacked a really affectionate nature;
so he always loved what he missed."
This was John Berryman's mother, not mine.

Alas, I can only tell my own story—
talking to myself, or reading, or writing,
or fearlessly holding back nothing from a friend,
who believes me for a moment
to keep up conversation.

I was surer, wasn't I, once . . .
and had flashes when I first found
a humor for myself in images,
farfetched misalliance
that made evasion a revelation?

Dr. Merrill Moore, the family psychiatrist,
had unpresentable red smudge eyebrows,

and no infirmity for tact—
in his conversation or letters,
each phrase a new
paragraph,
implausible as the million
sonnets he rhymed into his dictaphone,
or dashed on windshield writing-pads,
while waiting out a stoplight—
scattered pearls, some true.
Dead he is still a mystery,
once a crutch to writers in crisis.
I am two-tongued, I will not admit
his Tennessee rattling saved my life.
Did he become mother's lover
and prey
by rescuing her from me?
He was thirteen years her junior . . .
When I was in college, he said, "You know
you were an unwanted child?"
Was he striking my parents to help me?
I shook him off the scent by pretending
anyone is unwanted in a medical sense—
lust our only father . . . and yet
in that world where an only child
was a scandal—
unwanted before I am?

That year Carl Jung said to mother in Zurich,
"If your son is as you have described him,
he is an incurable schizophrenic."

In 1916
father on sea-duty, mother with child
in one house with her affectionate mother-in-law,
unconsuming, already consumptive . . .
bromidic to mother . . . Mother,
I must not blame you for carrying me in you
on your brisk winter lunges across
the desperate, refusey Staten Island beaches,

their good view skyscrapers on Wall Street . . .
for yearning seaward, far from any home, and saying,
"I wish I were dead, I wish I were dead."
Unforgivable for a mother to tell her child—
but you wanted me to share your good fortune,
perhaps, by recapturing the disgust of those walks;
your credulity assumed we survived,
while weaklings fell with the dead and dying.

That consuming love,
woman's everlasting *cri de coeur*,
"When you have a child of your own, you'll know."
Her dowry for her children . . .

One thing is certain—compared with my wives,
mother was stupid. Was she?
Some would not have judged so—
among them, her alcoholic patients,
those raconteurish, old Boston young men,
whose fees, late in her life
and to everyone's concern,
she openly halved with Merrill Moore.
Since time out of mind, mother's gay hurting
assessments of enemies and intimates
had made her a formidable character
to her "reading club," seven ladies,
who since her early twenties
met once a week through winters
in their sitting rooms for confidence and tea—
she couldn't read a book . . .
How many of her statements began with,
But Papá always said or *Oh Bobby* . . .
if she Byronized her father and son,
she saw her husband as a valet sees through a master.

She was stupider than my wife . . .
When I was three months,
I rocked back and forth howling
for weeks, for weeks each hour . . .

Then I found the thing I loved most
was the anorexia Christ
swinging on Nellie's gaudy rosary.
It disappeared, I said nothing,
but mother saw me poking strips of paper
down a floor-grate to the central heating.
"Oh Bobby, do you want to set us on fire?"
"Yes . . . that's where Jesus is." I smiled.

Is the one unpardonable sin
our fear of not being wanted?
For this, will mother go on cleaning house
for eternity, and making it unlivable?
Is getting well ever an art,
or art a way to get well?

The Downlook

For the last two minutes, the retiring monarchy
of the full moon looks down on the first chirping sparrows—
nothing lovelier than waking to find
another breathing body in my bed . . .
glowshadow halfcovered with dayclothes like my own,
caught in my arms.

Last summer nothing dared impede
the flow of the body's thousand rivulets of welcome,
winding effortlessly, yet with ambiguous invention—
safety in nearness.

Now the downlook, the downlook—small fuss,
nothing that could earn a line or picture
in the responsible daily paper we'll be reading,
an anthology of the unredeemable world,
beyond the accumulative genius of prose or this—
a day that sharpens apprehension by dulling;
each miss must be a mile,
if one risk the narrow two-lane highway.

It's impotence and impertinence to ask directions,
while staring right and left in two-way traffic.

There's no greater happiness in days of the downlook
than to turn back to recapture former joy.

Ah loved perhaps before I knew you,
others have been lost like this,
yet found foothold
by winning the dolphin from the humming water.

How often have my antics
and insupportable, trespassing tongue
gone astray and led me to prison . . .
to lying . . . kneeling . . . standing.

Thanks-Offering for Recovery

The airy, going house grows small
tonight, and soft enough to be crumpled up
like a handkerchief in my hand.
Here with you by this hotbed of coals,
I am the *homme sensuel*, free
to turn my back on the lamp, and work.
Something has been taken off,
a wooden winter shadow—
goodbye nothing. I give thanks, thanks—
thanks too for this small
Brazilian *ex voto*, this primitive head
sent me across the Atlantic by my friend . . .
a corkweight thing,
to be offered *Deo gratias* in church
on recovering from head-injury or migraine—
now mercifully delivered in my hands,
though shelved awhile unnoticing and unnoticed.
Free of the unshakable terror that made me write . . .
I pick it up, a head holy and unholy,
tonsured or damaged,
with gross black charcoaled brows and stern eyes
frowning as if they had seen the splendor
times past counting . . . unspoiled,
solemn as a child is serious—
light balsa wood the color of my skin.
It is all childcraft, especially
its shallow, chiseled ears,
crudely healed scars lumped out
to listen to itself, perhaps, not knowing
it was made to be given up.
Goodbye nothing. Blockhead,
I would take you to church,
if any church would take you . . .
This winter, I thought
I was created to be given away.

Epilogue

Those blessèd structures, plot and rhyme—
why are they no help to me now
I want to make
something imagined, not recalled?
I hear the noise of my own voice:
The painter's vision is not a lens,
it trembles to caress the light.
But sometimes everything I write
with the threadbare art of my eye
seems a snapshot,
lurid, rapid, garish, grouped,
heightened from life,
yet paralyzed by fact.
All's misalliance.
Yet why not say what happened?
Pray for the grace of accuracy
Vermeer gave to the sun's illumination
stealing like the tide across a map
to his girl solid with yearning.
We are poor passing facts,
warned by that to give
each figure in the photograph
his living name.

from

Last Poems

(1977)

Summer Tides

Tonight
I watch the incoming moon swim
under three agate veins of cloud,
casting crisps of false silver-plate
to the thirsty granite fringe of the shore.
Yesterday, the sun's gregarious sparklings;
tonight, the moon has no satellite.
All this spendthrift, in-the-house summer,
our yacht-jammed harbor
lay unattempted—
pictorial to me like your portrait.
I wonder who posed you so artfully
for it in the prow of his Italian skiff,
like a maiden figurehead without legs to fly.
Time lent its wings. Last year
our drunken quarrels had no explanation,
except everything, except everything.
Did the oak provoke the lightning,
when we heard its boughs and foliage fall? . . .
My wooden beach-ladder swings by one bolt,
and repeats its single creaking rhythm—
I cannot go down to the sea.
After so much logical interrogation,
I can do nothing that matters.
The east wind carries disturbance for leagues—
I think of my son and daughter,
and three stepdaughters
on far-out ledges
washed by the dreaded clock-clock of the waves . . .
gradually rotting the bulwark where I stand.
Their father's unmotherly touch
trembles on a loosened rail.

Notes

Chronology

Index of Titles

Index of First Lines

Notes

These are the abbreviations used in the Notes when referring to Lowell's books:

LOU	*Land of Unlikeness*
LWC	*Lord Weary's Castle*
MK	*The Mills of the Kavanaughs*
LS	*Life Studies*
IM	*Imitations*
FTUD	*For the Union Dead*
NTO	*Near the Ocean*
HIS	*History*
DOL	*The Dolphin*
FLH	*For Lizzie and Harriet*
SP	*Selected Poems* (revised)
DBD	*Day by Day*
CPR	*Collected Prose*
CPO	*Collected Poems*
L	*The Letters of Robert Lowell*

from LORD WEARY'S CASTLE (1946)

THE EXILE'S RETURN

The poem uses images and phrases from Thomas Mann's short story "Tonio Kröger" (*Stories of Three Decades*, trans. H. T. Lowe-Porter [1936]). The story begins, "The winter sun, poor ghost of itself, hung milky and wan behind layers of cloud above the huddled roofs of the town. In the gabled streets it was wet and windy and there came in gusts a sort of soft hail, not ice, not snow" (85).

2–3 Hôtel / De Ville: Town hall.
8 Holstenwall: " 'All right; let's go over the wall,' [Tonio] said with a quaver in his voice. 'Over the Millwall and the Holstenwall, and I'll go as far as your house' " (86).
15 The Yankee commandant: The first printing reads, "The bristling podestà" (podestà: Italian for a mayor or local administrative head).
21 Rathaus: Town hall.
24 Lasciate ogni speranza, voi ch'entrate (Abandon all hope, you who enter here); inscription over the Gate of Hell, Dante, *Inferno*, III.9.

The Holy Innocents: Herod slaughtered the children of Bethlehem, trying to destroy the infant Jesus; see Matthew 2:16–18. The Feast is celebrated on December 28.

1.1ff The setting of the poem is Damariscotta Mills, Maine, where Lowell lived in the winter of 1945 (Hugh B. Staples, *Robert Lowell: The First Twenty Years* [1962], 96); St. Patrick's Church, not St. Peter's (1.6), is nearby.

1.7 "These are they which were not defiled with women; for they are virgin" (Revelation 14:4). (All biblical references are to the King James version, unless otherwise specified.)

2.2 "[I]t out-Herods Herod, pray you avoid it" (Hamlet's instructions to the Players, *Hamlet*, III.ii. 13–14).

COLLOQUY IN BLACK ROCK

Black Rock and its mudflats, Black Mud, are situated near Bridgeport, Connecticut, on Long Island Sound; Lowell lived there after his imprisonment for draft resistance (1944), working "in a Catholic cadet nurses' dormitory, mopping corridors and toilets" (Lowell, *CPR* 279). Bridgeport's large Hungarian population, many of whom worked at the Sikorski helicopter factory, attended St. Stephen's Catholic Church. St. Stephen is Hungary's first king and patron saint; the first Christian martyr, who died by stoning, is also named Stephen (Acts 7:59). The poem was originally titled "Pentecost." About the composition of this poem, Lowell writes, "I hadn't written a line for a year, and had just come home one evening from mopping floors as a conscientious objector. I was strolling about and staring at the low-tide litter and wishing. That the War were over, and that the [transformative] event in the last stanza would lift me out of my pails of dirty water. Then the lyrical outline came" (Paul Mariani, *Lost Puritan: A Life of Robert Lowell* [1994], 116). A Black Rock neighbor writes that Lowell stayed at a "big yellow stucco [rooming] house sitting on the edge of the dump. . . . More often than not the residue of the dump actually came up to the doorstep. What is interesting is that standing on the steps of that house, one was in a position to see the spire of St. Stephen's to the right and the spire of St. Peter's to the left" (letter from Maureen Maguire, *Black Rock News*, 1 Jan. 1978).

2.1 T. S. Eliot (Lowell's editor at Faber) was bothered by "detritus," which makes this a four-beat line; in *Poems 1938–49* (Faber and Faber) Lowell made changes in response to Eliot, as well as other revisions in this and other poems. None of the changes were ever incorporated in later collections.

3.5 A year and a day: Lowell's sentence for refusing the draft, "the extra day making him in the eyes of the law a felon" (Mariani, *Lost Puritan*, 108).

5.1 Jesus—who fished for men's souls—walked on the sea (John 6:19).

5.2 kingfisher: A bird with a crested head, identified with "halcyon" (fabled bird "that was supposed to have had the power to calm the wind and the waves during the winter solstice while it nested on the sea," *American Heritage Dictionary*). See the final line of "Domesday Book" in *DBD*, 766.

5.2–3 Corpus Christi: Body of Christ. "Services at St. Stephen's are held in Hungarian, and on the Sunday following Corpus Christi Day the feast is celebrated by a special procession and mass. . . . [T]he 'drum-beat of St. Stephen's choir' is an echo of [a] religious parade" (Staples, *Robert Lowell*, 42).

5.4 *Stupor Mundi*: Wonder of the World (epithet of Frederick II [1194–1250], Holy Roman Emperor).

The body of Warren Winslow, Lowell's cousin, was never recovered after his Navy destroyer, *Turner*, sank from an accidental explosion in New York harbor during World War II (Alan Williamson, *Pity the Monsters: The Political Vision of Robert Lowell* [1974], 35, n. 14).

Epigraph: Genesis 1:26 (Douay version).

In 1963, Lowell spoke about *Moby Dick*: "If I have an image for [America], it would be one taken from Melville's *Moby Dick*: the fanatical idealist who brings the world down in ruin through some sort of simplicity of mind. I believe that's in our character and in my own personal character; I reflect that it's a danger for us. It's not all on the negative side, but there's power there and energy and freshness and the possibility of ruin" (Jeffrey Meyers, ed., *Robert Lowell: Interviews and Memoirs* [1988], 77). He later states, "I always think there are two great symbolic figures that stand behind American ambition and culture. One is Milton's Lucifer and the other is Captain Ahab: these two sublime ambitions that are doomed and ready, for their idealism, to face any amount of violence" (Meyers, *Interviews*, 105). See Herman Melville's *Moby Dick* (ch. 16): "Some of these same Quakers are the most sanguinary of all sailors and whale-hunters. They are fighting Quakers; they are Quakers with a vengeance." Lowell's comments on this poem quoted below are from a letter to Shozo Tokunaga, his Japanese translator, Jan. 10, 1969, unless another source is specified.

I.1–12 See "The Shipwreck," chapter one of Thoreau's *Cape Cod* (1864): "I saw many marble feet and matted heads as the clothes were raised, and one livid, swollen, and mangled body of a drowned girl . . . the coiled-up wreck of a human hulk, gashed by the rocks or fishes, so that the bone and muscle were exposed, but quite bloodless,—merely red and white,—with wide-open and staring eyes, yet lustreless, dead-lights; or like the cabin windows of a stranded vessel, filled with sand. . . ."

I.1 Madaket: A harbor on the western shore of Nantucket Island; during college, Lowell spent two summers there.

I.10 dead-lights: Heavy glass portholes.

I.14 barks: "'bark' means take the bark or skin off" (Lowell).

I.15 Ahab's void: In *Moby Dick*, Ahab is captain of the whaling ship the *Pequod*. "'Void' is Ahab's death or absence" (Lowell).

I.18 dreadnaughts: "pun on a heavy warship and the literal meaning of the words, implying hubris" (Lowell).

I.19 deity: "'Deity,' the devil, the god of war" (Lowell).

I.22 earth-shaker: Poseidon, god of earthquakes and of water.

I.22–23 "'Chaste,' in the sense of inhuman, sterile, 'steel' like a warship" (Lowell).

II.7 Large racing sailboats, called S-boats, sailed from Siasconset, Nantucket Island.

II.11 lead squids: Artificial bait.

III.5 westward: Many editors consider this a misprint for "eastward." "Someone in Nantucket once told me if I kept going east I'd come to Spain (enemy of England) maybe 'westward' should be 'eastward,' but I meant looking west toward New England! You know 'Castles in Spain' are illusory hopes or possessions" (Lowell).

III.7 "'Eelgrass' is grasslike seaweed growing mostly in the shoals, not weeds on ship; 'water-clock' is really the globe, a kind [of] round clock, touched by the hours, changes of season" (Lowell).

III.15 "'Wooden' etc. a cliché maybe: a simpler less complicated older time. . . . [I]t's also pre-stee[l] ships. Also, stiff" (Lowell).

III.18 Of IS, the whited monster: The magazine version and *LWC* first printing read: "Of Is, the swashing castle." In Exodus 3:14 God, from a burning bush, tells Moses: "I AM

THAT I AM"; Gerard Manley Hopkins writes "what Christ is, / . . . IS immortal diamond" ("That Nature is a Heraclitean Fire"); Etienne Gilson writes, "It is because God is beautiful that things are beautiful . . . because He IS that they are" (*The Spirit of Medieval Philosophy* [1936], 133). "I think Lowell also means to retain by the word IS a reference to Christ (*I*esus *S*alvator)" (Staples, *Robert Lowell*, 102).

IV.1.1 whaleroad: From the Old English kenning *hrónrad* ("riding place of the whale"); the ocean.

IV.1.10 *Clamavimus*: We have cried. "Out of the depths have I cried unto thee, O Lord" (Psalms 130:1).

IV.2.4 " 'Crabs' maybe Eliot, but I got it from Corbière in a poem about Paris. 'Quaker Graveyard' began as a translation of that poem, then black turned into blue and nothing but this is left of the original" (Lowell). Cf. Corbière, "Paris Nocturne," stanza 1. This is a translation by Kenneth Koch and Georges Guy:

> —It is the sea: dead calm—and the spring tide
> With a far-off roaring has departed.
> The surge will come back rolling in its noise—
> Do you hear the scratching of the crabs of night?

IV.2.8 "I am poured out like water" (Psalms 22:14).

IV.2.9 The mast-lashed master of Leviathans: "Ahab, who, however, becomes finally lashed to the white whale itself " (Staples, *Robert Lowell*, 102). Cf. Odysseus, lashed to a mast as he listens to the Sirens (*Odyssey*, XII).

V See *Moby Dick*, chapters 61 ("Stubb Kills a Whale") and 67 ("Cutting In").

V.3–4 Woods Hole, Martha's Vineyard: Other launching points for ships.

V.6 Jehoshaphat: In Hebrew, the valley of decision or judgment. "Let the heathen be wakened, and come up to the valley of Jehoshaphat: for there will I sit to judge all the heathen round about. . . . Multitudes, multitudes in the valley of decision: for the day of the Lord is near in the valley of decision" (Joel 3:12, 14). "The valley of judgment. The world, according to some prophets and scientists, will end in fire" (Lowell, "Author's Note," in *Modern Poetry*, ed. K. Friar and J. M. Brinnin [1951], 520).

V.9 "Stubb slowly churned his long sharp lance into the fish, and kept it there, carefully churning and churning" (*Moby Dick*, ch. 61).

V.10 swingle: A wooden, swordlike instrument.

V.15 "When the morning stars sang together, and all the sons of God shouted for joy" (Job 38:7).

V.17 "A red arm and hammer hovered backwardly uplifted in the open air, in the act of nailing the flag faster and yet faster to the subsiding spar" of the *Pequod* as it sank (*Moby Dick*, chapter 135, "The Chase—Third Day").

V.17 In *LWC*, "Hide,"; according to Lowell, the comma after "Hide" is a consistent misprint (Williamson, *Pity the Monsters*, 42, n.20). "No comma after 'hide'; Jonah a type of Christ, but Christ by my bitter jugglery becomes the whale not the Whaleman" (Lowell).

V.18 Jonas Messias: Jonas Messiah; "for as Jonas was three days and three nights in the whale's belly; so shall the Son of man be three days and three nights in the heart of the earth" (Matthew 12:40).

VI The Carmelite Monastery of Walsingham, in Norfolk, England, was a popular shrine to Mary in pre-Reformation days; it was destroyed in 1538. "The road to the shrine is a quiet country lane shaded with trees, and lined on one side by a hedgerow. On the other, a stream flows down beneath the trees, the water symbol of the Holy Spirit, 'the waters of Shiloah that go softly,' the 'flow of the river making glad the city of God' " (E. I. Watkin, *Catholic Art and Culture* [1947], 177).

VI.1.4 munching: "[T]his word is never used the way I use it. The grass or leaves by the lane could be munched, I guess by some twist I made the lane become its cows" (Lowell).

VI.1.8–10 Shiloah . . . Sion: "or if Sion hill / Delight thee more, and Siloa's brook that flowed / Fast by the Oracle of God" (Milton, *Paradise Lost*, I.10–12). Sion: "The name came to signify God's holy hill at Jerusalem (Psalms 2:6), Jerusalem itself (Isaiah 1:27), and allegorically the heavenly city (Hebrews 12:22, Revelation 14:1)" (*Oxford Dictionary of the Christian Church*, 1977).

VI.2.6 *Non est species, neque decor*: [There is] neither form nor comeliness. "[H]e hath no form nor comeliness; and when we shall see him, there is no beauty that we should desire him" (Isaiah 53:2). "[T]here is no comeliness or charm in that expressionless face with heavy eyelids" (Watkin, *Catholic Art and Culture*, 177).

VI.2.8 "Nostalgia locates desire in the past where it suffers no active conflict and can be yearned toward pleasantly. History is the antidote to this. . . . Warren Wilson drowns, the Quakers drown, the wounded whale churns in an imagination of suffering and violence which it is the imperative of the poem to find release from, and each successive section of the poem is an attempt to discover a way out. . . . What the Lady of Walsingham represents is past contention. She's just there. The method of the poem simply includes her among its elements, past argument, as a possibility through which all the painful seeing in the poem can be transformed and granted peace. She floats; everything else in the poem rises and breaks, relentlessly, like waves" (Robert Hass, *Twentieth Century Pleasures* [1984], 5, 6, 22–23).

VII.5 shoal-bell: A warning of shallow waters.

VII.8 "Dagon his name, sea monster, upward man / And downward fish" (Milton, *Paradise Lost*, I.462–63).

VII.10 clippers: Clipper ships (the fast sailing ships of the mid-nineteenth century).

VII.11 bell-trap: Bell-shaped fish trap (John Frederick Nims, *The Harper Anthology of Poetry* [1981], 679) or, according to Anzilotti's conversation with Lowell, the bell or ball discharging the water siphon in a toilet tank (Rolando Anzilotti, ed., *Robert Lowell: A Tribute* [1979], 64).

VII.17 "I will set my bow in the clouds, and it shall be the sign of a covenant between me and between the earth" (God's promise to Noah not to flood the earth again, Genesis 9:13, Douay version).

IN MEMORY OF ARTHUR WINSLOW

An elegy for Lowell's maternal grandfather. See "In Memory of Arthur Winslow," p. 11; and the first three poems in the sequence "Life Studies," pp. 105–13.

I.1.2 Phillips House: The private, posh wing of Massachusetts General Hospital in Boston.

I.1.3 crab: The Latin word for crab is "cancer."

I.1.9 coxes: The coxswains of the racing shells.

I.1.10 *resurrexit dominus*: The Lord has risen.

I.2.1 swanboats: Flat pleasure-boats with a front shaped like a swan, their back like a swan's wing and tail; they circle the pond in Boston's Public Garden.

MARY WINSLOW

Lowell's maternal grandmother (d. 1944), married to Arthur Winslow.

1.7 rigid Charles: The frozen Charles River.
2.9 Glass what they're not: our Copley ancestress: I.e., mirror or reflect "the portrait by John
Singleton Copley (who had married a Winslow) of our ancestor, Sarah Waldo" (Sarah
Payne Stuart, *My First Cousin Once Removed: Money, Madness, and the Family of Robert
Lowell* [1998], 204).

THE DRUNKEN FISHERMAN

1.3 Jehovah's bow: See note to "The Quaker Graveyard in Nantucket" VII. 17, p. 349.
5.3 Fisher's: Christ's. "Follow me and I will make you become fishers of men" (Mark 1.17).
5.4 peter: A pun on Peter, the chief Apostle, a fisherman before following Jesus.
5.5 I will catch Christ with a greased worm: "[T]he fish is a symbol of Christ. . . . It came into
use in the second century, but neither its origin nor its meaning have so far been com-
pletely elucidated" (*Oxford Dictionary of the Christian Church*, 514).
5.7 Stygian: Of the river Styx, the principal river of the Underworld, which the dead must
cross.
5.8 Man-Fisher: Christ, fisher of men, walked on the sea (John 6:19).

BETWEEN THE PORCH AND THE ALTAR

Joel 2:17 "Between the porch and the altar, the priests, the Lord's ministers, shall weep, and
shall say: Spare, O Lord, spare Thy people" (from the Epistle for the Mass of Ash Wednes-
day). The Revised Standard Version translates "porch" as "vestibule." See also Jean
Stafford's story "Between the Porch and the Altar" (first published in *Harper's*, June 1945).

I.12 Aeneas searching through the burning ruins of Troy (*Aeneid*, II.752ff).
II.1 The Farmer: "The statue of the Minute-Man" (Lowell quoted in Staples, *Robert Lowell*, 88).
Emerson in "Concord Hymn" calls the militiamen "embattled farmers" (1.3).
II.8 Never to have lived is best: Sophocles, *Oedipus at Colonus*, 1224.
II.9 Man tasted Eve with death: "According to ancient tradition, immediately after the fall,
Adam and Eve knew that they must die, and they performed the sexual act, these two be-
coming inextricably intertwined" (George P. Elliott, in Staples, *Robert Lowell*, 88).
II.15–16 St. Patrick banished the snakes from Ireland.
III " 'Katherine's Dream' was a real dream. I found that I shaped it a bit, and cut it, and alle-
gorized it, but still it was a dream someone had had" (Lowell, *CPR*, 241–42). "Details" of
"Stafford's story . . . recall 'Katherine's Dream' " (Stephen Yenser, *Circle to Circle: The
Poetry of Robert Lowell* [1975], 334 n.29).
IV According to Lowell, the opening scene takes place in an imaginary Boston nightclub, "in
which there is an ice-skating floorshow" (Staples, *Robert Lowell*, 88).
IV.25 *Dies amara valde*: Day bitter above all [others]; "the Day" (23) when God "shall come
to judge the world with fire." Latin from the Responsory of the Mass on Ash Wednesday.
(In the Requiem Mass, this text is not part of the opening "Dies irae" sequence, but ap-
pears in "Libera me.") See notes to "The Day" 4.4 on p. 403, and to "St. Mark's, 1933"
6.1 on p. 404.
IV.25–26 Here the Lord / Is Lucifer in harness: "The region where Lucifer is Lord is Hell; in
the Bible, harness usually means armor" (George P. Elliott, in Staples, *Robert Lowell*, 88).

Based on Sextus Propertius' *Elegies* 4.7. Propertius' lover is called "Cynthia" in his four books of poems (her real name was probably Hostia).

2.7 Lethe: The river of forgetfulness in the Underworld; souls that return to earth must first drink from it.

3.4 Rome has seven hills.

3.9 Notus: The southwest wind.

5.1 Pompilia's Chloris: Accused by Cynthia of being a poisoner, as is Nomas (5.4).

5.3 Pluto: King of the Underworld. He seized Persephone as she was gathering flowers and dragged her down to his realm, making her queen there.

5.8 Thracians: People from Thrace, in Asia Minor; considered barbaric outsiders in both Greece and Rome. "[T]heir savage methods of fighting, their human sacrifices, their habits of tattooing and of eating butter, made them appear barbarous to the Greeks" (*Oxford Classical Dictionary* [1949], 901).

5.8 my golden bust: Cynthia's image in gold.

8.3 Anio: A river rising in the Sabine country and joining the Tiber just north of Rome.

8.5 Herakles: Known for his prodigious strength, simple living, and valor; he also, in a fit of madness, killed his wife and children (in Latin, Hercules).

9.5 dog: Cerberus, the three-headed dog guarding the entrance to Hades.

IN THE CAGE

Lowell was imprisoned for draft resistance, 1943–1944. For background, see note to "Memories of West Street and Lepke" 2.3 on p. 366.

6 "In the poem, prison is seen as a coal-mine. . . . The canaries beating their bars are the canaries that miners used to take down the pit to detect dangerous escapes of gas" (Jonathan Raban, ed., *Robert Lowell's Poems: A Selection* [1974], 164).

10 Black conscientious objector, member of a religious group named "The Israelites." "They had found a text in the Bible which said, 'But I am black though my brother is white.' This convinced them that the people of the Old Testament were Negroes. The Israelites believed that modern Jews were imposters" (Lowell, *CPR*, 362).

AT THE INDIAN KILLER'S GRAVE

The "Indian killer" is in part Lowell's ancestor John Winslow, for whom (along with his wife, Mary Winslow) there is a cenotaph (2.18) in King's Chapel Burying Ground, Boston. But the Indian killer of the title is essentially generic, a collective figure—the "Pilgrim Fathers" (3.3) whose heritage Lowell ponders in Boston's oldest cemetery, "[t]his garden of the elders" (2.2).

Epigraph: From Nathaniel Hawthorne's "The Gray Champion" (par. 3) in *Twice Told Tales* (tenses slightly changed).

1.3 Jehoshaphat: See note to "The Quaker Graveyard in Nantucket" V.6 on p. 348.

1.4 King Philip: Metacomet, chief sachem of the Wampanoags; the colonists called him King Philip. On King Philip's War (1675–1676): "This war, caused by the colonists' territorial expansionism, was the bloodiest of all the wars between the newcomers and native Americans. . . . [T]he leader of the colonists' military forces was Josiah Winslow, commander-in-chief and governor of Plymouth Colony, and Lowell's direct ancestor on his mother's side. . . . Winslow and his men burned villages of men, women, and children, and caused the virtual annihilation of the Narragansetts" (Steven Gould Axelrod, *Robert Lowell: Life and Art* [1978], 69–70). In 1676 King Philip was killed. "After Philip's body was quartered and decapitated, his head was exhibited on a pole in Plymouth for twenty years. His wife and children were sold into slavery in the West Indies" (Richard J. Fein, *Robert Lowell* [1979], 195).

1.7 An old well in the graveyard is covered by a metal cage. "The diabolical-looking octagonal metal cage has nothing to do with burials; it's a vent shaft for the subway" (Harris and Lyon, *Boston* [1999], 92).

1.11 Grace-with-wings and Time-on-wings: Insignia on the top borders of tombstones.

2.7–8 "The chapel, founded in 1686, was the first Anglican church in Puritan Boston to serve the British officers dispatched to the city by the king. No Puritan would sell land to the crown, so the governor appropriated a corner of the cemetery" (Harris and Lyon, *Boston*, 92).

2.15 The Massachusetts State House has a golden dome.

2.19 John and Mary Winslow: John died in 1674, a year before King Philip's War, so cannot be among the "veterans" mentioned in Hawthorne's epigraph. The brother of Governor Edward Winslow, he became a wealthy merchant and shipowner; in 1637, helped raise money to support troops fighting the Pequin Indians; in 1638, served on a jury that condemned three white men to death for murdering an Indian; in 1653, served on Plymouth's "Council of War." (Josiah Winslow, his brother Edward's son, was the first commander-in-chief in King Philip's War.) In sum, Lowell chooses as his emblematic "Indian killer" not a famous soldier in the Indian Wars, but a successful Puritan businessman, a "good citizen" whose religious convictions and mercantile habits inevitably led to the near-extinction of New England's Native American tribes. Mary Chilton (later, John's wife) at age twelve was the first female *Mayflower* passenger to go ashore at Plymouth Rock.

3.5 dragon: At the Apocalypse.

3.8ff "The address of King Philip to the Indian killers in the poem is also the address of Lowell to his ancestors" (Fein, *Robert Lowell* [1979],196).

3.16 *raca*: Fool (Aramaic; see Matthew 5:22).

3.20 Your election: Predestination; here, Puritan belief in selection (by the Divine Will) for salvation.

4.1 man-hole: A grave.

5.2 the man who sowed: Like Cadmus, who killed a dragon, then sowed its teeth, from which an army sprang up. The army fought until only five warriors survived; with these five Cadmus founded Thebes.

5.6 The four writers of the Gospels.

5.8 "The image here of the magical mother twining flowers into the warlock of Philip's severed head—consoling and restoring—is both gothic and poignant" (Vereen Bell, *Robert Lowell: Nihilist as Hero* [1983], 26).

5.8–11 "The 'Cistercians' ['Cistercians in Germany'] wasn't very close to me, but the last lines seemed felt; I dropped the Cistercians and put a Boston graveyard in" (Lowell, *CPR*, 247).

MR. EDWARDS AND THE SPIDER

This poem employs passages from Jonathan Edwards' *Of Insects*, his sermons "Sinners in the Hands of an Angry God" (based on Ezekiel 22:14) and "The Future Punishment of the Wicked." The source of the stanzaic structure is Donne's "A Nocturnal on St. Lucy's Day."

1.8 "[S]o flying for Nothing but their Ease and Comfort they Suffer themselves to Go" ("The Habits of Spiders" in *Of Insects*, written when Edwards was eleven).

2.1 "Art thou in the hands of the great God, who . . . when fixed time shall come, will shake all to pieces?" ("The Future Punishment of the Wicked").

2.9 "Can thine heart endure, or can thine hands be strong, in the days that I shall deal with thee?" (Ezekiel 22:14).

3.2 The underside of the female Black Widow, a poisonous spider, has an hourglass design.

4.1–2 Windsor Marsh is near East Windsor, Connecticut, where Edwards grew up. "You have often seen a spider . . . when thrown into the midst of a fierce flame" ("The Future Punishment of the Wicked").

5.2 Josiah Hawley: Edwards' uncle (see note to line 4, next poem).

AFTER THE SURPRISING CONVERSIONS

"I hope that the source of 'After the Surprising Conversions' will be recognized" (Lowell's Note to *LWC*). The poem is mainly derived from the conclusion to Jonathan Edwards' letter known as "Narrative of Surprising Conversions" (November 6, 1736), describing the religious revival he had led in Northampton, Mass. The passage begins, "In the latter part of May, it began to be very sensible that the Spirit of God was gradually withdrawing from us, and after this time Satan seemed to be more let loose, and raged in a dreadful manner. The first instance wherein it appeared, was a person putting an end to his own life by cutting his throat." The passage ends, "And many who seemed under no melancholy, some pious persons, who had no special darkness or doubts about the goodness of their state—nor were under any special trouble or concern or mind about anything spiritual or temporal—had it urged upon them as if somebody had spoke to them, Cut your own throat, now is a good opportunity. Now! Now!"

3 Ascension Day is celebrated in May or early June, on the Thursday forty days after Easter.

4 sensible: Evident. A gentleman: probably Edwards' uncle Josiah Hawley, who committed suicide. "The Devil took the advantage, and drove him into despairing Thoughts" (from Edwards' letter).

THE DEATH OF THE SHERIFF

Epigraph: "Perhaps you ask what was the fate of Priam?" (*Aeneid*, II.506). King Priam, killed during the fall of Troy, was the son of Laomedon. Laomedon had hired Poseidon, god of the sea, to build the walls of Troy, but then ("like Lord Weary in the ballad" [Staples, *Robert Lowell*, 93]) refused to pay him. As Troy fell, Poseidon with his trident broke up the city's walls and foundations. See *Aeneid*, II.506–634.

I Noli Me Tangere: Touch me not; Christ's warning to Mary Magdalene (John 20:17). See also Thomas Wyatt's "Whoso List to Hunt" 13.

I.2.5 tabula rasa: clean slate.

I.3.6 Our aunt, his mother: "This seems to imply that the love affair is incestuous" (Staples, *Robert Lowell*, 93); the lovers are cousins of the dead sheriff.

WHERE THE RAINBOW ENDS

"Much of the imagery of the poem is taken from the book of Revelation. See especially Revelation 4:7–8; 6 (*passim*); 8:7–9; 9:3; 12:14; 15:6; 19:8–9" (Staples, *Robert Lowell*, 107). For the rainbow, see note to "The Quaker Graveyard in Nantucket" VII. 17, p. 349.

1.3 slates: Slate gravestones.

1.8 Ararat: Mountain where Noah's ark landed (Genesis 8:4).

1.10 The wild ingrafted olive and the root: See Romans 11:17.

2.2 Pepperpot: Longfellow Bridge, the "salt and pepper" bridge spanning the Charles River between Cambridge and Boston, whose towers resemble canisters used to hold salt and pepper.

3.9–10 Stand and live / The dove has brought an olive branch to eat: The dove bringing an olive branch signaled to Noah the end of the Flood (Genesis 8:11). These lines are engraved on Lowell's father's tombstone in Dunbarton, New Hampshire. See headnote to "Dunbarton," p. 363.

from THE MILLS OF THE KAVANAUGHS (1951)

THE MILLS OF THE KAVANAUGHS

A synopsis of this (in its original version) long and difficult poem: "[It] is told from the point of view of Anne, a poor girl from a family of thirteen children, who is first adopted by the Kavanaughs and then married to the youngest son, Harry. . . . Joining the Navy prior to Pearl Harbor, her husband returns from the war on the verge of a nervous breakdown; he attempts and fails to suffocate his wife in bed one night because she speaks aloud, while asleep, to a man in a dream; Harry fears that she has committed adultery. Shortly thereafter, greatly distraught, he [dies]. Anne, left alone in the Kavanaugh garden near her husband's grave amid Grecian statuary, reflects on the Kavanaugh myth, their heritage of success and failure, sometimes addressing her dead husband, sometimes not. . . . Ovid's mythological account of Persephone in *Metamorphoses* V [337–571] is brought into play by the poet's use of a four-part organization in imitation of Persephone's circle of seasons. Spring (stanzas 1–7) dates Anne's meeting with Harry; summer (8–15) recalls their courtship; autumn (16–22) reflects the course of their marriage; and winter (23–38) is the season of his manic depression and collapse" (C. David Heymann, *American Aristocracy: The Lives and Times of James Russell, Amy, and Robert Lowell* [1980], 381–82). "The [final] five stanzas record Anne's thoughts as she gets into her boat and rows down the millstream. Her quest for the meaning of her life is a coda that summarizes the meaning of the poem. It is a review of the history of the Kavanaughs, her marriage ('Even in August it was autumn') and her future ('Love, I gave / Whatever brought me gladness to the grave')" (Staples, *Robert Lowell*, 58).

Lowell shortened the poem in *Selected Poems* (1976), reducing it to its final five stanzas. The present text is that version.

1.12 John Adams: U.S. president (1797–1801).

1.12 Romish: Roman Catholic.

1.16 The quotation mark ending this stanza was inadvertently left out of all previous printings of the complete text; this was finally corrected in *Selected Poems*.

2.5 Fragonard: Jean-Honoré Fragonard (1732–1806), French rococo painter primarily of romance and garden scenes.

3.2–4 Matches are being thrown in the millpond, making "target-circles" near the "bobber" (the float on a fishing line).

4.10 Harry Tudor: King Henry VIII of England broke with Rome and established the Anglican Church; in Catholic eyes, he died "outside the church" (4.9).

5.3 After Napoleon's defeat (Waterloo, 1815), the Bourbon Louis XVIII ruled until his death (1824).

5.3–12 Death: Hades, "God's brother" (5.7) because he is the brother of Zeus (chief of the gods, father of Persephone).

5.8 Death whipped his horses through the startled sod: the moment when Hades, having seized Persephone, opens the route to the Underworld in his chariot.

5.12 Thracian field: See note to "The Ghost" 5.8, p. 351.

FALLING ASLEEP OVER THE AENEID

In this poem the dreamlike phantasmagoria of "an old man's" sleep merges with a version of the funeral of Pallas in the *Aeneid*, XI.22–99. The Trojans have arrived in Italy, after the fall of Troy and much deprivation; Pallas, the son of an Italian ally, has been killed in battle by Turnus, king of the Rutulians, who opposes the Trojan presence in Italy.

5 lictor: An attendant to a magistrate.

7 Ares: The Greek and Trojan god of war, identified by the Romans with Mars.

15 Dido: Queen of Carthage who, in love with Aeneas, killed herself when he sailed for Italy (*Aeneid* IV.663).

17 Punic: Carthaginian.

22 Child of Aphrodite: Aeneas' mother is Aphrodite (Venus).

45 bitter river: Styx.

65 elephants of Carthage: Prefiguring the Carthaginian Hannibal's march on Rome, using elephants (218–211 B.C.).

66 Turms: Troops of thirty or thirty-two horsemen.

76 My Uncle Charles: Lowell's distant cousin, Charles Russell Lowell, killed in the Civil War.

77 Phillips Brooks: Brooks (1835–1893) was an Episcopal bishop, minister of Boston's Trinity Church, and an author. Grant: Ulysses S. Grant, Civil War general, later U.S. president.

85 young Augustus: Many Romans, including Virgil, were grateful for the peace the grand-nephew of Julius Caesar brought to the Empire after many years of civil war. When Octavian, after the defeat of Antony and Cleopatra, became Augustus (27 B.C.), he was thirty-six years old.

HER DEAD BROTHER

I.1.1 Lion of St. Mark's: A great winged lion on a pillar guards St. Mark's Square, Venice; emblem of the power of the Venetian Republic.

I.1.10 Achilles dead: "I would rather follow the plow as thrall to another / man, one with no land allotted him and not much to live on, / than be a king over all the perished dead" (*The Odyssey of Homer*, trans. Lattimore [1967], XI. 489–91).

I.2.4 crocking: Soiling with color.

I.2.5 Sheepscot: A river in southern Maine.

I.2.8 scotching: Crushing.

I.3.3 Stowe: A town in Vermont.

I.3.6 As false as Cressid: Shakespeare, *Troilus and Cressida*, III.ii.183. Cressid (Cressida) was a Trojan woman who pledged fidelity to Troilus, then betrayed him.

I.3.10 Packard: A car.

MOTHER MARIE THERESE

The young nun who speaks the poem remembers Mother Marie Therese, drowned Mother Superior of her convent. (The Austrian Empress Maria Theresa [1717–1780] was Marie Antoinette's mother; Mother Marie Therese, also aristocratic, is fictional.) "I don't believe any-body would think my nun was quite a real person. She has a heart and she's alive, I hope, and she has a lot of color to her and drama, and has some things that Frost's characters don't, but she doesn't have their wonderful quality of life" (Lowell, *CPR*, 265).

1 Maris Stella House: Presumably their convent. Maris Stella: Star of the sea.

2 Mother's: The Mother Superior's.

4 Pio Nono: Pope Pius IX (1792–1878).

8 Carthage: A (fictional) nearby coastal town.

18 friends of Cato: I.e., friends of the rulers of this world.

24 Probationers: Those preparing to become nuns.

28 Bourbon: The ruling family of France and Spain.

38 In *The Mills of the Kavanaughs*, this line ends with a comma.

46 Proserpina: Daughter of Zeus and Demeter who, picking flowers, was carried off by Hades and made queen of the Underworld; Greek name, Persephone. After the intervention of Demeter, she returned to the earth six months each year.

48 Candle, Book and Bell: A phrase signifying the ceremony of excommunication from the Roman Catholic Church; here, the nun expels (half-expels) "flowers and fowling pieces" from her life.

52 Canuck: French Canadian patois.

54 *Action Française*: A right-wing nationalist French daily newspaper.

55 soi-disant: Self-styled; here, the King is pretender to the throne.

57 Bridegroom: When a nun makes final vows, she becomes a Bride of Christ; a gold ring is placed on her finger.

59 Hohenzollern: The ruling family of Prussia and imperial Germany until 1918.

66 An émigrée in this world and the next: Kafka, "The Hunter Gracchus" (Staples, *Robert Lowell*, 55).

71 The Feast of (Saint) Louis IX (1214–1270), king of France, celebrated on August 25.

76 Saint Denis' Head and Queen Mary's Neck (81) seem to be Canadian promontories. Al-though there is a Queen Mary's Church in Herring Neck, Newfoundland, "certainly the geography is fictional; indeed, there is a kind of grisly humor attached to such formations as *St. Denis' Head* and *Queen Mary's Neck*, when the manner of death of St. Denis and Marie Antoinette is taken into consideration" (Staples, *Robert Lowell*, 99). St. Denis (died c. A.D. 250) reportedly walked with his head in his hands after his beheading.

83 Montcalm: Louis-Joseph de Montcalm-Gozon, French general who successfully led French forces in the French and Indian War, until 1759, when the British under General James Wolfe (86) defeated him; both Montcalm and Wolfe were killed.

83–84 on Abraham's / Bosom: I.e., in heaven. The site of the battle in which Montcalm and Wolfe were killed was called the Plains of Abraham.

86 The Huron tribe, converted by French Jesuit missionaries in the early seventeenth century, were decimated by the Iroquois in 1649, then dispersed (Jesuit priests [87] were also killed).

95 Boom: Floating barrier of logs.

96 Frontenac: Louis de Buade, Comte de Frontenac (1622–1698), French soldier and twice colonial ruler of New France (Great Lakes region and Eastern Canada); in the first French and Indian War, he attacked Boston.

108 *Contra naturam*: Against nature.

111 Advent: From Latin "Adventus," coming (i.e., of Christ).

128 venite: Come! "O come, let us sing unto the Lord" (Psalms 95:1).

129 Cf. the final line of "The Servant" in *IM*, 248: "My nurse's hollow sockets fill with tears."

THE FAT MAN IN THE MIRROR

Based on Werfel's poem "Der Dicke Mann im Spiegel."

3.4 pursey: Short-winded, swollen, heavy, puckered (*OED*).
5.2 meerschaum: A kind of clay, used in making the bowl of a pipe.
6.2 beaver: A visor on a helmet.

THANKSGIVING'S OVER

Lowell radically shortened this poem for *Selected Poems*, printing only its opening fourteen lines and its final stanza. This is the *Selected Poems* version.

1.3 the El: An elevated train line.
2.4 St. Francis of Assisi (1182–1226) once preached to the birds.
2.10 *Come unto us, our burden's light*: Matthew 11:30, "My yoke is easy, and my burden light."
2.15 beads: Rosary beads.
2.16 *Miserere*: Have mercy. From Psalms 51:1: *Miserere mei Deus* (Have mercy on me, O God).

LIFE STUDIES (1959)

About *Life Studies*, Lowell said in 1964: "I wanted to see how much of my personal story and memories I could get into poetry. To a large extent, it was a technical problem, as most problems in poetry are. But it was also something of a cause: to extend the poem to include, without compromise, what I felt and knew" (Meyers, *Interviews*, 85).

PART ONE
BEYOND THE ALPS

This poem symbolically encapsulates Lowell's journey from *Lord Weary's Castle* to *Life Studies*. "Crossing the Alps," as early as 1953, is an emblem: reviewing Robert Penn Warren's long poem *Brother to Dragons*, Lowell says that modern poetry "could absorb everything—everything, that is, except plot and characters, just those things long poems usually relied upon." Now Warren "has crossed the Alps and, like Napoleon's shoeless army, entered the fat, populated river bottom of the novel" (*CPR*, 68).

In *For the Union Dead*, Lowell cites Napoleon as the source of the title "Beyond the Alps." (Lowell first uses the phrase in "Falling Asleep over the Aeneid," line 68 [1947].)

Prefatory note: *Mary's bodily assumption*: On November 1, 1950, Pope Pius XII "declared it as a matter of divinely revealed dogma that the Blessed Virgin Mary 'having completed her earthly course was in body and soul assumed into heavenly glory,' to deny which would incur the wrath of Almighty God and the Holy Apostles" (*Oxford Dictionary of the Christian Church*, 949).

1.2 The Swiss made this attempt in 1952.
1.5 O beautiful Rome!
1.7 Life: "Man" in the Faber and Faber version. Lowell returned to "Man" in *FTUD* but retained "Life" in *SP*.
1.8 City of God: Rome. The phrase echoes Augustine's book *The City of God* (A.D. 413–426).

1.13 "I accept the universe": Attributed to Margaret Fuller (1810–1850). Carlyle's reported response: "By God! she'd better." (For Margaret Fuller, see headnote to "Margaret Fuller Drowned," p. 387.

2.2 San Pietro: The square before St. Peter's Basilica in Vatican City. *Papa*: "Pope" (Italian); "papá" means "father," and was printed in *SP* in error.

2.10 Saint Peter's brazen sandal: Part of the bronze statue of St. Peter in the Basilica, kissed in reverence by the faithful.

2.11 The Duce: Mussolini; caught escaping after his government fell, he and his mistress were gunned down and hanged head downward from a streetlamp in Milan (1945).

2.12 *coup de grâce*: A mortal, killing stroke.

2.13 Switzers: The Pope's official guards, from Switzerland.

3.4 Apollo plant his heels: Phoebus Apollo, the sun god, at dawn.

3.6 Parthenon: A temple honoring Minerva (in Greek, Athena), the "Goddess" of 3.9; she helped Odysseus blind the Cyclops (*Odyssey* IX). "Minerva was the goddess of both arts and war" (Raban, *Selection*, 165).

3.9 Hellas: Greece; here, ancient Greece.

3.10 golden bough: The branch carried by Aeneas that allowed him to pass safely through the underworld (*Aeneid*, VI.136ff).

3.12 Minerva, the miscarriage of the brain: Minerva was born, clothed in full armor, directly from the head of Zeus.

4.1 Now Paris, our black classic, breaking up: The train's destination. Rome was the symbolic home of Lowell's early Roman Catholicism, as well as of the universalist politics underlying the city's ecclesiastical and imperialist past; now Lowell arrives at a new city, "our black classic"—no less violent, but secular, the home of radical, fragmenting political and artistic revolution.

4.2 "The 'killer kings on an Etruscan cup' are the black-figure paintings on the vases which the Etruscans buried with their dead in ceremonial tombs. Great battles and scenes from mythology were recorded in a frieze around the body of the vase; and the black paint was subsequently scored with an awl to reveal details" (Raban, *Selection*, 166). "Etruscan art, formally dependent upon Greek art, is equally complex for, while the forms are recognizably Hellenized, the underlying spirit still retains a barbaric energy quite opposed to the Greek search for perfection in harmony" (*New Columbia Encyclopedia*, 1975). Etruscan civilization predated the Roman.

THE BANKER'S DAUGHTER

Marie de Médicis (1573–1642), daughter of Florentine banker Francesco de' Medici, in 1600 married Henri IV (1553–1610), king of France and Navarre; her son ruled as King Louis XIII (1610–1643). She was twice excluded from court (1617–1622 and 1631–1642) for attempting to control government policy.

5.2 Finisterre: Literally, "land's end," the promontory of northwest Spain extending into the Atlantic.

5.6 Saint Denis: The royal abbey in the town of Saint-Denis, north of Paris, where most of the kings and queens of France are buried, including Henri IV and Marie de Médicis.

5.7 Carrara: Sculpted from Carrara marble.

INAUGURATION DAY: JANUARY 1953

1.1 Stuyvesant: A square in New York City named after Peter Stuyvesant, Dutch colonial governor who surrendered New Amsterdam to the British (1664).

1.3 El: An elevated train line.

1.8 Cold Harbor: Site in Virginia of Ulysses S. Grant's victory over Robert E. Lee (June 1864); Grant, however, lost five times as many soldiers.

2.4 Ike: Like Grant, Dwight Eisenhower ("Ike") became president after serving as commander of the Army.

2.5 mausoleum: The most popular memorial to Grant is his tomb, in New York City.

A MAD NEGRO SOLDIER CONFINED AT MUNICH

1.2 Kraut DP: German displaced person.

2.2 Koenigsplatz: King's square.

3.2 outing shirts: made from outing flannel.

PART TWO
91 REVERE STREET

Lowell lived here with his parents, on Boston's Beacon Hill, from age eight to ten (1925–1927). In 1927 the family moved to 170 Marlborough Street; in 1930 he became a boarding student at St. Mark's School in Southborough, Massachusetts.

61 *ci-devant*: Former; an aristocrat who lost his title in the French Revolution. *Parvenu*: Upstart.

62 motto: Cf. "For the Union Dead" 10.4, p. 374.

62 wandering Jew: Condemned to wander the earth until Judgment Day, for mocking Christ on the day of Crucifixion (medieval legend).

62 *homo lupus homini*: Man [is] wolf to man.

63 *parti pris*: Prejudice or bias.

63 Jordan Marsh: Boston department store.

63 *chasseurs d'Alpine*: Mountain soldiers of the French army.

64 *pro tem*: Short for *pro tempore*: temporary.

64 Brahmin: Member of an old, patrician Boston family.

64 Hub of the Universe: Local nickname for Boston.

65 Tommies: British soldiers.

66 plebe: Naval Academy freshman.

66 *hors de combat*: Outside the fight or contest; disabled.

67 Siegfried . . . Valhalla: In Richard Wagner's opera tetralogy *Der Ring des Nibelungen* (1853–1874), the body of the German warrior Siegfried is not carried to the stronghold of the gods, Valhalla, by Brunnhilde. In the final opera, Brunnhilde joins Siegfried's body on his funeral pyre; the fire god then travels to Valhalla, which he destroys by flame.

67 Abbé Liszt: Franz Liszt (1811–1886), the most famous piano virtuoso of his time, as well as composer; Wagner's father-in-law. He took minor orders (therefore "Abbé") in 1861.

67 Mother's hero: Siegfried, who kills the dragon guarding the hoard of the Rheingold.

67 Sarah Bernhardt: In 1901 the French stage actress starred in Edmond Rostand's *L'Aiglon*, about Napoleon's son.

69 Ludendorff: Erich Ludendorff (1865–1937), German general and military strategist of World War I.

69 *sturm und drang*: "Storm and stress," German Romantic literary movement (c. 1765–1785).

69 Japanese hotel: Frank Lloyd Wright designed the Imperial Hotel (constructed 1916–1922) in Tokyo; it was famous not only for its architectural design but for withstanding the 1923 earthquake.

70 swan boats: See note to "In Memory of Arthur Winslow" I.2.1 on p. 349.

70 *Ein, zwei, drei*: one, two, three. *BEER* rhymes with *vier*, four.

72 pirates' chorus: From Gilbert and Sullivan's *The Pirates of Penzance* (1879).

72 Scollay Square: A shabby area of "tattooing parlors, shooting galleries, and burlesque" (Walter Muir Whitehill, *Boston: A Topographic History* [1968], 201).

73 my first school: Potomac School, near Washington, D.C.

73 Riverside Press: Publisher and printing house in Cambridge, Massachusetts. Rudy Vallee: American crooner. Hampton Institute: A historically black college in Virginia.

74 Admiral William Sims (1858–1936), American commander of operations in European waters, World War I.

76 *Beau Geste*: A silent film with Ronald Colman (1926).

76 *in ovo*: Unformed ("in the egg").

77 Sacco and Vanzetti: Italian immigrants to Massachusetts convicted (1927) for robbery and murder; many felt that the evidence was insufficient, and that they were persecuted for being anarchists. Lowell's cousin Abbott Lawrence Lowell, president of Harvard, was asked by the governor of Massachusetts to head a committee to review the case. The committee concluded that Sacco and Vanzetti's trial had been fair; their executions followed.

78 King Log: A fable in which frogs, asking Jupiter for a king, are sent a log. When they complain of its inertness, they are sent a stork, which devours them.

78 Filene's Basement: The discount portion of a department store in Boston.

78 Bill Tilden: tennis champion. Capablanca: José Raúl Capablanca, Cuban chess grand-master.

78 Sir Thomas Lipton: British tea merchant and yachtsman (1850–1931). His ships, all named *Shamrock*, raced five times unsuccessfully in the America's Cup sailing race ("Cup Defender races").

79 Harkness: Cf. Lowell, *CPR*, 357.

80 Mahan: Alfred Thayer Mahan (1840–1914), American naval officer, influential naval historian.

81 skipper a flivver: Be the commander of (drive) an old or cheap car.

83 *climacteric*: See note to " 'To Speak of Woe That Is in Marriage' " 13, p. 367.

83 remember the *Maine*: Rallying cry of the Spanish-American War, prompted in part by the blowing up of the U.S. destroyer *Maine* (1898).

83 cigar-chawing: Amy Lowell smoked cigars.

83 *Patterns*: Amy Lowell's most famous poem.

84 the Duse: Eleonora Duse (1858–1924), celebrated Italian actress.

84 *cits*: Citizens, i.e., civilians.

84 broking gangs: Stockbrokers.

84 Harkness: "With [Harvard President Abbott Lawrence] Lowell's encouragement a New York oil magnate, Edward S. Harkness, donated $12 million to Harvard . . . for the establishment of seven Georgian residence centers" (Heymann, *American Aristocracy*, 44).

84 Bull Moose Party: Theodore Roosevelt's Bull Moose Party, formally called the Progressive Party (1912), advocated many social reforms.

84 Curley: Four-time Mayor James Michael ("Boss") Curley ran the Irish political machine in Boston.

84 Bolshies: Bolsheviks, the Communist forces who won the Russian Revolution (1917).

85 Béla Kun-Whon: Hungarian Communist leader (1886–1937); he ruled Hungary for four months in 1919.

85 Etretat: A town on the Normandy coast of France.

85 *vers de société*: Urbane, ironic verse.

85 Somerset Club: An exclusive men's club on Beacon Hill.

87 Oyez: Hear ye!

88 *bête noire*: Someone or something especially disliked or avoided.

89 *coup de théâtre*: An unexpected dramatic event that overturns the given.

89 patroon: A landholder (under the original Dutch system) in New York.

89 Robert Livingston: A patrician New York lawyer and diplomat (1746–1813), minister to France who helped negotiate the Louisiana Purchase (1803).

PART THREE
FORD MADOX FORD

Lowell served informally as Ford's personal secretary (August–September 1937). In 1962, Lowell wrote: "Something planned and grand, and something helter skelter and unexpected seemed to come together in this poem. I thought for a long time I would never catch the tone and the man; now I think I have perhaps" (*Poet's Choice*, ed. Engle and Langland [1962], 164).

1.2 birdie: In golf, for any hole, one stroke under par.

1.3 Lloyd George: David Lloyd George (1863–1945), prime minister of Great Britain (1916–1922).

1.5 Hueffer: Ford Madox Ford's original surname; his father was a German music critic, Francis Hueffer. After serving with the British Army in World War I (during which he was gassed and shell-shocked), in 1919 he changed "Hueffer" to "Ford." Niblick: Nickname for a nine iron, inappropriate for putting.

1.14 Georgian Whig magnificoes: Aristocrat reformers.

1.15 Somme: French battleground in World War I, as were Nancy and Belleau Wood (1.18).

1.34–35 Washington Square and Stuyvesant Square, New York City.

1.41 Brevoort: A hotel in New York, frequented by artists. In Dutch, "voort" means "ford" (shallow place where a body of water can be crossed).

FOR GEORGE SANTAYANA

George Santayana (1863–1952), philosopher, novelist, poet. Born in Spain, educated largely in the United States, Santayana taught philosophy at Harvard from 1889 until 1912, when he returned to Europe. "I used to visit George Santayana in 1950 and 1951 in Rome. He was just under ninety, I was just over thirty. He took a fancy to my craggy, dark, apocalyptic poetry because I was both an old Bostonian and an apostate Catholic" (Lowell, *CPR*, 205). Before they met, Santayana praised Lowell's poems; there was an extensive correspondence between them. For Lowell's brief essay on Santayana, see *CPR*, 205–6.

1.11–14 Santo Stefano Rotondo is the church on the grounds of the convent of the Blue Sisters of the Little Company of Mary, in Rome. Santayana lived in a nursing home attached to this convent.

2.3 Ser Brunetto: Brunetto Latini (c. 1212–1294) was a diplomat and scholar, whose didactic poem *Il Tesoretto* (*The Little Treasury*) may have served as a model for Dante's *Commedia*.

2.3–5 These lines are based on Dante's *Inferno*, XV.121–24.

2.7 Alcibiades: Handsome, traitorous Athenian soldier and politician, who professes his love for the philosopher Socrates in Plato's dialogue *The Symposium* (215b ff.). As implied by the references both to Brunetto Latini and to Santayana's "long pursuit" of Alcibiades, Santayana was homosexual.

2.9 fleeting virgins: Like Daphne, who when pursued by Apollo was changed into a laurel tree (as a wreath, once conferred on poets, heroes, victors).

2.15 galleys: Printer's proofs.

TO DELMORE SCHWARTZ

The time of this poem is the year that Lowell and his wife Jean Stafford lived with Delmore Schwartz in Cambridge, Massachusetts. In later years Schwartz's mental problems increasingly alienated him from friends and jobs. A few days after Schwartz's death in 1966, Lowell wrote to Elizabeth Bishop that 1946 had been

> an intimate gruelling year . . . Jean and he and I, sedentary, indoors souls, talking about books and literary gossip over glasses of milk, strengthened with Maine vodka. . . . Delmore in an unpressed mustard gaberdeen, a little winded, husky-voiced, unhealthy, but with a carton of varied vitamin bottles, the color of oil, quickening with Jewish humor, and in-the-knowness, and his own genius, every person, every book—motives for everything, Freud in his blood, great webs of causation, then suspicion, then rushes of rage. He was more reasonable then, but obsessed, a much better mind, but one already chasing the dust—it was like living with a sluggish, sometimes angry spider—no hurry, no motion, Delmore's voice, almost inaudible, dead, intuitive, pointing somewhere, then the strings tightening, the roar of rage—too much, too much for us! Nothing haunts me more than breaking with friends. I used to think he was the only one I broke with. (*L*, 472)

2.16–17 "Freude" in German means "joy."

2.25–26 Schwartz is quoting and changing lines from Wordsworth's "Resolution and Independence": "We Poets in our youth begin in gladness; / But thereof come in the end despondency and madness" (48–49). After reading Lowell's poem, Schwartz wrote to Lowell that he had looked up what he had written in 1946: "We poets in our youth begin in sadness / But thereof come, for some, exaltation, / ascendancy and gladness" (Mariani, *Lost Puritan*, 475, n.93).

2.27 In 1946, Stalin had not yet suffered cerebral hemorrhages.

WORDS FOR HART CRANE

Hart Crane: American poet (1899–1932).

1.8 *Catullus redivivus*: Catullus restored to life.

PART FOUR: LIFE STUDIES

MY LAST AFTERNOON WITH UNCLE DEVEREUX WINSLOW

" 'Rock' was my name for Grandfather Winslow's country place at Rock, Massachusetts. An avenue of poplars led from the stable to the pine grove. . . . The letter paper at Rock bore the name 'Chardesa,' taken from the names of my grandfather's three children—Charlotte [Lowell's mother], Devereux, and Sarah" (*CPR*, 359–60). Devereux was "named for the North Carolina Devereuxs on their mother's side" (Mariani, *Lost Puritan*, 28). For the prose genesis of this poem, see *CPR*, 359–61.

I.1.5 Fontainebleau: town on the Seine, with former royal residence. Mattapoisett: "Fashionable summer watering spot" (Mariani, *Lost Puritan*, 34), on Buzzards Bay, southern coast of Massachusetts. Puget Sound: inlet of the Pacific, Washington State ("Father['s] ten years' dream of moving from Boston to Puget Sound," *CPR*, 354).

I.1.8 Norman: "Just like those poplars one sees in Normandy, was [Lowell's] explanation" (Anzilotti, *Tribute*, 64).

I.2.7 root-house: A half-sunken storage shed for root vegetables and bulbs.

I.2.12 silver mine: See headnote to "Grandparents," below.

I.2.13 *Stukkert am Neckar*: Stuttgart, Germany, on the Neckar River.

III. For drafts of this section, see Axelrod, *Life*, 247.

III.1.4 Great Aunt Sarah (Winslow), the sister of Lowell's grandfather, Arthur Winslow.

III.1.6 dummy piano: A soundless piano for practicing.

III.1.12 "Auction": Auction bridge.

III.1.15 Tauchnitz: Inexpensive editions of American and British authors.

IV.1.7 troubling the waters: "For an angel went down at a certain season into the pool, and troubled the water" (John 5:4).

IV.2.9 Mr. Punch: Cartoon figure from the cover of the London satiric magazine *Punch, or, The London Charivari*.

IV.2.11 *La Belle France*: France personified as the toga-clad figure of a woman.

IV.2.18 veldt: Open country. The poster depicts a scene from the South African Boer War (1899–1902), between the British and the Dutch-descended Afrikaners.

IV.3.8 Agrippina: mother of Nero, murdered by Nero. "I would beg my Uncle Devereux to read me more stories about that Emperor, who built a death barge for his mother, one that collapsed like a bombarded duck blind!" (*CPR*, 361).

IV.3.9 Golden House: Nero's Domus Aurea, palace built after the great fire of Rome (A.D. 64).

DUNBARTON

In the Faber and Faber edition (published before the American), the present first stanza is printed as the final stanza. Dunbarton, New Hampshire, is where Lowell's maternal ancestors, the Winslows and Starks, are buried. After the first publication of this poem, the cemetery was moved to a different location in Dunbarton; Lowell is buried there. For information on and photo of the Stark cemetery, see William Corbett, *Literary New England* (1993), 156–58, 86. Lowell describes the original cemetery in *CPR*, 348.

7.5 fauve: Violent, intense colors (as used by the Fauvist painters, 1898–1908).

GRANDPARENTS

Lowell's maternal grandparents: "Arthur Winslow [was] a six-foot self-made millionaire who had gone as a youth to Stuttgart, Germany, instead of to Boston Latin, for his schooling. . . . Back home, he went west to Colorado as a mining engineer to rip his fortune from the mountains, marry Mary Devereux of Raleigh, North Carolina, and return east" (Mariani, *Lost Puritan*, 28).

1.9 Pierce Arrow: An elegant large automobile.

1.13 "They Are All Gone into the World of Light!," title and first line of a poem (1655) by Henry Vaughan.

2.6 The song "Summertime," from the opera *Porgy and Bess*, by George and Ira Gershwin and DuBose Heyward (1935).

2.8 *Ancien Régime*: The old order (term for the aristocracy overturned by the French Revolution).

COMMANDER LOWELL

Lowell's father, the third Robert Traill Spence Lowell. "At twenty, Bob had graduated Annapolis with the class of '07. He was an engineer, a sliderule man, a wizard in math and the nascent science of radio" (Mariani, *Lost Puritan*, 30).

Lowell said of the genesis of this poem: "[W]hen I was writing *Life Studies*, a good number of the poems were started in very strict meter, and I found that, more than the rhymes, the regular beat was what I didn't want. . . . ['Commander Lowell'] is largely in couplets, but I originally wrote perfectly strict four-foot couplets. With that form it's hard not to have echoes of Marvell. That regularity just seemed to ruin the honesty of sentiment, and became rhetorical; it said, 'I'm a poem'—though it was a great help when I was revising, having this original skeleton. I could keep the couplets where I wanted them and drop them where I didn't; there'd be a form to come back to" (*CPR*, 243).

1.7–8 The archduchess Marie-Louise Hapsburg married Napoleon in 1810.
4.9 Menninger: Karl Menninger (1893–1990), psychiatrist and author.
4.13 *à la clarté déserte de sa lampe*: "In the deserted light of his lamp"; adapted from Stéphane Mallarmé's poem "Brise Marine." The passage, in Roger Fry's translation, reads:

> Nothing, not old gardens reflected in eyes
> Will keep back this heart that is plunged in the sea
> O nights! Nor the deserted light of the lamp
> On the empty paper which its whiteness protects
> Nor even the young woman suckling her child.

> (Staples, *Robert Lowell*, 91)

5.12 Yangtze: River in China; Lowell's father served there during the Chinese Civil War (Mariani, *Lost Puritan*, 30).

TERMINAL DAYS AT BEVERLY FARMS

Beverly Farms, a seaside town on Boston's North Shore.

FATHER'S BEDROOM

See *CPR*, 355, for another version of this scene.

FOR SALE

4–10 See *CPR*, 354, for another description of this cottage.

SAILING HOME FROM RAPALLO

Rapallo: Resort on the Italian Riviera, where Charlotte Winslow Lowell died. For Lowell on his mother's last days, see *CPR*, 349–50, and Ian Hamilton, *Robert Lowell: A Biography* (1983), 202–3.

2.2 *Golfo di Genova*: Gulf of Genoa.

2.6 *spumante*: Sparkling wine.

2.9 *Risorgimento*: A style characteristic of the period of Italy's national revival and consolidation (mid-nineteenth century); heavy, showy, with much sculpted detail.

2.10 the *Invalides*: The army mausoleum housing Napoleon's tomb in Paris.

3.16 *Occasionem cognosce*: Recognize the opportunity, or, more colloquially, "Seize your chance."

4.4 *panettone*: A tall, sweet Italian holiday bread. Lowell writes that his mother's body "shone in her bridal tinfoil" (*CPR*, 350); Mariani claims that "her body [was] wrapped in cellophane" (*Lost Puritan*, 22). Anzilotti gives a paraphrased exchange between himself and Lowell: "The *panettone* that we know in Italy is not wrapped in tinfoil. Perhaps [Lowell] meant *panforte*? Yes, this is what he had in mind, the dark and hard Sienese panforte I had sent him as a Christmas present" (*Tribute*, 64).

DURING FEVER

2.8 Triskets: Triscuits, thrice-baked crackers.

3.1ff For a prose version, see *CPR*, 355–56.

3.9 *putti*: Cupid-like children in Italian art.

4.3–8 Lowell describes this scene in *CPR*, 297–98.

WAKING IN THE BLUE

For an early draft of this poem, see Hamilton, *Robert Lowell*, 244–46. For Lowell's prose about another psychiatric hospital (Payne Whitney Clinic), see *CPR*, 346–63 *passim*.

1.1 B.U.: Boston University. A draft of the poem was seen by Donald Junkins while Lowell was a patient at McLean's, mid-December 1957; during this period Lowell taught in the B.U. English Department, and Junkins was his student (Mariani, *Lost Puritan*, 262).

1.3 *The Meaning of Meaning*: A book co-authored by critic I. A. Richards and linguist C. K. Ogden.

1.8 Cf. John Crowe Ransom, "Winter Remembered": "A cry of Absence, Absence, in the heart" (3).

3.1 McLean's: A private psychiatric hospital in Belmont, Massachusetts.

3.3 Porcellian: An exclusive student club at Harvard College.

HOME AFTER THREE MONTHS AWAY

2.2 In 1954, when Lowell was confined in a Cincinnati hospital, Elizabeth Hardwick wrote to him from New York: "I hope you are feeling well. We all think of you constantly, darling, and long to have 'Richard himself again so that we may resume the even tenor of our ways.' (I've never learned where that comes from or even if it is correctly quoted.)" (April 19, 1954). Lowell may also possibly have known this passage from Colley Cibber's adaptation of Shakespeare's *Richard III* (V.3.118–21):

> Hence babbling Dreams, you threaten here in vain;
> Conscience avant, *Richard's* himself again:
> Hark! the Shrill Trumpet sounds, to Horse, away,
> My Soul's in Arms, and eager for the Fray.

2.4 levee: A reception held by an eminent person upon rising from bed.

3.1 "Consider the lilies of the field, how they grow; they toil not, neither do they spin" (Matthew 6:28).

1.4 "hardly passionate Marlborough Street": "William James once gave his classes this example of understatement: 'Marlborough Street is hardly a passionate street' " (letter from Lowell to W. C. Williams, April 19, 1957, *L*, 275).

2.2 seedtime: "fair seed-time had my soul" (Wordsworth, *The Prelude*, I.301).

2.3 C.O.: Conscientious objector. Lowell refused to register for the armed services in 1943 and was jailed for five months in Danbury, Connecticut, after spending ten days in New York City's West Street Jail. In an interview twenty-five years later, Lowell said to V. S. Naipaul: "I was a Roman Catholic at the time, and we had a very complicated idea of what was called 'the unjust war.' This policy of bombing German cities seemed to be clearly unjust. So I refused to go to the army and was sent to jail" (Mariani, *Lost Puritan*, 106). For Lowell's public letter announcing his refusal to register, see *CPR*, 367–70.

3.2 At West Street, Louis "Lepke" Buchalter (the head of Murder Incorporated) and two extortion racketeers from a theatrical union, William Bioff and George Browne, were imprisoned. Browne had earlier been convicted of pandering. Buchalter (1897–1944) was convicted of murder in 1941 and electrocuted three years later. "Lepke" is from the Yiddish word "Lepkeleh" ("Little Louis").

4.7 *Murder Incorporated*: The public nickname for Lepke's "murder for hire" syndicate. As inmate Jim Peck recalls, "Lowell was in a cell next to Lepke, you know, Murder Incorporated, and Lepke says to him: 'I'm in for killing. What are you in for?' 'Oh, I'm in for refusing to kill.' And Lepke burst out laughing" (Hamilton, *Robert Lowell*, 91). Peck's story may be apocryphal, mistaking Robert Lowell for fellow war-resister Lowell Naeve; see Philip Metres, "Confusing a Naive Robert Lowell and Lowell Naeve: 'Lost Connections' in 1940s War Resistance at West Street Jail and Danbury Prison," *Contemporary Literature*, 41, no. 4, 661–92.

4.13 lobotomized: Metaphorical; Buchalter was not physically lobotomized.

4.15 agonizing reappraisal: A phrase made famous by John Foster Dulles, President Eisenhower's secretary of state (1953–1959). "[H]is insistence upon the establishment of the European Defense Community (EDC) threatened to polarize the free world, when in 1953 he announced that failure to ratify EDC by France would result in an 'agonizing reappraisal' of the United States' relations with France" (*Encyclopædia Brittanica*).

1.1 *Miltown*: a popular tranquilizer in the 1950s.

1.17 the Rahvs: Philip Rahv, editor of the *Partisan Review*, and his wife, Nathalie.

The title is from the Wife of Bath: "Experience, though noon auctoritee / Were in this world, is right y-nogh for me / To speke of wo that is in mariage" (opening of "The Wife of Bath's Prologue," Chaucer, *The Canterbury Tales*). The epigraph is a spliced quotation from Schopenhauer's *The World as Will and Idea*, trans. Haldane and Kemp [1909]:

[I]s not the definite determination of the individualities of the next generation a much higher and more worthy end than those exuberant feelings and supersensible soap bubbles of theirs? . . . For it is the future generation, in its whole individual determinateness, that presses into existence by means of those efforts and toils. ("The Metaphysics of the Love of the Sexes," vol. 3, ch. 44, p. 342)

" 'To Speak of Woe That Is in Marriage' . . . started as a translation of Catullus's *siqua recordanti benefacta* [LXXVI]. I don't know what traces are left, but it couldn't have been written without Catullus" (Lowell, *CPR*, 254). When first published (*Partisan Review* 25 [1958]), the poem was not enclosed in quote marks.

13 climacteric: A period or critical moment when physiological changes take place in the body; here, the male equivalent of menopause.

SKUNK HOUR

Lowell writes: "The dedication is to Elizabeth Bishop, because rereading her suggested a way of breaking through the shell of my old manner. Her rhythms, idiom, images, and stanza structure seemed to belong to a later century. 'Skunk Hour' is modelled on Miss Bishop's 'The Armadillo.' . . . Both 'Skunk Hour' and 'The Armadillo' use short line stanzas, start with drifting description, and end with a single animal." The setting is Castine, "a declining Maine sea town [near Nautilus Island]. I move from the ocean inland" ("On 'Skunk Hour,' " *CPR*, 226). Lowell's essay discusses other sources, poems by Hölderlin and Annette von Droste-Hülshoff; the essay as a whole is of extraordinary interest, but too long to be reproduced here. Axelrod (*Life*, 247) prints a draft.

3.6 Lowell writes that the "red fox stain" is "meant to describe the rusty reddish color of autumn on Blue Hill, a Maine mountain near where we were living. I had seen foxes playing on the road one night, and I think the words have sinister and askew suggestions" (*CPR*, 229).

5.1–6 Lowell: "This is the dark night. I hoped my readers would remember John of the Cross' poem ['The Dark Night of the Soul']. My night is not gracious, but secular, puritan, and agnostical. An Existential night" (*CPR*, 226).

5.2 Tudor Ford: A two-door sedan (Ford named the four-door model the Fordor).

5.2 the hill's skull: Golgotha, the hill where Jesus was crucified, is Hebrew for "skull" (from the shape of the hill).

5.3 I watched for love-cars: Lowell writes that the anecdote of "watching the lovers was not mine," but "about Walt Whitman in his old age" (*CPR*, 228). In the early 1970s, Elizabeth Bishop told Frank Bidart that the source of the anecdote was Logan Pearsall Smith's *Unforgotten Years* (1939):

> Almost every afternoon my father would take Walt Whitman driving in the Park; it was an unfailing interest to them to drive as close as they could behind buggies in which pairs of lovers were seated, and observe the degree of slope towards each other, or "buggy-angle," as they called it, of these couples; and if ever they saw this angle of approximation narrowed to an embrace, my father and Walt Whitman, who had ever honored that joy-giving power of nature symbolized under the name of Venus, would return home with happy hearts. (99)

6.2 careless Love: The blues song "Careless Love" has many verses; we have no information regarding which version or performance Lowell might have had in mind. Here is a verse recorded by Big Joe Turner in February 1941:

> Love, O Love, O careless Love . . .
> You worried my mother until she died
> You caused my father to lose his mind
> You worried my mother until she died
> You made my father lose his mind.

6.3 "The 'sob in each blood cell' is meant to have a haggard, romantic profilish exaggerated qual-ity—true, but in the rhetoric of destitution, here the more matter of fact descriptive style gives out, won't do, and there's only the stagey for the despair. Then one leaves it for the skunk vision. Most people take the skunks as cheerful [but] they are horrible blind energy, at the same time . . . a wish and a fear of annihilation, i.e., dropping to a simpler form of life, and a hopeful wish for that simpler energy" (Lowell, letter to John Berryman, March 18, 1962, *L*, 400).

6.5 "Which way I fly is hell; my self am hell" (Satan, in Milton's *Paradise Lost*, IV.75).

Regarding the ending Lowell writes, "Somewhere in my mind was a passage from Sartre or Camus about reaching some point of final darkness where the one free act is suicide. Out of this comes the march and affirmation, an ambiguous one, of my skunks in the last two stanzas" (*CPR*, 226).

from FOR THE UNION DEAD (1964)

In an interview, Lowell said: "In *For the Union Dead*, I modified the style of *Life Studies*—free-verse stanzas, each poem on its own and more ornately organized. Then came metrical poems, more plated, far from conversation, metaphysical. My subjects were still mostly realism about my life. I also wrote one long public piece, the title poem" (*CPR*, 269). Elsewhere he said: "*For the Union Dead* is more mixed, and the poems in it are separate entities. I'm after invention rather than memory, and I'd like to achieve some music and elegance and splendor, but not in any programmatic sense. Some of the poems may be close to symbolism" (Meyers, *Interviews*, 85).

WATER

Addressed to Elizabeth Bishop.

THE OLD FLAME

Addressed to Lowell's first wife, Jean Stafford. The setting is Damariscotta Mills, Maine.

MIDDLE AGE

3 Cf. the Lord's Prayer: "[F]orgive us our trespasses, As we forgive those who trespass against us" (from *The Book of Common Prayer*, 1929).

4.2 Mount Sion: Or Zion, hill in Jerusalem conquered by King David, the City of David; symbolic of Jerusalem, the Promised Land, God's holy hill.

2.2–4 Lowell drew this image from his memory of imprisonment during World War II. He writes: "we would sit around barrels filled with burning coke and roast wheat seeds" (*CPR*, 361–62). The Israelites mentioned in "In the Cage" were part of this group; see Mariani, *Lost Puritan*, 113 and 472, n.9.

FALL 1961

For an early draft of this poem, see Patrick K. Miehe, *The Robert Lowell Papers at the Houghton Library* (1990), 122.

2.3 "Across the nation last week, there was endless conversation about the threat of nuclear war" between the United States and the Soviet Union (*Time*, September 29, 1961; 13); opposing troops engaged in a stand-off as the Berlin Wall was built, and both countries resumed nuclear testing. (For more on the "historical moment," see Steven Axelrod, "Robert Lowell and the Cold War," *New England Quarterly*, September 1999, 349–52.)

4.1 shield: The North American Air Defense Command engaged in an exercise called "Sky Shield II" against a simulated Russian nuclear attack on October 14, 1961.

5.1 "The purpose of playing . . . is, to hold as 'twere the mirror up to nature" (Hamlet's instructions to the Players, III.ii.20–22).

FLORENCE

Among her many books, novelist and critic Mary McCarthy wrote *The Stones of Florence* (1959).

1.1 black ink: "When disturbed, cuttlefish eject a cloud of dark brown ink from an ink sac for protection. . . . The ink . . . has been used as the artist's pigment, sepia" (*New Columbia Encyclopedia* [1975]).

3.6 Perseus, David and Judith: Great decapitators. Perseus beheaded Medusa ("the Gorgon," 3.20); David beheaded Goliath; Judith beheaded Holofernes. Statues of Perseus, David and Judith are in the Piazza della Signoria in Florence ("Where the tower of the Old Palace / pierces the sky" [3.3–4]).

EYE AND TOOTH

1.2 the old cut cornea: Lowell had suffered a corneal abrasion from a contact lens. He described this poem as "my farewell to contact lenses" (Hamilton, *Robert Lowell*, 293).

1.3 "now we see through a glass, darkly; but then face to face" (I Corinthians 13.12).

3.1ff "When I woke up this morning, something unusual for this summer was going on!—pinpricks of rain were falling in a reliable, comforting simmer. Our town was blanketed in the rain of rot and the rain of renewal. New life was muscling in, everything growing moved on its one-way trip to the ground. I could feel this, yet believe our universal misfortune was bearable and even welcome. An image held my mind during these moments and kept returning—an old-fashioned New England cottage freshly painted white. I saw a shaggy, triangular shade on the house, trees, a hedge, or their shadows, the blotch of decay. The house might have been the house I was now living in, but it wasn't; it came from the time when I was a child, still unable to read, and living in the small town of Barnstable on Cape Cod. Inside the house was a bird book with an old stiff and steely engraving of a sharp-shinned hawk. The hawk's legs had a reddish-brown buffalo fuzz on them; be-hind was the blue sky, bare and abstracted from the world. In the present, pinpricks of rain were falling on everything I could see, and even on the white house in my mind, but the hawk's picture, being indoors I suppose, was more or less spared. Since I saw the pic-ture of the hawk, the pinpricks of rain have gone on, half the people I once knew are dead, half the people I now know were then unborn, and I have learned to read. An im-age of a white house with a blotch on it—this is perhaps the start of a Williams poem" (Lowell, *CPR*, 37–38).

7.3–4 "Eye for eye, tooth for tooth, hand for hand, foot for foot" (Exodus 21:24).
8.1ff See Deuteronomy 28:65.

ALFRED CORNING CLARK

A classmate at St. Mark's School.

THE PUBLIC GARDEN

1.9 swanboats: See note to "In Memory of Arthur Winslow" I.2.1, p. 349.

GOING TO AND FRO

"And the Lord said unto Satan, Whence comest thou? Then Satan answered the Lord, and said, From going to and fro in the earth, and from walking up and down in it" (Job 1:7). A draft of this poem (Houghton Library bMS Am 1905 2745) is titled "For Nerval or Someone."

5.4 Mary, Myrtho, Isis: Myrtho is a name, derived from "myrtle," invented by Gérard de Ner-val (1808–1855) in his sonnet "Myrtho" (*Gérard de Nerval: Selected Writings*, trans. Sieburth [1999], 403); wreaths of myrtle crowned the victors in the ancient Olympic games. Isis is the wife of Osiris, the slain god of Egyptian mythology; to restore him to life, she reassembled the scattered bits of his dead body. From Nerval's "Aurélia":

> I turned my thoughts to the eternal Isis, sacred mother and bride; all my aspira-tions, all my prayers gathered into her magic name; I felt myself come back to life in her, and at times she appeared to me in the guise of the ancient Venus, at times she took on the features of the Christian Virgin. (Sieburth, *Gérard de Ner-val*, 308)

Mary the mother of Jesus is "the Christian Virgin."
5.6–6.1 The love that moves the stars/moved you!: "[T]he magnetic rays that emanate from me or from others flow directly through the infinite chain of creation whose transparent network is in continuous communication with the planets and the stars" (Sieburth, *Gérard de Nerval*, 307). Also cf. the final line of Dante's *Commedia* (Paradiso, XXXIII.143).
6 Nerval was hospitalized several times for severe mental breakdowns. During the final weeks of his life he lived on the streets of Paris without fixed address; at the age of forty-six, he hanged himself in the rue de la Vieille-Lanterne.

MYOPIA: A NIGHT

3.1 the morning star: Lucifer, another name for Satan (4.1ff).

For Lowell on Hawthorne, see *CPR*, 188–91.

Many details of the first two stanzas are drawn from "The Customs House," Hawthorne's introduction to his novel *The Scarlet Letter*.

5.2 Lowell: James Russell Lowell. Henry Wadsworth Longfellow (1807–1882), Oliver Wendell Holmes (1809–1894) and John Greenleaf Whittier (1807–1892) were prominent New England "men of letters." For Lowell on J. R. Lowell and Longfellow, see *CPR*, 194–96.

6.2–5 From Hawthorne's romance *Septimus Felton* (1871).

JONATHAN EDWARDS IN WESTERN MASSACHUSETTS

Several passages use phrases from works by Edwards: "Of Insects," "Personal Narrative," "Sarah Pierrepont," and "Sinners in the Hands of an Angry God"; and from Sir Francis Bacon's essays (as cited below).

5.3 *Whitehall*: "Whitehall, the Royal Palace, becomes the metaphor for any country house imbued with the presence of God" (Jerome Mazzaro, *The Poetic Themes of Robert Lowell* [1965], 132).

6 "And because, the *Breath* of Flowers, is farre Sweeter in the Aire, (where it comes and Goes, like the Warbling of Musick) then in the hand" (Bacon, "Of Gardens").

7.3 *when he fell*: In 1621, Bacon pleaded guilty to accepting bribes as Lord Chancellor; he spent the next five years, until his death, writing in retirement.

7.4 "In Fame of Learning, the Flight will be slow, without some Feathers of *Ostentation*" (Bacon, "Of Vaine-Glory").

11.1 George Berkeley (1685–1753), philosopher and divine. Berkeley "held that, when we affirm material things to be real, we mean no more than that they are perceived (*esse est percipi*). Material objects, on Berkeley's view, continue to exist when not perceived by us solely because they are objects of the thought of God" (*The Oxford Dictionary of the Christian Church*, 161).

11.4 Sarah Pierrepont: Edwards' wife.

12.1ff "They say there is a young lady who is beloved of that Great Being, who . . . comes to her and fills her mind with exceeding sweet delight, and that she hardly cares for anything. . . . She will sometimes go about from place to place, singing sweetly, and . . . loves to be alone, walking in the fields and groves, and seems to have some one invisible always conversing with her" (Edwards, "Sarah Pierrepont," quoted in Mazzaro, *Themes*, 132).

16.2 Great Awakening: A widespread series of religious revivals in the American Colonies, mid-eighteenth century; begun in New England (1734–1735) by Edwards' preaching in Northampton, Massachusetts.

16.2–4 "Alas, how many . . .": From Edwards' "Sinners in the Hands of an Angry God."

17.3 you fell from your parish: In 1750 Edwards' congregation dismissed him from Northampton.

17.4 "All rising to *Great Place*, is by a winding Staire" (Bacon, "Of Great Place").

23.2ff From Edwards' letter to the Board of Trustees of the College of New Jersey (now Princeton University).

TENTH MUSE

There are nine Muses in Greek mythology.

1.1 Sloth: one of the seven Deadly Sins. In 1964, Stanley Kunitz said: "Only once did he ever complete a poem in a day. That was 'The Tenth Muse,' a poem about sloth!" (Meyers, *Interviews*, 89). Lowell writes: "sloth is the safest cure of all vices" (*CPR*, 132).
2.1ff Moses brought the Ten Commandments, the "old law" inscribed on stone, down from Mt. Sinai (Exodus 20).

CALIGULA

"Cal" was Lowell's nickname, the name used by his closest friends. Lowell to Bishop: "Dear Elizabeth; (You must be called that; I'm called Cal, but I won't explain why. None of the prototypes are flattering: Calvin, Caligula, Caliban, Calvin Coolidge, Calligraphy—with merciless irony)" (August 21, 1947, *L*, 69). Many details in this poem are drawn from the portrait of Caligula by Suetonius, *Lives of the Caesars*. Caligula: "little boots" in Latin.

1.3 "The whole poem unfolds that altogether convincing hesitation in 'like you'—a verb or not?" (Christopher Ricks, in Jonathan Price, ed., *Critics on Robert Lowell* [1972], 99).
3.10 Adonis was gored by a boar.
3.13 Caligula declared himself a god.

JULY IN WASHINGTON

1.1 this wheel: Pierre-Charles L'Enfant planned Washington, D.C. (1791), so that federal buildings are in a central location and broad, diagonal avenues radiate out from this center.
4.1 circles: Traffic circles, with statues and greenery in the center.
5.2 Cf. "the meek shall inherit the earth" (Psalms 37:11).
6.1 " 'The Elect,' the old American Calvinist doctrine of a community of saints existing by divine grace, have turned into 'the elected' " (Raban, *Selection*, 174).
8.2 delectable mountains: Cf. "il dilettoso monte" (Dante, *Inferno*, I.77).

BUENOS AIRES

Lowell visited Brazil in summer 1962, then in September briefly went to Argentina. On December 24, 1962, Lowell wrote Bishop from the United States: "I guess I was beginning to go off during the last two weeks in Brazil, and this must have been painful for you to watch or at least sense. When I got to Buenos Aires, my state zoomed sky-high and I am glad you didn't see it. It's hard for the controlled man to look back on the moment of chaos and claim. I shan't try, but it was all me, and I am sorry you were touched by it" (*L*, 402).

Some months before Lowell's visit to Argentina, Dr. Arturo Frondizi, the Argentine president, had been arrested by the military, who then assumed power.

SOFT WOOD

1.2 Scholar Gypsy: In Matthew Arnold's poem, the title figure leaves Oxford to join a band of gypsies; centuries later, he is seen, or perhaps seen.
6.1 my window: Lowell in this poem conjoins two Castine residences. His studio was a con-

verted seaside barn; he described it as being "right on the bay, which on one side looks like a print of Japan and other side like a lake in Michigan as the rocky islands with pine trees ease off into birches and meadows" (Corbett, *Literary New England*, 41). Harriet Winslow's "house" (7.1) was in the center of town; for photos, see Mariani, *Lost Puritan*, 320 and 224.

7.1 Harriet Winslow: Lowell's cousin Harriet was "completely incapacitated now by strokes and slowly dying" (Mariani, *Lost Puritan*, 315).

NEW YORK 1962: FRAGMENT

E.H.L.: Elizabeth Hardwick Lowell.

17–19 "Still, still, still. Whenever Lowell uses the word 'still' we know that something is about to change, if not for the character in the poem, then for the poet. 'Still' connotes a cross between persistence and despair. The dual meanings of the word seem to be at loggerheads" (Mark Rudman, *Robert Lowell: An Introduction to the Poetry* [1983], 22).

THE FLAW

"Like 'Eye and Tooth' and 'Flaw (Flying to Chicago)' this poem elaborates, in the style of a metaphysical conceit, the image of the hairline cut on the cornea of Lowell's eye. . . . The flaw [is] shaped like a question mark" (Raban, *Selection*, 174–75). "I kept seeing a little black nit or gnat worrying oddly over any white surface I looked at. At times it became a hair with little legs" (Lowell, letter, November 1, 1970, *L*, 555).

1.4 essence: French for "gasoline."
4.5 *Fête Champêtre*: A village festival.

NIGHT SWEAT

1.13–14 Cf. "May our heirs seal us in a single urn, / A single spirit never to return" (Yvor Winters' "The Marriage").
2 In the first *SP* Lowell eliminated the break between stanzas, which is restored here. See Introduction to *CPO* (p. xii) for discussion of this change.
2.1 Behind me! You!: "Get thee behind me, Satan" (Matthew 16:23).

FOR THE UNION DEAD

A brief recital of the poem's historical background: President Lincoln began admitting African-American soldiers into the Union forces in 1863. The 54th Regiment of Massachusetts Volunteer Infantry became the first black regiment recruited in the North. Robert Gould Shaw, a twenty-six-year-old white officer from a prominent abolitionist Boston family, volunteered for its command. The 54th Regiment became famous for leading an unsuccessful assault on Fort Wagner, South Carolina (July 18, 1863). In the hard-fought battle, the regiment lost more than 250 soldiers, including Shaw. The heroic charge, coupled with so many casualties, made the regiment a household name throughout the North, and helped spur black recruiting. Augustus Saint-Gaudens' bronze bas-relief monument commemorating Shaw and his men, which faces the Massachusetts State House, was dedicated in 1897.

Lowell's poem was originally titled "Colonel Shaw and the Massachusetts' 54th," and appeared as the final poem in the first paperback edition of *Life Studies* (Vintage, 1960). It was published under its present title in *The Atlantic Monthly* 206 (1960), no. 5. Lowell read the poem at the Boston Arts Festival, June 1960, held near the Augustus Saint-Gaudens monument. Lowell's great-grand-uncle, the poet James Russell Lowell, had written a poem about Robert Gould Shaw, "Memoriae Positum R.G.S.," published in 1864; a passage from it is inscribed on the Shaw monument:

> Right in the van of the red rampart's slippery swell
> With heart that beat a charge he fell forward as fits a man
> But the high soul burns on to light men's feet
> Where death for noble ends makes dying sweet.

In 1928, Robert Lowell's mentor Allen Tate wrote "Ode to the Confederate Dead." For a list of prior poems, speeches, and other sources, see Axelrod, *Life*, 268–69, n.33; William Doreski adds several more (*Robert Lowell's Shifting Colors* [1999], 242, n.5). Doreski prints manuscript passages, a complete draft (97–109) and two statements about the poem made by Lowell (94–95, 109).

In 1960, reading the poem for the first time in public, Lowell began with a prepared statement: "My poem, *The Union Dead*, is about childhood memories, the evisceration of our modern cities, civil rights, nuclear warfare and more particularly, Colonel Robert Shaw and his Negro regiment, the Massachusetts 54th. I brought in early personal memories because I wanted to avoid the fixed, brazen tone of the set-piece and official ode" (Doreski, *Shifting Colors*, 109). In 1964, Lowell wrote in the *Village Voice*: "I lament the loss of the old Abolitionist spirit: the terrible injustice, in the past and in the present, of the American treatment of the Negro is of the greatest urgency to me as a man and as a writer" (letter to the editor, November 19, 1964, 4). In 1969, Lowell wrote: "In 1959 I had a message. Since then the blacks have perhaps found their 'break,' but the landscape remains" (Doreski, *Shifting Colors*, 95).

Relinquunt . . . Publicam: The inscription on Saint-Gaudens' sculpture reads: "Omnia relinquit servare rempublicam" ("he leaves all behind to protect [preserve, save] the state"). Lowell in his epigraph changes the Latin so that "he" becomes "they." "Omnia relinquit servare rempublicam" is the motto of the Society of the Cincinnati (Washington, D.C.); the phrase is attributed to Henry Knox.

1.3 cod: Until 1974, the unofficial symbol of Massachusetts; in that year it became official.

7.4 "so true to nature that one can almost hear them breathing" (from William James' speech at the dedication of the monument).

10.1 He is out of bounds now: "Our wall of circumstance / Cleared at a bound, he flashes o'er the fight" (J. R. Lowell, "Memoriae Positum R.G.S." III.2.7–8).

10.2 "choose life and die": cf. Deuteronomy 30:19 ("therefore choose life, that both thou and thy seed may live," KJV).

10.4 Cf. "91 Revere Street," p. 62, paragraph 2 (final sentence).

12.1 "the abstract soldiers'-monuments have been reared on every village green" (William James' speech).

13.4 After the charge, there were "many anonymous and widely circulated pieces of doggerel, one of which purported to describe Fort Wagner's commanding officer ordering his troops to bury Shaw 'with his niggers' " (Axelrod, *Life*, 164). "I am thankful they buried him 'with his niggers.' They were brave men and they were his men" (Colonel Charles Russell Lowell). Charles Russell Lowell, Jr., married Josephine Shaw, Colonel Shaw's sister, after Shaw's death; he also died in the Civil War. See "Colonel Charles Russell Lowell 1835–64" in *CPO*, 485.

15.1 Mosler Safe: An advertisement for this safe read: "The Hiroshima Story Comes to Life, with a Bang"; the first atomic bomb was dropped on Hiroshima, 1945.

15.4 The poem was written during the period of forced school desegregation in the South; nine African-American schoolchildren attempting to attend an all-white high school in Little Rock, Arkansas, had to be escorted by federal troops (September 1957).

17 "The poem . . . finally circles back to its memory of childhood, at which there dawns, un-voiced, the fear that the Aquarium's tanks are now dry because the sea-world has broken loose. . . . How right to eschew a hyphen in 'giant finned' " (Christopher Ricks, in Price, *Critics on Robert Lowell*, 98).

from NEAR THE OCEAN (1967)

Lowell writes: "My next book, *Near the Ocean*, starts as public. I had turned down an invita-tion to an Arts Festival at the White House because of Vietnam. This brought more publicity than poems, and I felt miscast, felt burdened to write on the great theme, private though al-most 'global.' . . . [T]he meter I chose, Marvell's eight-line stanza . . . hummed in my mind summer till fall. It's possible to have good meter yet bad intention or vice versa—*vers de so-ciété*, or gauche sprawl. All summer, as I say, the steady, hypnotic couplet beat followed me like a dog. I liked that. After two months, I had two poems, one a hopeless snakeskin of chimes. My last piece ['Near the Ocean,' section V of the sequence of the same title], my most ambitious and least public, was a 'Dover Beach,' an obscure marriage-poem set in our small Eastern seaboard America" (*CPR*, 269–70).

NEAR THE OCEAN

I. WAKING EARLY SUNDAY MORNING

2.5 I.e., a rainbow trout biting a fishing lure that sits on the water's surface. "A dry fly floats on the surface, that's the generic name for this kind of fly, unlike a *wet* fly" (Lowell, quoted in Anzilotti, *Tribute*, 62–63).

4.3–4 "They that go down to the sea in ships, that do business in great waters; These see the works of the Lord, and his wonders in the deep" (Psalms 107:23–24).

6.5 anywhere, but somewhere else!: Cf. Baudelaire's prose-poem "Any Where Out of the World" (he gave it this English title) in *Le Spleen de Paris* (1864; Axelrod, *Life*, p. 270, n.54).

8.3–8 This passage offers a sequence of things or representations that, though once useful, once powerful, now are remnants. Unexplicit, "wordless," their power is the power of things once believed, of again wearing "old clothes." The last line quotes St. Paul: "Though I speak with the tongues of men and of angels, and have not charity, I am be-come as sounding brass, or a tinkling cymbal" (I Corinthians 13:1). For those animated by conviction, such things or arts offer merely tantalizing, seductive surfaces, signs without substance like the graven images condemned in the Hebrew Bible. Paul, who damned the "unrighteous" (see I Corinthians 6:9–10), was himself banished, an "example" (Acts 19–20; Yenser, *Circle to Circle*, p. 347, n.10). According to Lowell, the pun on "cymbal-symbol" is found in Paul's Greek text (Williamson, *Pity the Monsters*, 122).

9.1–2 "[N]ow we see through a glass, darkly; but then face to face" (I Corinthians 13:12).

9.7 Lowell tried to use the china doorknobs as early as "Skunk Hour": "I began to feel that real poetry came, not from fierce confessions, but from something almost meaningless but imagined. I was haunted by an image of a blue china doorknob. I never used the doorknob, or knew what it meant, yet somehow it started the current of images in my opening stanzas" (written in 1964; *CPR*, 228).

10.2–8 Goliath: The Philistine giant slain by David. King Saul asked David to bring him one hundred foreskins of Philistines, instead of a dowry, to marry the king's daughter Michal (I Samuel 18:25–27).

12.3 President Lyndon B. Johnson.

12.6 bear-cuffed: I.e., playfully slapped with an open hand. "[T]he bear was Johnson, the President, who cuffed his aides" (Lowell in conversation, paraphrased by Anzilotti, *Tribute*, 65).

14.6 "Our official doctrine is that we must be prepared to police the world" (Walter Lippmann, *Newsweek*, May 24, 1965, 23).

14.8 Cf. "The Voyage" VII.1.2–4 in *IM*, 254. Perhaps "monotonous sublime" is an inversion of each term of Shelley's phrase "intense inane" (*Prometheus Unbound*, III.iv.204), spoken by the "Spirit of the Hour":

> The loftiest star of unascended Heaven
> Pinnacled dim in the intense inane.

2. FOURTH OF JULY IN MAINE

2.2 Clergy active in the civil rights movement (late 1950s and 1960s).

2.7 See Emerson's essay "Self-Reliance."

6.3 China trade: New England merchant ships carried American goods such as leather to China, Chinese tea, ceramic wares and silk back; the China trade flourished between the late eighteenth century and mid-nineteenth century.

6.5 Cotton Mather: American Puritan clergyman and writer (1663–1728). "Mather, the Salem witch hanger, was a professional man of letters employed to moralize and subdue. His truer self was a power-crazed mind bent on destroying darkness with darkness, on applying his cruel, high-minded, obsessed intellect to the extermination of witch and neurotic. His soft, bookish hands are indelibly stained with blood. . . . His face is not on a postage stamp" (Lowell, *CPR*, 183).

6.6 *bell'età dell'oro*: Golden age.

8.3 Trollope's Barchester: Many of Anthony Trollope's novels were set in the fictional town of Barchester; see, e.g., *Barchester Towers* (1857).

10.6 Nadia Boulanger (1887–1979), French conductor and teacher; here, her recordings are played on a Magnavox record player (10.8).

15.1 converted barn: See note to "Soft Wood" 6.1 on pp. 372–73.

16.1 This line rewrites the final line of John Crowe Ransom's "Of Margaret": "Of that far away time of gentleness." Lowell wrote Ransom that he had reworked his line (July 26, 1968).

16.5 Logos: Word. See John 1:1.

3. THE OPPOSITE HOUSE

2.5 José Antonio Primo de Rivera, the Falangist leader, appealed for clemency for his brother and brother's wife: "Life is not a firework one lets off at the end of a garden party" (Hugh Thomas, *The Spanish Civil War*, 1961, 352).

2.7 *casa*: Literally, "house"; but with some of the larger implications of the French *maison*.

3.9 *Viva la muerte!*: Long live death! (Falangist general Millán Astray's motto in the Spanish Civil War [Thomas, *Spanish Civil War*, 354]).

4. CENTRAL PARK

This poem carries echoes of William Carlos Williams' "Sunday in the Park" section of *Paterson* II (Axelrod, *Life*, 190; Mariani, *Lost Puritan*, 338–39).

4.6 Cleopatra's Needle: A stone obelisk in Central Park.

5. NEAR THE OCEAN

Lowell described this poem as "a nightmarish, obscure reverie on marriage, both vengeful and apologetic" (Mariani, *Lost Puritan*, 336). E.H.L.: Elizabeth Hardwick Lowell.

1.4 her once head: Decapitated head; like Perseus lifting Medusa's head in Bernini's statue (Florence).
1.7 old iron-bruises: A pun on "Old Ironsides," nickname of the U.S.S. *Constitution*, moored in Boston Harbor. "[A] sort of pun; the old lady is hard as iron, her complexion is like bruises from something hard, rather the color of old iron" (Lowell, quoted in Anzilotti, *Tribute*, 62).
2.5 gorgon head: The head of Medusa, the snake-haired monster whose gaze turned beholders to stone.
6.3 hardveined elms: "like us with hardening of the arteries" (Lowell, quoted in Anzilotti, *Tribute*, 62).

from HISTORY (1973)

After *Near the Ocean*, Lowell began writing unrhymed blank verse "sonnets"—stanzas of fourteen lines, some free-standing enough to be considered "poems," others clearly not. All were units of a larger project. At first he published them as *Notebook 1967–68* (1969; enlarged for a second printing the same year), then much enlarged, simply as *Notebook* (1970). The autobiographical sequence of sonnets ultimately published as *The Dolphin* was begun in 1970. In early 1972, the *Notebook* stanzas were split into two volumes: the sonnets about family became *For Lizzie and Harriet*, the others (with many new sonnets) *History*. *History, For Lizzie and Harriet*, and *The Dolphin* appeared together in 1973; Lowell never published another unrhymed sonnet.

In 1971, in the middle of this process, Lowell compared his new form with the Marvell stanza that he used in *Near the Ocean*:

> *Notebook* . . . is in unrhymed, loose blank-verse stanzas, a roomier stanza [than Marvell's], less a prosodist's darling. It can say almost anything conversation or correspondence can. . . . [It] allowed me rhetoric, formal construction, and quick breaks. Much of *Life Studies* is recollection; *Notebook* mixes the day-to-day with the history—the lamp by a tree out this window on Redcliffe Square . . . or maybe the rain, but always the instant, sometimes changing to the lost. A flash of haiku to lighten the distant. Has this something to do with a rhymeless sonnet? One poem must lead toward the next, but is fairly complete; it can stride on stilts, or talk. . . .
>
> I didn't find fourteen lines a handcuff. I gained more than I gave. It would have been a worry never to have known when a section must end; variation might have been monotony. Formlessness might have crowded me toward consecutive narrative. Sometimes I did want the traditional sonnet, an organism, split near the middle, and

building to break with the last line. Often a poem didn't live until the last line cleared the lungs. . . .

I wrote in end-stopped lines, and rewrote to keep a sense of line. I never wrote more, or used more ink in changes. Words came rapidly, almost four hundred sonnets in four years—a calendar of workdays. I did nothing but write; I was thinking lines even when teaching or playing tennis. Yet I had idleness, though drawn to spend more hours working than I ever had or perhaps will. Ideas sprang from the bushes, my head; five or six sonnets started or reworked in a day. As I have said, I wished to describe the immediate instant. . . . Things I felt or saw, or read were drift in the whirlpool, the squeeze of the sonnet and the loose ravel of blank verse. I hoped in *Life Studies*—it was a limitation—that each poem might seem as open and single-surfaced as a photograph. *Notebook* is more jagged and imagined than was desirable in *Life Studies*. It's severe to be confined to rendering appearances. (*CPR*, 270–72)

This is Lowell's prefatory Note to *History*:

About 80 of the poems in *History* are new, the rest are taken from my last published poem, *Notebook* begun six years ago. All the poems have been changed, some heavily. I have plotted. My old title, *Notebook*, was more accurate than I wished, i.e., the composition was jumbled. I hope this jumble or jungle is cleared—that I have cut the waste marble from the figure.

Alex Calder writes of the principles underlying *History*: "In *History*, the sonnets—or sonnet titles since time is often stacked 'ply on ply' in an individual sonnet—are arranged in rough chronological order yet they do not constitute a chronological series. Unlike the *Notebooks* or *For Lizzie and Harriet*, *History* does not rely on an exterior line of events, such as a real or supposed time of writing, to cohere as a long poem. . . . [A] more positive parallel for the method and structure of *History* can be found in what Foucault, echoing Nietzsche, describes as genealogy (see Foucault, *Language, Counter-Memory, Practice* [1977], 139–64). A genealogy, for Foucault, is a critical examination of patterns of descent and emergence. . . . First, as a study of descent, *History* is like a family tree in which a genealogy of 'the poet,' of the person of 'powerful vision,' traces tyrants as well as artists as ancestral types. As Foucault suggests, this form of genealogy might well parody the uses to which traditional history is put. . . . An author ought to be directing the lineup [of the powerful] but 'he' so often appears inside the procession, there can be no separating out of identities" (Steven Gould Axelrod and Helen Deese, eds., *Robert Lowell: Essays on the Poetry* [1986], 134–35).

Foucault's sentences describing Nietzschean "genealogy" describe the texture of discontinuities, refusals, surprises, reversals, and retrievals that Lowell has given *History*: "[I]f the genealogist refuses to extend his faith in metaphysics, if he listens to history, he finds that there is 'something altogether different' behind things: not a timeless and essential secret, but the secret that they have no essence or that their essence was fabricated in a piecemeal fashion from alien forms. . . . The body is the inscribed surface of events (traced by language and dissolved by ideas), the locus of a dissociated Self (adopting the illusion of a substantial unity), and a volume in perpetual disintegration. . . . History becomes 'effective' to the degree that it introduces discontinuity into our very being—as it divides our emotions, dramatizes our instincts, multiplies our body and sets it against itself. . . . Knowledge is not made for understanding; it is made for cutting" (142, 148, 154). Foucault finally asserts, however, that genealogy possesses a healing function: "Its task is to become a curative science" (156). This

Lowell's skepticism precludes; near the end of *History*, in "Reading Myself," he hopes not to cure, but to become food:

> the corpse of the insect lives embalmed in honey,
> prays that its perishable work live long
> enough for the sweet-tooth bear to desecrate—
> this open book . . . my open coffin.

The fact that in *History* there is, in Alex Calder's phrase, "no separating out of identities" follows the dictum of Emerson, in his essay "History": "Man is explicable by nothing less than all his history. Without hurry, without rest, the human spirit goes forth from the beginning to embody every faculty, every thought, every emotion which belongs to it, in appropriate events. . . . We, as we read, must become Greeks, Romans, Turks, priest and king, martyr and executioner; must fasten these images to some reality in our secret experience, or we shall learn nothing rightly. . . . The instinct of the mind, the purpose of nature, betrays itself in the use we make of the signal narrations of history. . . . [A]ll public facts are to be individualized, all private facts are to be generalized. Then at once History becomes fluid and true, and Biography deep and sublime" (*Essays, First Series*, 1841).

HISTORY

10 hunter's moon: Autumnal full moon (technically, the full moon following the harvest moon).
10–14 As the poet looks out, first at the moon, then at the landscape, what he sees is his own face.

MAN AND WOMAN

9 authentic Mother: The ideal Mary, the idea of Mary; as in Renaissance paintings.
10 Berenson: Bernard Berenson (1865–1959), American art historian and connoisseur of Italian art, especially Renaissance art; famous for his authentications and as advisor to great collections, he lived in Tuscany, near Florence.

ALEXANDER

3 Demosthenes delivered the "Philippics" against Alexander's father, Philip of Macedon; Alexander, coming to power, demanded that Demosthenes be surrendered to him, then relented.
6 On his conquests, Alexander carried a copy of the *Iliad* annotated by Aristotle (who had been his teacher).
11 Medius: Medius of Larissa. Arrian writes that a few days before Alexander's death "[a]ccording to some accounts, when he wished to leave his friends at their drinking and retire to his bedroom, he happened to meet Medius, who at that time was the Companion [the Companions were Alexander's best cavalry] most closely in his confidence, and Medius asked him to come and continue drinking at his own table, adding that the party would be a merry one. The royal Diaries confirm the fact that he drank with Medius after his first carouse. Then (they continue) he left the table, bathed, and went to sleep, after which he supped with Medius and again set to drinking, continuing till late at night. Then, once more, he took a bath, ate a little, and went straight to sleep, with the fever [that killed him] already on him. . . . Next day he bathed again and offered sacrifice as

usual, after which he . . . chatted to Medius" (*The Campaigns of Alexander*, trans. de Sélin-court [1971], 391–92).

DEATH OF ALEXANDER

"Lying speechless as the men filed by, [Alexander] yet struggled to raise his head, and in his eyes there was a look of recognition for each individual as he passed. . . . The Diaries say that [seven of his friends] spent the night in the temple of Serapis and asked the God if it would be better for Alexander to be carried to the Temple himself, in order to pray there and perhaps recover; but the God forbade it, and declared it would be better for him if he stayed where he was. The God's command was made public, and soon afterwards Alexander died—this, after all, being the 'better' thing" (Arrian, 393–94).

14 Perhaps Lowell is thinking of Alexander's response after murdering his friend Cleitus: "With a roar of pain and a groan, Cleitus fell, and immediately the king's anger left him. When he came to himself and saw his friends standing around him speechless, he snatched the weapon out of the dead body and would have plunged it into his own throat if the guards had not forestalled him by seizing his hands and carrying him by force into his chamber. There he spent the rest of the night and the whole of the following day sob-bing in an agony of remorse" (Plutarch, *Alexander*, trans. Scott-Kilvert [1973], sec. 51–52, p. 309).

HANNIBAL I. ROMAN DISASTER AT THE TREBIA

Based on José-Maria de Heredia's "La Trebbia."

    The scene (218 B.C.) is the river Trebia in northern Italy, not long after Hannibal crossed the Alps with his troops and elephants. Sempronius (Roman consul for this year, along with Scipio) has just won a skirmish against Hannibal; now he advances across the river Trebia and allows himself to be drawn into an ambush by Hannibal's hidden cavalry and infantry. (See Livy, *History*, XXI.51–56.)

10 Gallic villages: Cisalpine Gaul.

MARCUS CATO 234–149 B.C.

Proverbial for fearless independence, honesty, and a hard-edged frugal practicality. "In 184 [Cato the Elder] held the censorship, the office that made him famous. He applied himself to the reformation of the lax morals of the Roman nobility, and to checking the luxury and ex-travagance of the wealthy. His ideal was a return to the primitive simplicity of a mainly agri-cultural State" (*Oxford Companion to Classical Literature*, 94).

5 jumping her in thunderstorms: "For his own part, Cato declared, he never embraced his wife except when a loud peal of thunder occurred, and it was a favorite joke of his that he was a happy man whenever Jove took it into his head to thunder" (Plutarch, *Cato the El-der*, trans. Scott-Kilvert [1965], 139).
5 *Juppiter Tonans*: Jupiter the Thunderer.
11 "Late in life he went as a commissioner to Carthage, and was so impressed by the danger to Rome from her reviving prosperity that he never ceased impressing on the Senate the ne-cessity for her destruction: 'Carthago delenda est' [Carthage must die]" (*Oxford Compan-ion to Classical Literature*, 94).

MARCUS CATO 95–46 B.C.

Great-grandson of Cato the Elder (see above). "[A] man of unbending character, and absolute integrity, narrow, short-sighted, impervious to reason as to bribery. . . . He is one of the heroes of Lucan's *Pharsalia*. Dante devotes to him a great part of the first canto of his 'Purgatorio' " (*Oxford Companion to Classical Literature*, 94).

1 Sulla: General Sulla (138–78 B.C.) "inaugurated the period of military dictatorships by marching on Rome with his legions. . . . The quasi-regal character of Sulla's dictatorship, unlimited in power and duration, set the model for the undisguised monarchies of Caesar and the second Triumvirate" (*Oxford Classical Dictionary*, 866–67).

5 wasn't invited back: "Sarpedon hearing [Cato's threat to kill Sulla], and at the same time seeing his countenance swelling with anger and determination, took care thenceforward to watch him strictly, lest he should hazard any desperate attempt" (Plutarch, *Cato the Younger*, trans. Dryden-Clough [1924], 416–17).

7 stoned like Paul: St. Paul. After Cato persuaded the senate to order that those newly elected must account, in court under oath, for their actions to gain office, he was stoned by a crowd (Dryden-Clough, 462).

9 saved Caesar: "He was the chief political antagonist of Caesar and the triumvirate" (*Oxford Companion to Classical Literature*, 94), in the name of saving the Republic.

CICERO, THE SACRIFICIAL KILLING

A modern-dress version of the events just before the assassination of Cicero, or someone like Cicero; the poem begins with the poet trying to remember a "scarlet patch" from his reading.

2 Tacitus: Roman historian and statesman (A.D. c. 55–c. 117).

3 Pound, whose *Cantos* is an attempt to write a twentieth-century epic poem, said: "An epic is a poem including history" (*Social Credit: An Impact* [1935]).

5 Cicero (106–43 B.C.), one of the most powerful men of his time (as orator, writer, politician), repeatedly attacked Mark Antony in the "Philippics," defending the Republic. Antony demanded the death of Cicero as the price of joining the second Triumvirate (with Lepidus and Octavian, who later became Augustus). Octavian, though he had earlier been helped by Cicero, reluctantly "sacrificed" Cicero.

5 Marius: Gaius Marius (c. 157–86 B.C.), low-born Roman general, "the people's soldier" ("Rome," *CPO*, 438). In 89 B.C. Marius fled Rome as Sulla's armies approached; he was captured alone hiding in a marsh, but escaped to Africa.

10 Aware that he was on the list of those condemned to death, Cicero fled to one of his estates. As he was being carried from the house to the sea, assassins found him. "Cicero heard [Herennius] coming and ordered his servants to set the litter down where they were. He himself, in that characteristic posture of his, with his chin resting on his left hand, looked steadfastly at his murderers. He was all covered in dust; his hair was long and disordered, and his face was pinched and wasted with his anxieties—so that most of those who stood by covered their faces while Herennius was killing him" (Plutarch, *Cicero*, trans. Rex Warner [1972], 360).

NUNC EST BIBENDUM, CLEOPATRA'S DEATH

Based on Horace's *Ode* I.37.

1 *Nunc est bibendum, nunc pede liberum:* Line two translates this line. Lowell (in what probably is a memory slip) changes the final word of Horace's first line from "libero" to "liberum."

JUVENAL'S PRAYER

Based on Juvenal's Tenth Satire (346–66), which Lowell, following Samuel Johnson, translated as "The Vanity of Human Wishes."

ATTILA, HITLER

Attila the Hun, barbarian "Scourge of God," invaded the Roman Empire with perhaps half a million Huns and allies (A.D. 451–52).

9 in this coarsest, cruelest . . . : That is, in Hitler.

MOHAMMED

1 Henry VIII: Refused a divorce from Catherine of Aragon, Henry declared himself the ecclesiastical authority in England, dissolved the monasteries, and remarried.
6 *schrecklichkeit*: Frightfulness, horror.

DEATH OF COUNT ROLAND

Scenes from the *Chanson de Roland* (c. 1098–1100), which Lowell renders almost as Pre-Raphaelite tableaux. Roland is a Frankish Christian hero, the nephew of Charlemagne; left to guard the rear of Charlemagne's troops as they return to France after seven years fighting the Saracens in Spain, Roland and his friends are ambushed.

1 King Marsilius: Saracen leader, also called King Marsile. Saragossa: In northeast Spain.
6 it did to spark the Franco-Moorish War: The king's speech sparks the battles of the *Chanson de Roland*. In *HIS*, the line reads: "it did not spark the Franco-Moorish War. . . ."

JOINVILLE AND LOUIS IX

Jean de Joinville (c. 1224–1317), governor of Champagne, accompanied Louis IX of France (St. Louis) on the Seventh Crusade (1248–1254); in old age (1304–1309) he dictated a memoir of Louis. The poem is based on paragraphs 122 and 422–37 of Natalis De Wailly's text (*The Life of St. Louis*, trans. Hague [1955]).

7 Acre: A coastal city in Palestine.
8 Sore of heart then: This follows a confrontation between Joinville and the other nobles. The King and nobles had been imprisoned by the Saracens; the King arranged their ransom. He then asked his council of nobles whether he should sail back to France. Joinville angered his elders, including Philip de Nemours (11), by saying that if the King leaves, the "meaner folk" (8) who are imprisoned never will be freed. The King then put off a decision. The scene at the "barred window" (9) follows.
14 Spoken by the King.

The source is the *Purgatorio*, V.85–129.

1 Giovanna: Buonconte's widow.
4 Casentino: The upper valley of the river Arno.

DAMES DU TEMPS JADIS

An abbreviated version of Villon's "Ballad for the Dead Ladies."

COLERIDGE AND RICHARD II

2–4 Coleridge on Shakespeare's *Richard II*: "[York's] species of accidental weakness is brought into parallel with Richard's continually increasing energy of thought, and as constantly diminishing power of acting. . . . It is clear that Shakespeare never meant to represent Richard II as a vulgar debauchee, but merely [as a man with] a wantonness in feminine shew, feminine *friendism*, intensely woman-like love of those immediately about him, mistaking the delight of being loved by him for a love for him. . . . Constant overflow of feelings; incapability of controlling them; waste of that energy which should be reserved for action in the passion and effort of resolves and menaces, and the consequent exhaustion. . . . Exhaustion counterfeiting quiet; and yet the habit of kingliness, the effect of flatteries from infancy, constantly producing a sort of *wordy* courage that betrays the inward impotence" (*Shakespearean Criticism*, ed. Raysor [1960], I, 136–40).
5 Richard unkinged saw shipwreck in the mirror: In *Richard II*, when Richard abdicates he asks for a mirror, "That it may show me what a face I have" (IV.1.256). Then he smashes it: "For there it is, cracked in an hundred shivers. / . . . How soon my sorrow hath destroyed my face."

BOSWORTH FIELD

Richard III (Dickon, the Duke of Gloucester) was defeated and killed at Bosworth Field (1485), ending the line of Yorkist kings.

8 we have dug him up past proof: The negative portrait of Richard III in Thomas More's biography is the basis for Shakespeare's *Richard III*; some recent historians have charged that his evil reputation is unjustified, the result of propagandists for Henry Tudor, who usurped Richard's crown.

SIR THOMAS MORE

Sir Thomas More (1478–1535) became Lord Chancellor in 1529, resigned in 1532. He refused to subscribe to the Act of Supremacy, which made Henry VIII the head of the English Church, and was beheaded in the Tower. The Roman Catholic Church canonized him in 1935. Anecdotes in the poem are versions of episodes in the biography by William Roper, his son-in-law.

1–4 These lines describe the celebrated portrait (1527) by Hans Holbein.
5 executioner: An accusation made by historians John Foxe (1563) and J. A. Froude

(1856–1870); Anthony Hecht "believe[s] they have been convincingly refuted by R. W. Chambers (1935)" (Hecht, in Meyers, *Interviews*, 346).

ANNE BOLEYN

Despite its title, this poem is essentially about two kinds of painting and art: the art of Potter and Cuyp, naturalistically focused on landscape, farming, farm animals, the world that continues indifferent or untouched by the vicissitudes and fashions of court life, or the history of thought; and the art of Giorgione, focused on the "great world," myth, literature, the court's fascination with a bucolic dreamworld, where the ostensible subject is a pretext for exploration and self-discovery, emphasizing human invention surpassing nature.

1 Potter . . . Cuyp: Paul Potter (1625–1654); Aelbert Cuyp (1620–1691). Helen Deese "associates Potter's famous and massive *Young Bull* with Henry VIII" (Deese, in Axelrod and Deese, *Essays*, 183).
3 Hegel: The German philosopher.
4 our rear-guard painters: Twentieth-century artists who rebel against departures from representation, "haters of abstraction"; their art nonetheless lacks Potter and Cuyp's "art of farming," their weight, mystery, inwardness ("tonnage and rumination of the sod," 8).
9 Henry VIII's second wife (1533–1536), Boleyn was tried on charges of adultery and incest, then beheaded. The rule-breaking abandon of her life, the whiteness of her throat, become emblems here of the Renaissance refusal to be bound by "nature" (12).
10 *raison d'état*: Reason of state; justification based on the needs of the state.
11 Giorgione: Renaissance Venetian painter (c. 1477–1510).
13 the Venetian: Giorgione.

DEATH OF ANNE BOLEYN

Anne Boleyn: see note to "Anne Boleyn" 9, above.

3 Wolsey: In order to marry Anne Boleyn, Henry VIII demanded a divorce from Catherine of Aragon; Archbishop Wolsey, Lord Chancellor, fell from power (1529) for failing quickly to procure Henry's divorce. (He had incurred Anne Boleyn's enmity by urging a French marriage on the king.)
3 J. A. Froude (1818–1894) wrote *The History of England from the Fall of Wolsey to the Defeat of the Spanish Armada* (1856–1870).

CHARLES V BY TITIAN

Charles V (1500–1558), Holy Roman Emperor, King of Spain. Born at Ghent, raised in Flanders, he inherited a vast empire. The Venetian painter Titian's equestrian portrait is titled *Charles V at the Battle of Mühlberg* (he defeated John of Saxony there in 1547) or *Portrait of Charles V on Horseback*. In 1554 he began a series of abdications, giving countries and dominions to his brother and son; in 1558 he formally abdicated as emperor. His plans for a universal empire had been thwarted by the French, the Ottomans, the spread of Protestantism. Although he retired to the monastery of Yuste, he remained active in politics. See "Charles the Fifth and the Peasant," *CPO*, 40.

10 Saturn was so fearful of usurpation that he attempted to eat each of his children.

MARLOWE

Christopher Marlowe, author of *Tamburlaine the Great*, *Doctor Faustus*, *The Jew of Malta*, *Edward II*, accused by Thomas Kyd of holding and disseminating heretical, lewd religious and moral principles, suspected by others of being a government agent, at twenty-nine was stabbed by a drinking companion in Deptford.

5 "Marlowe's mighty line" (Ben Jonson, "To the Memory of My Beloved, the Author, Mr. William Shakespeare" [1623], 30).

7 hits: Hit plays.

10 Jesus spoke Aramaic, not Hebrew, Greek, or Latin; the earliest form of the New Testament as we have it is in Greek.

MARY STUART

Mary Queen of Scots was accused of complicity in the murder of her husband, Henry Stuart, Lord Darnley. The Earl of Bothwell was widely suspected of the murder; three months after the death of Darnley, Mary Stuart and Bothwell were married. Something like this situation becomes the premise of a modern-dress nightmare.

REMBRANDT

Rembrandt van Rijn (1606–1669), Dutch painter, etcher, draftsman.

1 "The first line reminds us of how old paint looks on a canvas, finely crackled" (Helen Deese, in Axelrod and Deese, *Essays*, 194).

2 *The Jewish Bridegroom* (painting, c. 1665), usually called *The Jewish Bride*.

4 flayed steer: *The Slaughtered Ox* (painting, 1655); a young woman, half in shadow, looks up at a hanging carcass.

8 The model for *Bathsheba with King David's Letter* (painting, 1654) was his housekeeper (and, for many years, lover) Hendrickje Stoffels. Kenneth Clark: "[T]his ample stomach, these heavy, practical hands and feet, achieve a nobility far greater than the ideal form of, shall we say, Titian's *Venus of Urbino*. Moreover, this Christian acceptance of the unfortunate body has permitted the Christian privilege of a soul" (*The Nude*, 439–41).

13 Lowell struggled to find the right word for the characteristic light in Rembrandt: in *Notebook*, "a red mist"; in *History*, "a brown mist"; in *Selected Poems* (rev.), "a copper mist."

14 idol: "Line fourteen derives from Francis Bacon's third class of idols. Bacon's 'Idols of the Marketplace' are not, as we moderns might assume, the ambitions of merchants. Rather they are words, abstract signifiers that create unsubstantial images or 'false notions,' words that 'wonderfully obstruct the understanding . . . throw all into confusion, and lead men away into numberless empty controversies and idle fancies' " (Deese, in Axelrod and Deese, *Essays*, 195–96).

THE WORST SINNER, JONATHAN EDWARDS' GOD

See "Mr. Edwards and the Spider," pp. 26–27, "After the Surprising Conversions," pp. 28–29, and "Jonathan Edwards in Western Massachusetts," pp. 160–63.

14 Cf. Voltaire, characterizing the philosophy of Leibniz and his followers: "All is for the best in the best of all possible worlds" (*Candide*, ch. 1).

11 René Descartes (1596–1650), French philosopher and scientist. William Paley (1743–1805), English theologian.

ROBESPIERRE AND MOZART AS STAGE

The poem contrasts revolution as theater with opera as theater. Robespierre was the dominant member of the Committee of Public Safety that began (1793) the Reign of Terror ("*la terreur*," 2) during the French Revolution. The National Convention in 1794 rose against him; he was summarily guillotined.

3 Saint Antoine: District of the poor in Paris.
5 *mort à Robespierre*: Death to Robespierre.
10 blue movie: pornographic movie.
11 Louis Seize: Louis XVI of France, executed in 1793. Living theater: in the 1960's, Julian Beck and Judith Malina's Living Theatre performance group became fashionable; it emphasized improvisation, spontaneity, audience participation during performance.
13–14 Mozart's insolent slash: Mozart's opera *The Marriage of Figaro* (1786), libretto by Lorenzo Da Ponte, questions the practices and prerogatives of the aristocracy; its popularity has been seen as prefiguring the French Revolution. Figaro is a barber, about to be married. He is in the service of a count who schemes to seduce his bride. Figaro in his first aria declares his militant will to defy the count.

SAINT-JUST 1767–93

Louis-Antoine-Léon de Saint-Just (1767–1794), French Revolutionary leader and writer, an associate of Robespierre; he was guillotined with Robespierre.

1 Missal: Book containing the prayers and responses used in celebrating the Roman Catholic Mass.
6 Sparta: The militaristic city-state of ancient Greece.
14 Je sais où je vais: I know where I go.

NAPOLEON

3 *Lives*: Biographies of Napoleon.
7 *sang-froid*: Literally, "cold blood"; composure, imperturbability.
10 The Jacobins grew increasingly radicalized as the Revolution proceeded; under their leader Robespierre, they instigated the Reign of Terror. With his fall (1794) they fell.
14 "And what was the result of this vast talent and power, of these immense armies, burned cities, squandered treasures, immolated millions of men, of this demoralized Europe? It came to no result. All passed away like the smoke of his artillery, and left no trace" (Emerson, "Napoleon; Or, the Man of the World").

WATERLOO

14 *Glory* fading to *run for your life* and *shit*.

BEETHOVEN

1 *Leaves of Grass* is Whitman's lifework, endlessly revised throughout his lifetime.

7 Othello dies onstage; Lincoln was assassinated while president.

10 Beethoven dedicated his Third Symphony, the *Eroica* (composed 1803–1804), to Napoleon, but erased the dedication when Napoleon made himself emperor.

13 In Beethoven's opera *Fidelio* (begun 1805, completed 1814), a chorus of prisoners is released from their dungeon and briefly allowed light and open air ("Nur hier, nur hier ist Leben, / Der Kerker eine Gruft" [Only here, only here is life; / The prison is a tomb]; Act I).

14 As early as 1801, Beethoven realized he was going deaf.

COLERIDGE

9 positive negation: See the final lines of Coleridge's "Limbo":

> A lurid thought is growthless, dull Privation,
> Yet that is but a Purgatory curse;
> Hell knows a fear far worse,
> A fear—a future state;—'tis positive Negation!

THE LOST TUNE

The title echoes Sir Arthur Sullivan's once-popular song "The Lost Chord."

4 *vivace*: Lively, animated (a marking indicating speed and expression in music).

13 Franz Schubert wrote many songs, using poems as texts. See "Death and the Maiden" and "Die Forelle," *CPO*, 479, 480.

14 greenroom: A waiting room or lounge where performers gather offstage.

MARGARET FULLER DROWNED

Margaret Fuller (1810–1850), American writer and feminist. In Rome she married the Marchese Ossoli, a follower of Mazzini, and took part in the Revolution of 1848–1849. As she returned to the United States with husband and child, the ship went down.

2 Fuller: "It does not follow because many books are written by persons born in America that there exists an American literature" (*New York Tribune*, 1846).

ABRAHAM LINCOLN

"One smiles, not without envy, at the ease and assured precocity with which these young men [Henry Adams and Charles Francis Adams], still in their twenties, could rip to shreds the policies of Lincoln and Secretary Seward" (*CPR*, 202). See *CPR*, 165–66, 192–93, for essays on Lincoln.

3 "War is not merely a political act, but also a political instrument, a continuation of political relations, a carrying out of the same by other means" (Carl von Clausewitz, *On War*).

9 *J'accuse*: I accuse; title and refrain of Emile Zola's famous letter to the president of the French Republic, defending Alfred Dreyfus (1898).

VERDUN

After a combined loss of nearly 700,000 men, neither the French nor German armies gained strategic advantage from the eleven-month Battle of Verdun (1916).

DREAM OF FAIR LADIES

11 *Pace*: Peace.

SERPENT

In 1907 Hitler moved to Vienna, where twice he applied for admission to the Academy of Fine Arts, and twice was rejected.

WORDS

7 blind mouths: Milton, "Lycidas," 119.

8 Chicago: Here, gangster. Mussolini and Clara Petacci were gunned down and hanged from a streetlamp; Hitler committed suicide with Eva Braun as enemies closed in.

14 word: Here, Logos (Greek for "word"); "in Greek and Hebrew metaphysics, the unifying principle of the world" (*New Columbia Encyclopedia*, 1604). In St. John's Gospel, Jesus is the Word made flesh (John 1:14).

SUNRISE

In 1944, Vice Admiral Takijiro Onishi, commander of Japan's First Air Fleet in the Philippines, created the Special Attack Groups of suicide dive-bombing pilots, the kamikazes. He committed hara-kiri when Japan surrendered.

RANDALL JARRELL 1. OCTOBER 1965

In October 1965 Jarrell died at the age of fifty-one. For Lowell on Jarrell, see *CPR*, 90–98.

RANDALL JARRELL 2

9–14 Jarrell's death. Lowell to Bishop: "He was undergoing treatment of an injured wrist at Chapel Hill, and 'lunged' in front of a car on a main highway near a bypass. He had a bottle of pain-killer in his pocket. It cannot be told for certain whether the death was suicide or an accident. I think suicide, but I'm not sure, and Mary [Jarrell]'s version, the official version, is accident. . . . Poor dear, he wanted to take care of himself!" (October 19, 1965, *L*, 463).

13 "Child," used here as an epithet, implies a young hero; cf. Byron's "Childe Harold's Pilgrimage" or Browning's "Childe Roland to the Dark Tower Came." "In 13th and 14th centuries 'child' appears to have been applied to a young noble awaiting knighthood" (*OED*).

14 Jarrell "had the harsh luminosity of Shelley" (*CPR*, 91).

RANDALL JARRELL 3

11 In the months before his death, Jarrell's hand (cut smashing a window) would not, even after surgery, uncurl (Mariani, *Lost Puritan*, 339). *Kitten*: The name of Jarrell's cat.

For Lowell on Eliot, see *CPR*, 48–52, 210–12.

EZRA POUND

Ezra Pound was committed to St. Elizabeth's Hospital for the criminally insane in Washington, D.C., after arrest for making radio broadcasts from Italy during World War II; Lowell visited him at St. Elizabeth's. Released after twelve years, he left America for Rapallo, Italy, where he lived with Olga Rudge. (Lowell first wrote Pound as a freshman at Harvard, in May 1936. After writing poetry for a year, he tells Pound: "If the 20th century is to realize a great art comparable to that of Chaucer and Shakespeare, the foundation will have to be your poems. . . . I would like to bring back momentum and movement in poetry on a grand scale" [*L*, 5–6].)

3 Social Credit: An economic theory developed by C. H. Douglas, espoused by Pound.
4 I.e., Eliot was ". . . here with a black suit and black briefcase."
5 Possum: Eliot's nickname. In "Milton II" (1947), Eliot recanted many of his earlier strictures against Milton.
14 Oedipus means "swollen foot."

WILLIAM CARLOS WILLIAMS

For Lowell on Williams, see *CPR*, 37–44.

ROBERT FROST

For Lowell on Frost, see *CPR*, 8–11, 206–8.

1 A pun on Coleridge's poem "Frost at Midnight."
7 Frost's son Carol committed suicide.
8 Merrill Moore: A psychiatrist, poet, and close friend of Lowell's mother; see note to "Unwanted" 5.1, p. 405.

STALIN

Text from *SP*.
    See also Lowell's translation of Mandelstam's "Stalin," p. 223.

CARACAS I

6 jerry skyscrapers: I.e., "jerry-built," flimsy.
7 El Presidente Leoni: Raúl Leoni was elected president of Venezuela in 1963. After a few years of political stability, in 1966 his government suppressed a military uprising; throughout the year, it fought guerrillas in the countryside and capital.

THE MARCH I

The Pentagon March in Washington, D.C., against the Vietnam War on October 21, 1967. Dwight Macdonald: editor and writer.

10 The First Battle of Bull Run (1861) was the first important engagement of the Civil War; Union troops were routed, and their flight did not end until they reached Washington.

13 Martian: Of Mars, god of war; also, like a space-alien, a "Martian" in a science-fiction film.

THE MARCH 2

1 "For where two or three are gathered together in my name, there am I in the midst of them" (Jesus' words in Matthew 18:20).

8 MP: Military police.

14 Lowell's reaction to the march: "It was mainly the fragility of a person caught in this situation . . . as in that poem of Horace's where you throw away your little sword at the battle of Philippi and get out of the thing" (Meyers, *Interviews*, 144).

WORSE TIMES

1–9 Plato's *Republic* argues against democratic rule; in *Statesman* (303b), he says that if the constitution is lawful and ordered, democracy is the least desirable form of government. Both Marx and Calvin (*Institutes of the Christian Religion* [1536–1559]) argue species of determinism (Marx, historical determinism; Calvin, predestination). Both Marxist governments and American Puritan communities (following Calvinist principles) suppressed some forms of artistic representation. The Scandinavian god Thor and the Hebrew King Saul (after Samuel withdrew religious sanctions from his monarchy) exerted power through physical force, elemental assertions of violence and military strength, not dialectical discussion.

14 Lowell wrote in *Commentary*, April 1969: "[T]he other morning, or some morning, I saw a newspaper photograph of students marching through Rome with banners showing a young Clark-Gable-style Stalin and a very fat old Mao—that was a salute to the glacier. No cause is pure enough to support these faces. We are fond of saying that our students have more generosity, idealism and freshness than any other group. Even granting this, still they are only us younger, and the violence that has betrayed our desires will also betray theirs if they trust to it" (Hamilton, 382).

ULYSSES

9 Nausicaa: The young girl who discovers Odysseus (Ulysses) naked and shipwrecked, fearlessly greets him and shows him how to enter the palace of her father the king (*Odyssey*, VI–VII). She would marry him, and her father agrees, but Odysseus is already married.

FEVER

3 Pavlov's dogs: The Russian physiologist Ivan Pavlov did experiments on dogs (1898–1930), studying the conditional (or "conditioned") reflex.

14 "I woke up one morning and found myself famous" (Lord Byron, reported by Thomas Moore, *Letters and Journals of Lord Byron, with Notices of His Life* [1829] I, 258).

TWO WALLS

8 In the final scene of Mozart's opera, Don Giovanni meets the father of a woman he seduced; the father, now a statue made of stone, drags him to hell.

13 The Greek biographer and essayist Plutarch (A.D. 46?–120) is the source of much of what we know about the heroes and masters of the ancient world.

14 your maturity: In all earlier versions, including *HIS*, "our maturity." When the poem first appeared, poet and Kennedy supporter Donald Junkins criticized the phrase, suggesting "your" instead of "our." Lowell answered that "*Our* is not an editorial we," that "the secondary meaning[,] the only possible one, would give *our* the meaning of *man's* or *mankind's*, or the future of our country." Kennedy "may have been our hero; he was never mature; nor would anyone who knew him well and love[d] him, have thought so. To say that he was our maturity robs him of most of his true seriousness and pathos" (Mariani, *Lost Puritan*, 363).

FOR EUGENE MCCARTHY

Lowell was an informal advisor to Senator McCarthy during his campaign for the Democratic nomination for president, at times traveling with McCarthy's entourage.

14 In 1968 McCarthy challenged the sitting president, Lyndon Johnson, in early primaries for the presidential nomination of Johnson's own party; the central issue was Johnson's prosecution of the Vietnam War. McCarthy did so well that Johnson decided not to run for re-election.

PUBLICATION DAY

Based on a letter to Lowell from the poet Marcia Nardi. In *Paterson*, Williams used her letters to him; she is "the 'Cress' of Williams's *Paterson*" (Mariani, *Lost Puritan*, 370).

12 In Mailer's *The Armies of the Night*.

LÉVI-STRAUSS IN LONDON

Claude Lévi-Strauss (b. 1908), French anthropologist.

2 ammonites: Extinct marine mollusks; "they often link the rock layer in which they are found to specific geological time periods" (*Encarta Encyclopedia* [2002]).

10 *structuralism*: "In cultural anthropology, the school of thought developed by . . . Lévi-Strauss, in which cultures, viewed as systems, are analyzed in terms of the structural relations among their elements. According to Lévi-Strauss's theories, universal patterns in cultural systems are products of the invariant structure of the human mind" (*Encyclopædia Britannica* [2002]).

11–13 Here, Cézanne stands for the earnest artist whose work submits to the elemental nature of its subject and in embodying it becomes one with it; Picasso, the artist as virtuoso, whose work encounters and tames its subject.

14 "There is a crack in everything God has made" (Emerson, "Compensation").

THE NIHILIST AS HERO

3 Paul Valéry (1871–1945), French poet, writer, aesthetician. "Valéry in paraphrase is speaking for the primacy of craft and 'intelligent labor' against mere inspiration, which is acciden-

tal. To the extent that discipline in craft serves the ends of 'la poésie pure,' the Satan here must be Valéry's Satan of 'Ébauche d'un serpent,' whom Alan Williamson quotes Lowell as calling 'the spirit that insists on perfection' " (Bell, *Nihilist as Hero*, 3–4).

13–14 The final couplet changed with each volume in which it appeared.

Notebook 1967–68:

> Only a nihilist desires the world
> to be as it is, or much more passable.

Notebook:

> A nihilist has to live in the world as is,
> gazing the impossible summit to rubble.

History:

> A nihilist has to live in the world as is,
> gazing the impassable summit to rubble.

READING MYSELF

6 Parnassus: A mountain consecrated to Apollo and the Muses.

FOR ELIZABETH BISHOP 4

3 *plein air*: Painting "en plein air" is "in its strictest sense, the practice of painting landscape pictures out-of-doors; more loosely, the achievement of an intense impression of the open air (*plein air*) in a landscape painting" (*Encyclopædia Britannica* [2002]).

4 Albert Pinkham Ryder, American painter of seascapes and mystical allegorical scenes (1847–1917). His works are pervaded by thick, yellow light, usually moonlight; by rapidly applying thick layers of pigment and then varnish, he created crackled surfaces. His lifework is about 150 paintings.

DEATH AND THE BRIDGE

Text from *SP*.

ICE

11 Cro-Magnon: Early man; the first prehistoric people to produce art, they buried their dead.

END OF A YEAR

8 The Rosetta Stone, found in Egypt by Napoleon's engineering corps (1799), displayed the same message in Greek, Egyptian demotic, and Egyptian hieroglyphic; by comparing the texts, for the first time scholars deciphered hieroglyphics.

9 annus mirabilis: Year of wonders. *Hero demens*: Mad hero, echoing the title of Seneca's play *Hercules Furens*.

14 carbon: Lowell's final image for the relation between writing and world has, since the demise of the typewriter, become unfamiliar. A "carbon" (or "carbons," line 6) is carbon

paper: "A lightweight paper faced on one side with a dark waxy pigment that is transferred by the impact of typewriter keys or by writing pressure to any copying surface, as paper" (*American Heritage Dictionary*). In line 14, sunset abruptly becomes the night sky. Hard to decipher as a palimpsest, carbon-black and fragile, re-used carbon paper becomes the bright night sky: where a key struck, a gap shows light.

from FOR LIZZIE AND HARRIET (1973)

PART ONE

HARRIET (Born January 4, 1957)

Lowell's daughter, Harriet Lowell.

1 Lowell writes in the "Afterthought" to *Notebook*: "My opening lines are as hermetic as any in the book. The 'fractions' mean that my daughter, born in January, is each July, a precision important to a child, something and a half years old. The 'Seaslug etc.' are her declining conceptions of God."

9–10 Diogenes Laertius on Thales (c. 625–c. 546 B.C.): "It is said that once, when he was taken out of doors by an old woman to observe the stars, he fell into a ditch. To his cry for help the old woman retorted, 'How can you expect to know all about the heavens, Thales, when you cannot even see what is just before your feet' " (*Lives of the Philosophers*, trans. Caponigri, 1969).

11–14 "The 'Harriet' poems were written a few months after the first production of Lowell's version of *Prometheus Bound*, and Lowell echoes Prometheus at the end of the first sonnet" (Raban, *Selection*, 182). From Lowell's *Prometheus Bound*: "Around some bend, under some moving stone, behind some thought, if it were ever the right thought, I will find my key. No, not just another of Nature's million petty clues, but a key, *my key, the* key, the one that must be there, because it can't be there—a face still friendly to chaos" (52–53).

HARRIET (A repeating fly)

6 "[T]he 'Arabs on the screen' were to be seen during the six-day war in June 1967 between Israel and Egypt" (Raban, *Selection*, 182).

ELIZABETH

Lowell's second wife, Elizabeth Hardwick ("Lizzie").

6 *Pace*: Peace.

7 Heart's-Ease: A name for several plants, such as the "wild pansy" and a mint plant also called Heal-all.

HARRIET (Spring moved to summer)

9 Shakespeare's Juliet was fourteen.

PART TWO

DAS EWIG WEIBLICHE

"The eternal feminine" (Goethe, *Faust* II.12110); penultimate line of the "Chorus Mysticus" that ends *Faust*.

OUR TWENTIETH WEDDING ANNIVERSARY   (ELIZABETH)

6 Still lifes by Jean-Baptiste-Siméon Chardin (1699–1779).

WORDS FOR MUFFIN, A GUINEA-PIG

9 Cromwell wanted to be painted with "all those roughnesses, pimples, warts, and everything as you see me, otherwise I will never pay a farthing for it" (quoted in Horace Walpole, *Anecdotes of Painting in England* [1762–1771]).

END OF CAMP ALAMOOSOOK   (HARRIET)

8 Acadians: "In 1755 the British fell upon the peaceful Acadian farms and, seizing most of the Acadians, deported them to the more southerly British colonies, scattering them along the Atlantic coast from Maine to Georgia" (*New Columbia Encyclopedia* [1975]).

GROWTH   (HARRIET)

10 *Boris*: Mussorgsky's opera *Boris Godunov*.

THE GRADUATE   (ELIZABETH)

1 Transylvania University, in Lexington, Kentucky.

NO HEARING

4–5 Cf. Spenser's "Epithalamion" (1595): "So I unto my selfe alone will sing, / The woods shall to me answer and my Eccho ring" (17–18).
6 Penobscot River, Maine.
8–9 Dante was forced into exile at age thirty-seven.

NO HEARING

8 The Maine Maritime Academy keeps this ship anchored at Castine.
13 Melville's "Bartleby, the Scrivener" (1856). Elizabeth Hardwick: "On the third day of copying, he is asked to collaborate in the matter of proof-reading. The laconic, implacable signature is at hand, the mysterious utterance that cannot be interpreted and cannot be misunderstood. Bartleby replies, 'I would prefer not to' " (*Herman Melville* [2000], 107).

3 *entremets chinois et canadiens*: Chinese and Canadian sweets (desserts).

14 we were kind of religious, we thought in images: "[W]ise men . . . fasten words again to
visible things; so that picturesque language is at once a commanding certificate that he
who employs it is a man in alliance with truth and God. The moment our discourse rises
above the ground line of familiar facts and is inflamed with passion or exalted by thought,
it clothes itself in images" (Emerson, "Nature," sec. IV).

OBIT

In the "Afterthought" to *Notebook* (1970), Lowell writes that "ideas and expressions in 'Obit'
and another poem [come] from Herbert Marcuse" (263).

2.3 During Lyndon Johnson's presidency, copper was added to silver coins.

from THE DOLPHIN (1973)

The text is from *SP* (1976).

The Dolphin fictionalizes the end of Lowell's marriage to Elizabeth Hardwick and his mar-
riage to Caroline Blackwood. As in all his autobiographical poems, fact and fiction are mixed.
In the early spring of 1972, for the first time, he arrived at a version of the manuscript that he
considered a whole: this he widely circulated among friends (Elizabeth Bishop, Stanley Ku-
nitz, William Alfred, among others). Bishop responded to this "*Ur-Dolphin*" in a letter that
has become famous: the book is "a great poem (I've never used the word 'great' before, that I
remember)," "magnificent poetry," but must not be published as it stands (Bishop, *One Art*,
1995, 561).
    Bishop's central objection is to the book's use of Elizabeth Hardwick's letters:

> There is a "mixture of fact & fiction," and you have *changed* her letters. That is "in-
> finite mischief," I think. . . . *Art just isn't worth that much*. I keep remembering Hop-
> kins's marvelous letter to Bridges about the idea of a "gentleman" being the highest
> thing ever conceived—higher than a "Christian," even, certainly than a poet. It's not
> being "gentle" to use personal, tragic, anguished letters that way—it's cruel. (562)

Lowell responded by fundamentally changing the book. Several of the poems in Hard-
wick's voice were muted by taking them out of direct quotation, placed in italics, their anger
and anguish softened. Lowell wrote to Stanley Kunitz: "Most of the letter poems—E.B.'s
[Elizabeth Bishop's] objection they were part fiction offered as truth—can go back to your old
plan, a mixture of my voice, and another voice in my head, part me, part Lizzie [Elizabeth
Hardwick], italicized, paraphrased, imperfectly, obsessively heard" (Kunitz, *New York Review
of Books*, October 16, 1977). In response to Bishop's objection that the chronology of the final
part of the book was confusing, and to make "Lizzie more restful and gracious," Lowell
placed Sheridan's birth before "Flight to New York" (reversing the actual chronology). Low-
ell wrote to Bidart:

> I've read and long thought on Elizabeth [Bishop]'s letter. It's a kind of masterpiece of
> criticism, though her extreme paranoia (for God's sake don't repeat this) about reve-
> lations gives it a wildness. Most people will feel something of her doubts. The terri-

ble thing isn't the mixing of fact and fiction, but the wife pleading with her husband to return—this backed by "documents." So far I've done this much: 1) most important—shift *Burden* [the section announcing Caroline's pregnancy and Sheridan's birth] before *Leaving America* and *Flight to New York*. This strangely makes Lizzie more restful and gracious about the "departure." . . . 2) Several of the early letters, From My Wife, are now cut up into Voices (often using such title) (changing mostly pronouns) as if I were speaking and paraphrasing or repeating Lizzie. Most of the later letters I haven't been able to change much or at all. . . . Now the book must still be painful to Lizzie, and won't satisfy Elizabeth. As Caroline says, it can't be otherwise with the book's donnée. (*L*, 592–93)

These changes, along with much rewriting during the summer of 1972, significantly changed the book's dynamics—without (as Lowell predicted) satisfying its critics. For a description of some manuscript changes, see Gewanter, "Child of Collaboration: Robert Lowell's *Dolphin*," *Modern Philology* 93 (1995), 178–203. The *Ur-Dolphin* is catalogued at the Harry Ransom Research Center in Austin, Texas, as Box 5 folder 9 (*The Dolphin* Draft F); in the Elizabeth Bishop Papers at Vassar College, Box 82, Folder 82.5.

FISHNET

2 trouvailles: Finds, discoveries, strokes of inspiration.
13 the net will hang on the wall: Cf. Horace, *Odes*, I.5.13–16 ("*Quis multa gracilis te puer in rosa*"), "The votive tablet on the temple wall / Is witness that in tribute to the god / I have hung up my sea-soaked garment there" (Ferry, trans., *Odes of Horace* [1997]).
14 illegible bronze: Cf. Horace, *Odes*, III.30.1 ("*Exegi monumentum aere perennius*"), "Today I have finished a work outlasting bronze" (Ferry).

THE SERPENT

11 "I see me—a green hunter who leaps from turn to turn" (*SP*, second printing).
12–13 "hang my bugle in an invisible baldrick" (Shakespeare, *Much Ado About Nothing* I.i.241–42/1.1.197–98) refers to being a cuckold; "groping for trouts in a peculiar river" (Shakespeare, *Measure for Measure* I.ii.90/1.2.0.6) refers to illegal or forbidden sexual intercourse.

SYMPTOMS

4 bag of waters: Bag of amniotic fluid.
7 my old infection: Manic-depression (bipolar illness). Until the advent of lithium treatment in 1967, Lowell for many years (each year, as fall became winter) had a manic breakdown. From spring 1967 until the time of this sonnet, early summer 1970, he was well.

OLD SNAPSHOT FROM VENICE 1952

4 Vittore Carpaccio (c. 1450–1522), narrative painter of Venetian pageantry and religious subjects, including *St. Jerome Leading the Tame Lion into the Monastery* (1502).
5 Jerome: St. Jerome (c. 347–420?), scholar, translator of the Bible, whose texts were the basis of the Vulgate. The lion is associated with Venice (the Lion of St. Mark), as well as Jerome: in a popular fable, Jerome pulled a thorn from the paw of a lion, which then became devoted to him.

6 Torcello: An island in the Lagoon of Venice.
7 *venti anni fa*: Twenty years ago.

FALL WEEKEND AT *MILGATE*

Milgate: Caroline Blackwood's country home in Kent, England, "early eighteenth-century Palladian and very old-South messy" (Lowell, quoted in Hamilton, *Robert Lowell*, 415). Once owned by mystical philosopher and Rosicrucian Robert Fludd (1574–1637), the house was rebuilt and enlarged in the eighteenth century.

1.6 the painter, your first husband: Lucien Freud.

MERMAID

3.3 *bel occhi grandi*: "Beautiful large eyes."
3.4 This photograph is reproduced in Hamilton (*Robert Lowell*) following p. 404.
4.9 Via Veneto: A fashionable street in Rome.
4.13 *inside-right*: Front-line position in British football (soccer).

PLOTTED

7–9 Hamlet is enjoined by his father's ghost to avenge his murder, stuck in a plot whose shape has become a convention (the Revenge Play); he becomes "scatological" in the "country matters" scene with Ophelia (III.ii.101–9) just before his play *The Mousetrap* is performed. Elizabethan theaters were open-air, under the "London sky."
14 Wittgenstein: "Death is not an event of life. Death is not lived through" (*Tractatus Logico-Philosophicus*, trans. Ogden [1922], 6.4311).

ARTIST'S MODEL

1.1 "If it were done when 'tis done, then 'twere well / It were done quickly" (Shakespeare, *Macbeth*, I.vii.1–2).

IVANA

Ivana: Daughter of Caroline Blackwood.

SICK

12 over-limit: I.e., while fishing.

PLANE-TICKET

6 I.e., Ford's novel *The Good Soldier* (1915), which begins, "This is the saddest story I have ever heard."
9 book of life: Psalms 69:28; Revelations 3:5; etc.

1.2 In 1961, Lowell published a translation of Jean Racine's neoclassical tragedy *Phèdre* (1677). Racine's version of Euripides' *Hippolytus* (428 B.C.), written in alexandrines, respects the neoclassical ideal of the "unities" that dominated contemporary French drama; Racine is "the man of craft." There is a contrast in the play between this formal decorum, and the passion that drives the title character, the "wandering voice" (4) to which the decorum gives ferocious utterance. Phèdre loves her stepson; rejected by him, she tells her husband that he tried to seduce her; the husband kills his son; Phèdre then kills herself.

2.1 my eyes have seen what my hand did: Until the summer of 1972, the final line of the book was "Why should shark be eaten when the bait swim free?" (This later became the final line of "Leaving Home, Marshal Ney" in *CPO*, 476.) Late one night at Milgate, Lowell asserted that Shakespeare had been lucky in his first editors, Heminge and Condell. In the preface to the First Folio, they had said one of the best things ever said about Shakespeare: "His eyes saw what his hand did." He quoted this from memory. He then tried to find the preface in his library, and couldn't; his books were still in New York, and at Milgate he mostly had paperbacks. Next morning at breakfast, Lowell with sly, bemused pleasure showed everyone a revision of "Dolphin" with its present final line—a line which resonates throughout his work. When I returned to America, I looked up Heminge and Condell. Lowell's memory had invented the line. Heminge and Condell say something altogether more commonplace, that Shakespeare revised very little: "His mind and hand went together: And what he thought, he uttered with that easiness, that we have scarce received from him a blot in his papers." [F.B.]

from SELECTED POEMS (1976)

NINETEEN THIRTIES

This sequence Lowell excerpted from *History* (*CPO*, 501–14), with revisions.

FIRST LOVE

14 In *Notebook*: "The mania for phrases dried his heart" (p. 38). Jonathan Raban identifies the *Notebook* version as a quotation from Flaubert's mother (Hamilton, *Robert Lowell*, 431). Anthony Hecht comments: "[T]here is in this revision of the Flaubert poem an allegory of what Lowell must have felt about himself: if to others it appeared that his heart had dried, to the artist, to Lowell/Flaubert, it was clear that his heart was enlarged by the very act of finding words, by the very mania for phrases that so obsessed them both" (Meyers, *Interviews*, 340). An "enlarged" heart is also a medical term, a condition that can cause heart failure.

1930'S

The stanzas titled "1930's" for the most part adapt stanzas from the sequence "Long Summers" in *Notebook*. In 1974 Lowell wrote to Robert Boyers that he now thought that this had been a mistake: "I put a section [of] 14 poems called 'Long Summer' in *Notebook*, into *History*. To do this I had to take immediate 1966 Maine experience and change it into recollections of boyhood. A symbolic solidity was lost. I intend to put this group in *Lizzie and Harriet* (with small changes from the original). It makes the whole book less delicate and more what I imagined" (January 22, 1974). But he never made these changes; for *Selected Poems* (1976), the majority of the stanzas remain titled "1930's" (though some sections return to *Notebook* texts).

3 Dealer's Choice: A variation of poker, which allows the dealer to choose how the hand is played.

1930's (The boys come)

10 Oskar Kokoschka (1886–1980), Austrian-born Expressionist painter.

1930's (My legs hinge)

6 Custer: George Armstrong Custer (1839–1876), American army officer killed by the Sioux in the Battle of the Little Bighorn; Sitting Bull (8) led the Sioux forces.

BOBBY DELANO

2 St. Mark's: A private secondary school (as is Groton). See "St. Mark's, 1933" in *DBD*, 800.
9 Both title and refrain of a popular song.
14 Ajax: Perhaps the Ajax known as "the Greater Ajax," a warrior of great stature and prowess, the Son of Telamon, king of Salamis: "In the *Odyssey* (XI.543ff.) mention is made of his death in consequence of the arms of Achilles having been adjudged to Odysseus and not to him after the death of their owner. The story is probably that found in later authors, e.g. Sophocles (*Ajax*), that he went mad with anger and disappointment and finally killed himself" (*Oxford Classical Dictionary*, 26). Delano, however, shares characteristics with Ajax the Lesser, the Son of Oïleus or Ileus, the Locrian chieftain: "of hateful character and on occasion grossly rude (as in *Iliad* XXIII.473ff.)" (ibid.).

1930's (The circular moon)

5 Great Mother: "She has the dual nature of creator and destroyer and is both nourisher, protector, provider of warmth and shelter, and the terrible forces of dissolution, devouring and death-dealing; she is the creator and nourisher of all life and its grave. . . . In Alchemy the Great Mother is dynamic as fire and heat, transforming, purifying, consuming and destroying; she is also the bearer of the embryo-ores in the earth-womb" (J. C. Cooper, *An Illustrated Encyclopaedia of Traditional Symbols*, 108).
6 Reichian prophets: Followers of psychiatrist and biophysicist Wilhelm Reich (1897–1957). "According to Reich's theories the universe is permeated by a primal, mass-free phenomenon that he called orgone energy; in the human organism the lack of repeated total discharge of this energy through natural sexual release is considered the genesis not only of all individual neurosis but also of irrational social movements and collective neurotic disorder" (*New Columbia Encyclopedia*, 2296).

ANNE DICK I. 1936

8 *Lycidas*: An elegy by Milton (1637).

ANNE DICK 2. 1936

2 *Anschluss*: The Nazi annexation of Austria (1938).
4 *Notebook* version: "I tasted first love gazing through your narrow" (p. 68).
7 Esplanade: A grassy park and promenade along the Charles River basin, Boston.
8 Claude: Claude Lorrain (c. 1600–1682), celebrated not only for his landscapes but also for scenes of harbors and seaports.
11 his unloved mother's death: Nero had his mother murdered. See note to "My Last Afternoon with Uncle Devereux Winslow" IV.3.8 on p. 363.

FATHER

8 Helios: The Sun-god. His son Phaethon "asked him a boon. The Sun granting him in advance anything he liked, he asked to guide the solar chariot for a day. But he was too weak to manage the solar horses, which bolted with him and were likely to set the world on fire till Zeus killed Phaethon with a thunderbolt" (*Oxford Classical Dictionary*). This narrative, with "old Helios" as father and a son whose lack of control results in destruction, hangs in the shadows as threat or prophecy: "a parental sentence on each step misplaced" (10).

MOTHER AND FATHER 1

2 Lowell's father died in 1950 and his mother in 1954.

MOTHER AND FATHER 2

10 *infantile*: Infantile paralysis, or polio; Dr. Jonas Salk developed the first vaccine that prevented it (1955).

MOTHER, 1972

11 See "Sailing Home from Rapallo," pp. 121–22.

WILL NOT COME BACK

An imitation of the nineteenth-century Spanish poet Gustavo Adolfo Bécquer's "Volverán las oscuras golondrinas."

MEXICO

MEXICO

For *SP*, Lowell excerpted this sequence from *For Lizzie and Harriet* (*CPO*, 624–29).

3.11 The Aztec emperor Montezuma, seized by Hernán Cortés (1520) as a hostage, was forced to speak against resistance to Spanish rule. When the Aztecs drove the Spanish out, he was killed—whether by the Aztecs or Spanish is uncertain. Cortés reconquered them in 1521.
4.6 bull and cow: Cuernavaca means "cow horn."

1. EIGHT MONTHS LATER

6 Lilith: Jewish female demon; in Jewish legend, Adam's first wife.

2. DIE GOLD-ORANGEN

Based on Goethe's "Mignon: Kennst du das Land."

from DAY BY DAY (1977)

Lowell writes of *Day by Day*: "I have been writing for the last three years in unrhymed free verse. At first I was so unused to this meter, it seemed like tree-climbing. It came back—gone now the sonnet's cramping and military beat" (from his final statement on his own work, "After Enjoying Six or Seven Essays on Me," *Salmagundi* 37 [Spring 1977], 112–15). On March 4, 1976, he writes to Elizabeth Bishop: "I have been writing furiously in my doldrums, and always feel on the edge of being too raw . . . and more than on the edge" (*L*, 645). On March 31, 1976, to Robert Boyers: "It is all in a very personal[,] in a solitary sublime style—no public events, no embarrassing personal references to friends, I hope." On July 27, to Steven Axelrod: "I fear [*Day by Day*] comes close to tragic, though that's not clear either in the book or life."

Helen Vendler, reviewing *Day by Day* (*New York Times Book Review*, August 14, 1977), says that the reader must "re-construct the scenario behind this book—Lowell's life in Kent, his hospitalization in England, his wife's sickness, their temporary stay in Boston, their separation, a reconciliation, a further rupture, a parting in Ireland, Lowell's return to America."

Francesco Rognoni, in the notes to his Italian translation (*Giorno per giorno*, Mondadori, 2001), offers the fullest annotation that these poems have received; our notes are indebted to his.

ULYSSES AND CIRCE

Ulysses is the Roman name for Odysseus, hero of the *Odyssey*; his arduous return from Troy to his wife Penelope is perhaps the dominant myth of middle-aged love in Lowell. King of Ithaca, he leaves wife and son to fight for ten years at Troy; on the ten-year journey back he has a long, absorbing dalliance with Circe; returned to Ithaca at last, he finds Penelope surrounded by suitors.

Lowell: "It's wonderful to write about a myth especially if what you write isn't wholly about yourself" (Hamilton, *Robert Lowell*, 459). "This Ulysses comes on as a man on the verge of being posthumous to himself, ventriloquizing (through the autobiographical voice of Robert Lowell) about his interlude with Circe, his sensual self-knowledge and his appeased curiosities. Ulysses begins the poem as a drowsy voluptuary and will end it as a killer about to strike, thus acting as a kind of correlative for the poet caught between his marriages and his manias. The poem is spoken in a middle voice, neither dramatic monologue exactly nor confessional lyric" (Seamus Heaney, *The Government of the Tongue* [1988], 143).

I.5 Cf. *Aeneid* II.3.
IV.2.8 Dante, *Inferno*, XXVI.117.
VI "In that history and science of feeling which poetry (according to Wordsworth) takes on as its task, Lowell has made a certain trajectory his own: the curve which begins in possibility and ends grimly in necessity. . . . We have come to the finale of the long effort. First

there was the naming of the world; then, in a search for new names, came the 'embarka-
tion and carnival of glory,' complete with marital triumph; next the war and the explo-
ration of the world, the folly of following the Circean moon, seeing 'the meanness and
beacons of men'; finally, 'bleak-boned with survival,' the return, drawn by the myth of
the unchanged home; what emotion is left to age but fury? Age finds in self the same
prison that Ulysses found, at the beginning of the poem, in Circe's bed" (Helen Vendler,
Salmagundi 37 [Spring 1977], 18, 21–22).
VI.2–4 Cf. Dante, *Inferno*, XXVI. 94–96.

OUR AFTERLIFE I

1.18 Ezra Pound died on November 1, 1972; Edmund Wilson, June 12, 1972; W. H. Auden,
September 29, 1973. Mariani rightly points out that Lowell's comments on Wilson's *Patri-
otic Gore* illuminate Lowell's purposes in his own historical portraits: "I am braced by
your portraits. I see now, I think, that all your life you have been writing a sort of
Plutarch's Lives. . . . One might use the phrase: moral aristocrats for them. By this, I mean
some queer tense twist of principle, changed to virtue by having been lived through the
undefinable multiplicity of experience. No two persons are alike, all are glaringly imper-
fect, still there are heroes. You can see I've just come from your [Oliver Wendell]
Holmes, whose principles mean nothing to me literally, but whose life seems so shining
and cantless. Pardon this sprawl, and let me salute you, dear old fellow questioning
Calvinist, on your triumphant book" (letter to Wilson, March 31, 1962, *L*, 405–6).

FOR JOHN BERRYMAN

1.12 *Les Maudits*: The damned; Verlaine titled his book about his fellow symbolists, including
Mallarmé and Rimbaud, *Les Poètes maudits* (1884).
1.16 grands maîtres: Great masters.
3.3–6 Lowell writes of the young Berryman's visit to Maine: "We gossiped on the rocks of the
millpond. . . . John could quote with vibrance to all lengths, even prose, even late Shake-
speare, to show me what could be done with disrupted and mended syntax. This was the
start of his real style" (*CPR*, 112).
3.10 this last *Dream Song*: That is, the final one written, beginning "I didn't. And I didn't"
(printed as the penultimate poem in *Henry's Fate*, 1977).
3.13 Berryman died by leaping from a bridge.
4 "Except Love's fires the virtue have / To fright the frost out of the grave" (song from Ben
Jonson's *The Sad Shepherd, or, A Tale of Robin Hood*, I.v.79–80).

SQUARE OF BLACK

For Lowell on Lincoln, see *CPR*, 165–66, 192–93, and "Abraham Lincoln," p. 217.

1.1 this book: *Poetry and Eloquence from the Blue and the Gray*, Part Nine of *The Photographic
History of the Civil War* (1911; Castle Books reprint, 1957).

IN THE WARD

Israel Citkowitz (1909–1974): composer; Caroline Blackwood's second husband. He was a
protégé of Aaron Copland and studied with Nadia Boulanger. For an earlier poem on Cit-
kovitz, see "Old Wanderer" in *CPO*, 426. The text is the magazine version (*CP*, p. 937).

7.3 Citkowitz championed modernism, but was unconventional enough also to celebrate Rachmaninoff; see "Orpheus With His Lute," *Tempo*, Winter 1951–1952. The *Tempo* piece gives a good sense of the humane learning, irony, and regard for the past that characterized Citkovitz's aesthetics: "Beethoven having a prophetic sense of the deteriorating effects of Czerny's methods, warned that the increasing mechanizing of technique would kill the spirit. . . . In our time, the progress of the aesthetic hero is apt to be measured by the corpses of vanquished traditions strewn along his path. . . . In this day of pianists with or without rubato—impossible to say which is worse—Rachmaninoff's rubato recreated the eloquence and sure musical instinct that must have characterized the rubato-practise of Mozart, Beethoven or Chopin" (9–11).

8.8 Schoenberg's twelve-tone system was both strict (with rule-laden "pedantry," 8.6) and revolutionary (its rejection of tonality was seen by many as "daimonic lawlessness," 8.7).

DAY BY DAY

THE DAY

4.4 *dies illa*: "That day" (Latin), from the *Requiem*, where "that day" is the day of wrath ("*Dies irae, dies illa*"), the day of tears ("*Lacrymosa dies illa*"), when all shall be judged; here, "in the marriage with nothingness" (5.2), its meaning is reversed. See note to "St. Mark's, 1933" 6.1 on p. 404.

DOMESDAY BOOK

William I, king of Normandy, defeated King Harold of England at the Battle of Hastings (1066); as William the Conqueror he ordered a detailed census of the economic resources of England, the Domesday Book (1085–1086), the better to tax. *Domesday* is a variant of *Doomsday*.

7.9 the Protector: Oliver Cromwell.
9 *Nulle terre sans seigneur*: No land without a ruler.
10.3 J.M.W. Turner, British painter.
11 kingfisher: See note to "Colloquy in Black Rock" 5.2, p. 348; here, an emblem both of the aristocracy and of those who sought to destroy it. (John Peck notes in the last line "the pun on Cromwell's role in the bird's name, and the flight of landed gentry" [*Salmagundi* 37 (Spring 1977), 35].)

MARRIAGE

I.2.13 he can choose both sides: Lowell wrote Peter Taylor of his son Sheridan, age four: "His bicentennial experiences in America have perhaps taught him . . . the ambivalence, which is really balance of power, of taking both sides. Here [England] people are a little bewildered when he stands up for King George" (September 11, 1975).
II.1.1 Jan Van Eyck's *The Arnolfini Marriage* (1434). Deese (building on Panofsky) mounts an elaborate and convincing argument that Van Eyck's painting itself functioned as a marriage certificate, and that (because Lowell and Blackwood were not legally married at the time of the photograph in section I) "Lowell's poetic formalization of their marriage, his verbal interplay of painting and photograph, had to take the place of a more ordinary le-

galization that circumstances made difficult. The photographer's flash becomes a 'miracle of lighting,' creating the 'sacramental instant' of marriage" (in Axelrod and Deese, *Essays*, 203).

II.3.8 *sang de boeuf*: Dark red (literally, ox blood).

ROBERT T. S. LOWELL

Lowell's father, Robert Traill Spence Lowell III. See "Commander Lowell," pp. 114–16; headnote to this poem, p. 364; and "Rebellion," *CPO*, 32.

FOR SHERIDAN

Lowell's son, Robert Sheridan Lowell.

2.1 negative: Photographic negative.
3.4 Stamp on silver cutlery.

ST. MARK'S, 1933

See headnotes to "91 Revere Street" on p. 359 and to "Bobby Delano," p. 399.

1.1 form: "Grade" in most American schools; "fourth form" is the equivalent of sophomore.
6.1 *Huic ergo parce, Deus*: "Spare then this [one], God"; or, "Spare him then, God." Line 4 from the "Lacrymosa" of the *Requiem*. ("Lacrymosa" is immediately preceded by "*Dies irae, dies illa*," a poem sometimes attributed to Thomas of Celano. "Lacrymosa" is modeled on it; "*Huic ergo*" echoes line 36: "*supplicanti parce, Deus*.")

SUBURBAN SURF

8.1 *méchants*: Spiteful, nasty, wicked.

NOTICE

1.2 Hamilton points out that "enthusiasm is a word [Lowell] regularly uses to describe his manic episodes" (*Robert Lowell*, 226).

SHIFTING COLORS

10.1–2 This is not the directness: Cf. "I want words meat-hooked from the living steer" ("The Nihilist as Hero," p. 229).
10.4 Mallarmé sought a "pure" poetry: "The pure work implies the disappearance of the poet as speaker, yielding his initiative to words, which are mobilized by the shock of their difference; they light up with reciprocal reflections like a virtual stream of fireworks over jewels, restoring perceptible breath to the former lyric impulse, or the enthusiastic personal directing of the sentence" (from "Crisis in Poetry," trans. Mary Ann Caws, *Selected Poetry and Prose* [1982]). The result was an extremely dense, packed style, usually at a remove from representational surfaces; at his death, much work was left uncompleted.

UNWANTED

1.2 *Antabuse*: An antidrinking drug that causes a violent reaction to alcohol, even occasionally death; Lowell at times took it because alcohol could trigger a brief manic attack.

5.1 Merrill Moore was not only a psychiatrist but "a poet of some reputation. He had been a fringe member of the Southern 'Fugitive' group led by John Crowe Ransom and Allen Tate and was famous for writing only—but voluminously—in sonnet form" (Hamilton, *Robert Lowell*, 28).

8.2 *cri de coeur*: Cry of the heart.

10.5–12 See *CPR*, 301–2.

THE DOWNLOOK

5 Cf. Dante, *Inferno*, V.120–23.

6.3–4 The semi-mythical poet Arion, surrounded by a murderous crew, sang to attract dolphins to his ship, then leapt into the sea. A dolphin carried him safely to shore.

7.2 insupportable, trespassing tongue: In 1966 Pound said to Lowell, "Didn't Frost say you'd say anything once?" (Lowell, letter to James Laughlin, August 31, 1966, *L*, 473).

THANKS-OFFERING FOR RECOVERY

5 *homme sensuel*: Sensual man.

11 *ex voto*: Latin, "from a vow"; "the replica of the afflicted part of the body which Latin Catholics give to the saint believed responsible for the cure" (Alan Williamson, in Meyers, *Interviews*, 272). Elizabeth Bishop to Lowell: "Frank [Bidart] was also here for a drink just before he left for England his last visit—and at the very last moment I picked up that weird balsa-wood head & thrust it on him . . . I've been thinking I wanted to send you *something*, but hadn't been able to think of anything. I have—had, that is—two of those heads, picked up by Lota years ago—they are *ex-votos*—someone cured of a head injury or violent headaches, etc., gave one to his church or the shrine where he'd prayed for recovery. The remaining one is different wood, much heavier, and very neatly painted, with a pert little moustache, etc.—rather like a hairdresser's sign. It wasn't until Frank had taken off that I suddenly thought, 'Oh dear!—I was just looking around frantically for a souvenir for Cal—I hope to goodness he doesn't think I *meant* anything by it . . . !' (Because I certainly didn't—or certainly not consciously) Then last night Frank told me you've already written a poem about it—which of course I'm dying to see . . ." (April 16, 1976).

14 *Deo gratias*: Thanks to God.

EPILOGUE

"[I]n paintings, [we feel] the artist's mothering work of hand and mind. I once asked the master photographer Walker Evans how Vermeer's *View of Delft* (that perhaps first trompe l'oeil of landscape verisimilitude) differed from a photograph. He paused, staring, as if his eye could not give the answer. His answer was [John Crowe] Ransom's—art demands the intelligent pain or care behind each speck of brick, each spot of paint" (*CPR*, 27).

9 "with dim eyes and threadbare art" (*Salmagundi* 37 [Spring 1977], 115).

15 Lowell, in 1963: "I started one of these poems [for *Life Studies*] in Marvell's four-foot couplet and showed it to my wife [Elizabeth Hardwick]. And she said 'Why not say what really happened?' (It wasn't the one about her.)" (Meyers, *Interviews*, 75).

17 "Among the Dutch painters, Jan Vermeer [1632–1675] was the most accurate in rendering the natural appearances of things and persons, in representing the effects of light passing from objects to retina, in recording compositionally what the eye has seen" (Helen Deese, in Axelrod and Deese, *Essays*, 185). Deese argues that the Vermeer painting embedded in Lowell's poem is *Woman in Blue Reading a Letter* (187). When Derek Walcott asked Lowell "what painter he imagined to be his complement," Lowell replied "Vermeer" (180).

from LAST POEMS (1977)

SUMMER TIDES

Addressed to Caroline Blackwood. This is Lowell's final completed poem, finished August 31, 1977, thirteen days before his death.

11 your portrait: See "Mermaid" 3.4–6, p. 256, and corresponding note, p. 397.
30 rotting the bulwark: "Literally, the front part of the lawn gave onto a precipice and there was a railing there and this was being eaten away and the whole thing was about to fall down" (Hamilton, *Robert Lowell*, 469).

Chronology

1917 Robert Traill Spence Lowell IV born March 1 in Boston, the only child of Robert Traill Spence Lowell III, USN, and Charlotte Winslow Lowell. Maternal ancestors include Pilgrim leader Edward Winslow (1595–1655), Plymouth colony governor Josiah Winslow (1629–1680), and Revolutionary War general John Stark (1728–1822); paternal ancestors include author Robert Traill Spence Lowell (1816–1891), poet James Russell Lowell (1819–1891), astronomer Percival Lowell (1855–1916), Harvard president A. Lawrence Lowell (1856–1943), and poet Amy Lowell (1874–1925).

1924 Lowell family settles permanently in Boston after periods in Philadelphia and Washington, D.C.

1924–30 Brimmer School in Boston.

1930–35 St. Mark's School in Southborough, Mass. Studies with Richard Eberhart, befriends Frank Parker.

1935–37 Harvard University. Meets Anne Dick. Fight with father.

1937 Spring and summer with Allen Tate at Clarksville, Tenn.

1937–40 Kenyon College. Studies with John Crowe Ransom, befriends Randall Jarrell and Peter Taylor. Graduates *summa cum laude* in Classics.

1940 Marries writer Jean Stafford on April 2.

1940–41 Converts to Roman Catholicism. Graduate study in English at Louisiana State University with Cleanth Brooks and Robert Penn Warren.

1941–42 Move to New York. Editorial assistant at Sheed & Ward.

1942–43 Writes poetry during year's stay with Allen Tate and Caroline Gordon at Monteagle, Tenn.

1943 Refuses military induction, sentenced in October to a year and a day for violating Selective Service Act. Serves five months in West Street detention center in New York and federal prison at Danbury, Conn. Parole in Black Rock, Conn.

1944 *Land of Unlikeness.* Jean Stafford's novel *Boston Adventure.* Move to Damariscotta Mills, Maine.

1946 *Lord Weary's Castle* (Pulitzer Prize). Befriends Delmore Schwartz and John Berryman. Separates from Stafford, moves to New York.

1947 Guggenheim Fellowship and American Academy grant. Befriends William Carlos Williams and Elizabeth Bishop.

1947–48 Poetry Consultant to the Library of Congress.

1948 Divorce from Jean Stafford. Leaves Roman Catholic Church.

1948–49 Yaddo Writers' Colony.

1949 Returns to New York. Member of committee awarding the Bollingen Prize to Ezra

Pound for *Pisan Cantos*. Hospitalized for mental disturbance in March. Marries writer Elizabeth Hardwick, July 28.

1950 Teaches creative writing at the University of Iowa in spring and at Kenyon College in summer. Father dies in August.

1950–53 Lowell and Hardwick live in Europe.

1951 *The Mills of the Kavanaughs* (Harriet Monroe Prize).

1952 Teaches at the Seminar in American Studies at Salzburg.

1953 Teaches at the University of Iowa. Students include W. D. Snodgrass and Philip Levine. Teaches summer session at the University of Indiana.

1954 Lectures at the University of Cincinnati. Mother dies in Italy in February. Lowell and Hardwick relocate to Boston. Manic-depressive breakdown. Begins drafting autobiography.

1954–60 Lowell and Hardwick live on Marlborough St. in Boston.

1955–60 Teaches at Boston University. Students include Sylvia Plath, Anne Sexton, and George Starbuck.

1957 Daughter Harriet Winslow Lowell born, January 4. West Coast speaking tour in March–April. Drafts "Skunk Hour" at summer home in Castine, Maine. Bipolar illness.

1958 Hospitalized in January. Meets Ann Adden. Continues work on *Life Studies*.

1959 *Life Studies* (National Book Award, Guinness Poetry Award).

1960 Reads "For the Union Dead" at Boston Arts Festival, June 5. Move to New York. Supports Kennedy for president.

1960–70 Residence on Upper West Side in Manhattan.

1961 *Imitations* (Harriet Monroe Prize, Bollingen Prize). *Phaedra*.

1962 Summer in South America.

1963–77 Teaches at Harvard (on leave 1970–72, commutes from England for one semester yearly 1973–76).

1964 *For the Union Dead*. "My Kinsman, Major Molineux" and "Benito Cereno" premiere in New York. November 1 (Obie Award). Ford grant for drama.

1965 *The Old Glory*. Protests Vietnam War by publicly declining President Johnson's invitation to the White House Festival of the Arts. *Phaedra* premieres at Wesleyan University.

1966 Defeated for Oxford Chair of Poetry by English poet Edmund Blunden. Wins Sarah Josepha Hale Award.

1967 *Near the Ocean*. Joins Allen Ginsberg, Denise Levertov, Norman Mailer, and others in March on Pentagon. *Prometheus Bound* premieres at Yale University.

1968 *The Old Glory*, revised edition. "Endecott and the Red Cross" premieres in New York, April 18. Campaigns for Eugene McCarthy in primaries, refuses to vote for president in November.

1969 *Notebook 1967–68*. *Prometheus Bound*. Visits Israel.

1970 *Notebook*. Visiting Fellow, All Souls' College, Oxford.

1970–76 Residence in England with writer Caroline Blackwood.

1970–72 Teaches at Essex University. Befriends Seamus Heaney.

1971 Son Robert Sheridan Lowell born to Blackwood and Lowell.

1972 Divorce from Elizabeth Hardwick, marriage to Caroline Blackwood in October.

1973 *The Dolphin* (Pulitzer Prize). *For Lizzie and Harriet*. *History*.

1974 Copernicus Award for lifetime achievement in poetry.

1976 *Selected Poems*.

1977 *Day by Day* (National Book Critics Circle Award). *Selected Poems*, revised edition. American Academy Medal for Literature. Returns to Elizabeth Hardwick in the

United States. Dies of heart failure in New York, September 12. Episcopalian funeral service in Boston, September 16. Burial in family plot at Dunbarton, N.H.

1978   *The Oresteia of Aeschylus* published posthumously.
1987   *Collected Prose* published posthumously.
2005   *The Letters of Robert Lowell* published posthumously.

—STEVEN GOULD AXELROD

(adapted from *The Critical Response to Robert Lowell*, 1999).

Index of Titles

Index of First Lines